LORNA

Journey to
JOY

Stories to Inspire Hope and Courage

Xulon Press Elite
555 Winderley Pl, Suite 225
Maitland, FL 32751
407.339.4217
www.xulonpress.com

© 2024 by Lorna Hardy

Illustrated by Lorna Hardy

All rights reserved solely by the author. The author guarantees all contents are original and do not infringe upon the legal rights of any other person or work. No part of this book may be reproduced in any form without the permission of the author.

Due to the changing nature of the Internet, if there are any web addresses, links, or URLs included in this manuscript, these may have been altered and may no longer be accessible. The views and opinions shared in this book belong solely to the author and do not necessarily reflect those of the publisher. The publisher therefore disclaims responsibility for the views or opinions expressed within the work.

Unless otherwise indicated, Scripture quotations taken from the Holy Bible, New International Version (NIV). Copyright © 1973, 1978, 1984, 2011 by Biblica, Inc.™. Used by permission. All rights reserved.

Scripture quotations taken from the King James Version (KJV) – public domain.

Scripture quotations taken from The Message (MSG). Copyright © 1993, 1994, 1995, 1996, 2000, 2001, 2002. Used by permission of NavPress Publishing Group. Used by permission. All rights reserved.

Scripture quotations taken from the New King James Version (NKJV). Copyright © 1982 by Thomas Nelson, Inc. Used by permission. All rights reserved.

Paperback ISBN-13: 978-1-66289-108-3
Ebook ISBN-13: 978-1-66289-109-0

Journey to JOY

Stories to Inspire Hope and Courage

LORNA HARDY

To

....

From

....

....

Date

....

I am delighted to dedicate this book with
deep love and gratitude to Norm and our
precious blended family of sons and daughters.
And, most of all to God who calls us all
"Family"!

Contents

Section 1: The Egg – Origin, Miracle, Wonder .10

Section 2: The Caterpillar – Identity, Curiosity, Growth 17

Section 3: The Cocoon – Part 1 Loss and Grief .92

       The Cocoon – Part 2 Resilience, Renewal, and Healing 174

       The Cocoon – Part 3 Transformation, Integrity, and Purpose. . 261

Section 4: The Butterfly – Vision, Significance, Legacy 312

Section 5: Interlude – Security, Rest, Hope .442

Section 6: Eternity – Awe, Love, Joyful Celebration. 467

References 491

List of Topics 505

Books You May Enjoy 512

A Final Blessing 517

Welcome,
I have written this book
for you.

For the days when you
Feel brave and strong and
The days when you don't,
For there will be some of both.

This book tells our story and celebrates our shared humanity in vivid color.

Like caterpillars, we naturally adapt again and again in a bid to survive. We nibble this and that, hoping to create a secure identity. We long for many things: purpose, belonging and someone to love. For safe spaces to curl up in, meadows and mountains to stretch our legs, and snuggly places to rest.

Like butterflies, we also have fun soaring above the mundane things of life, playing with big questions and complex ideas, and weaving adventure into each day.

So, here's to us. To the wonder of life and exploring it together.

Cheering you on!

What is this book about?

The inner life.
The shared life.
The eternal purpose of life.

For these three are one.

Section 1: The Egg

Origin, Miracle, Wonder

If a butterfly could talk, what a splendid story he would tell about change and resilience, about wriggling out of his egg, nibbling leaves, and snuggling up in a cocoon, then soaring into the sky for the first time.

But,

Your own life story is far more inspiring. It's filled with quiet miracles and breathless wonder, especially if we tell it from the very beginning . . .

Womb

Even before you were born,
you lived for an eternity in
your mother's mind.

From the start, you were *an aquatic creature*. You swam in the warm, watery
world of your mother's womb in blissful comfort.

Sometimes your world swayed from side to side, but if it did, you simply sucked
your thumb and drifted off to sleep, rocked and soothed by the liquid lullaby.
Day and night, you languidly floated in darkness, unconcerned and unafraid.
For your eyes had never seen light or glimpsed a playful sunbeam. Nor had
you witnessed, with a sense of holy awe, the glory of a moon-washed sky.

Because your growing intellect harbored no fear of miracles, you were free to
revel in becoming a miracle yourself. You spun flesh out of energy and created
delicate earlobes in humming silence. You shaped tiny toenails before your feet
could dance and formed eyes before you could see. You grew slender eyelashes,
then amused yourself by fluttering them until ripples formed.

Curled up in your mother's womb, your whole body throbbed to the drumbeat
of her heart. She was everything to you, *but you had no idea she even existed or
that her very being gave you life.*[1]

Until the day things changed . . .

Birth

The tragedy of birth is
that it always requires
loss before gain.
This, too, is its glory.

One day or night, before you knew how to tell the time, the hour came for
you to be born.

As the hour approached, your mother's heart rate changed, and deep in your soul you sensed its shifting rhythm. But you had no idea that your mother was in labor or the price she was paying as she sweated and stretched to bring you into the world.

But even then, life's irony teased your senses, because, as she risked her life for you, you thought your life was ending. The walls of your home closed in. They squeezed you without mercy and tightened around your tender face, flesh pressing on flesh. Even your nice warm bathwater abandoned you. Streaming past your ears, it fled, gurgling into space, and left you to languish in a strange, slippery silence pregnant with throbbing questions.

In those timeless, eternal, hours when your mother was in labor, it must have felt as if everything in the universe was conspiring to push you down, to cast you out, to banish you from all that was safe, secure, and familiar. And it was, for it was your time to be born, to be expelled forever from your mother's womb.

To be lifted free
or slide with a primal cry of protest,
naked and defenseless into the unknown,
where, for the first time in your life,
you saw your mother's face.[2]

CHANGE

Life beckons us forward
through a shining portal
curtained by fear yet
gilt-edged with hope.

After you were born, did you miss your solitary confinement? The certainty of
secure boundaries? The known? Did you grieve for the dark comfort of the
watery womb and long to hide from sight once more?

Or were you too entranced by the light to feel regret?

Too thrilled by your first glimpse of sense-rich beauty? Too captivated by
a world of wonder beyond anything your aquatic self could even imagine?
An enchanted world of tastes and textures where warm milk, like liquid life,
flowed over your tongue? Where home-baked bread crusted your mother's
fingers with crumbs for you to lick off? Where warm water bathed your silky
skin and soft towels lulled you to sleep in their soap-scented embrace?

Do you remember how you loved to explore then?

How you caressed the crinkles of your mother's smile with curious fingers?
How your eyes sparkled when dust diamonds danced above your cot in summer
and winged songbirds sang at dawn?

Do you remember stroking a kitten's soft fur for the first time? Or rising on
wobbly legs to toddle after a puppy's red ball on the lawn?

As the years flew by, did you ever stop to wonder about the miracle of your
birth? Or pause to consider with deep gratitude the splendid gift God gave
you as your first *birth day* present? A gift so profound that your aquatic self
could not even dream it existed;

your ability to breathe.[3]

THE GREATEST GIFT

Joy dances first in the heart
and then in the feet.
Or is it the other way around?

On the day you were born, God gently placed His most precious treasure in your tender palm, and you instinctively curled your fingers around it, even before you knew that it was:

The Gift of Life.

Every day since then, you have clung tightly to your treasure. Through storm and sunshine, doubt and fear, and every other challenge under the sun, you have held on. With all the energy and skill you possess, *you have tried to preserve your life*. You have looked both ways when you crossed each road. You have learned to eat your vegetables and get to bed on time (more or less). You have swum with care in deep water.

Even on days when your courage faltered or your will to live wavered, you have held on, held on to life.

I bow to your tenacity.
To your resilient hope.

To the gratitude you are showing the Life-Giver by honoring the precious gift he gave you.

Your very own gift of life
to nurture, shape, and treasure.

WONDER

Untamed by familiarity,
innocence is free to see
miracles everywhere.

You do not know its name yet. All you can do is watch it dance.

Entranced, your eyes follow it as it dips and sways to the rhythm of the wind. This glowing shaft of emerald light: creator of air and bringer of food.

One day, you will learn it is a common blade of grass, then you will trample over it as one who is blind to its beauty. But today, today you will see it as the first human being saw it at the dawn of time when God sang a love song to the earth, and the meadow grass heard His call and invited the flowers to dance.

Section 2: The Caterpillar

Identity, Curiosity, Growth

The caterpillar's garden home has everything he needs to thrive. Clusters of ruby tomatoes decorate his walls, and green beans curl up the pillars of his banqueting hall.

Each day the caterpillar weaves his wandering way through grass-high forests, where sunlight stripes his skin with flickering bands of emerald light. Wherever he wanders, he comes head-to-head with other wide-eyed bugs and stakes out his leafy territory one nibble at a time. Sometimes, on spring mornings, when sunshine fills his head, he goes a little loopy.

After lunch, the caterpillar naps among the flowers and listens to the hum of drowsy bees. As he snoozes, rose-pink petals whisper down to blanket him in fragrance.

When the sun farewells the sky, his home is filled with shifting shadows. A soft breeze begins to blow among the cabbages. One leaf rises and falls to the rhythm of the wind, and the caterpillar rides it like a magic carpet. He gazes at the gold and crimson canvas of the sky until the colors fade. Then, yawning, curls up in the crease of a leaf to dream. High above his head, trees stretch their silvered branches toward the moon and send their ebony leaves to dance for him among the stars.

THE SECRET NURSERY

In the eyes of a child,
the world is still
full of surprise
and delight.

I first noticed caterpillars when I was three or four years old, and our family lived in a red brick house in a small English village.

Our home was surrounded by a large garden, and I loved to watch my father digging in the rich earth and planting vegetable seedlings in neat rows. Sometimes I helped him poke holes in the dirt ready for their tiny roots. Or I held a ball of string for him so he could tie our pink climbing rose to a trel-lised arch.

One morning, no doubt, to get me from under her feet in the kitchen, my mother sent me out to play. Because my father was at work, I had the whole garden to myself. The summer sun was just beginning to filter through the large walnut trees as I set out to explore the world, alive with bouncy curls and curiosity. I paused to watch a shiny red ladybug climbing up a fence, then I said, "Hello," to the chickens scratching in the dirt.

Near the edge of a flower bed I spied a furry black caterpillar. So I squatted down to watch it looping lazily across a carpet of tiny pink and blue forget-me-nots.

When a few village folks wandered down our lane, I ran across our lawn to see them. The lawn was beaded with liquid diamonds, and the dew made my bare toes tingle. My footsteps left a glistening track all the way to our small wooden gate. Wedging my feet between the white palings, I leaned over the gate and watched the plump matrons bustle by chatting. Some herded reluctant children to school, and others carried wicker baskets on their way to the local shop.

When no one passed for a while, I hopped off the gate and began to explore the privet hedge on either side. The hedge was taller than me and covered in glossy green and yellow leaves. Pulling off a leaf, I laid it on my palm and idly stroked it with one finger. I wiggled it in the sunshine and watched the light playing along the golden veins. After a while, I grew bored and dropped the leaf. On a whim, I parted the hedge itself to look inside. Immediately, I glimpsed another world.

As my eyes adjusted to the gloom, I saw a tangle of twiggy brown stems looped with gossamer spider webs. Creepy crawly bugs were scurrying along the slender branches, and small black ants were waving their antennae at each other. Some ants paused to chat as if they were sharing the latest gossip before they hurried on their way.

After I had watched the ants for a while, I spied some strange lumpy things hanging from small twigs. Unlike the ants, these lumps didn't appear to be doing anything at all, just hanging there like tiny parcels wrapped in frayed grey bandages. Fascinated, I ran back inside the house and called, "Mom, come and see what I've found." Catching her hand in mine, I skipped beside her, and we made double tracks back across the lawn all the way to the hedge.

Releasing her hand, I parted the leaves and urged her to look inside. She bent down to my height, and we pressed our cheeks together to peer into the gloom. I pointed a chubby finger at one of the lumps and asked, "What's that?" My mother explained that the hedge was like a secret butterfly nursery, and tucked inside each *cocoon*, a wriggly caterpillar was lying very still, patiently trusting that God could transform it, day by day, into a butterfly.

Hiding there in the dusty shadows,
each caterpillar was forming wings.

FAMILY TREE

You did not choose your family
or the time and place of your birth,
so your lineage is neither
to your credit nor to your shame.

You may have been born at home or in a hospital ward, but when your eyes were bright with curiosity and your ears were finely tuned to every sound, no one took you shopping for parents. (Though, perhaps, you wish they had.) Instead, you received the parents you were given.

Your parents may have been happy or grumpy, indulgent or distant. They may have been steady as rocks, as flighty as butterflies, or just plain ordinary. But whatever they were like, *how you remember them* will influence your emotions as you draw your family tree. When you pick up a pencil to scribble down their names, you may smile warmly and sit up a little straighter in your chair. Or you may slump lower with a sigh and begin to scratch holes in the paper.

When I looked at my family tree, with all its ancestral foliage at the top of the page, I began to wonder if this top-heavy structure was symbolic. Did my relatives shelter me or cast long shadows across my life? As I wondered, I began to doodle, and gradually, a new family tree took shape.

In contrast to the old one, the new tree was

Up
Side
Down.

The difference this made was profound.

It affected how I saw my parents and how I viewed my own potential.

In the first picture, my ancestors dominated my life. But in the second, like the roots of a great tree, they anchored me in time and place. Each ancestor contributed something to my life, some because they were loving and kind, and others because they made mistakes, which taught me valuable life lessons.

I have no idea what your parents were like or who raised you, but my guess is that they brought you as far as their:

Circumstances
Resources
Skills
Hopes
Fears, and
Vision allowed

Whoever they were, a million large and small factors influenced the childhood they had, the kind of people they became, and the childhood they gave you.

If you were especially blessed, your parents poured all their resources into giving you a happy childhood, filling you to the brim with love and good memories while setting a few healthy boundaries in place for good measure. But your experience may have been the reverse of this. You may have suffered abuse or neglect and stumbled into adulthood feeling abandoned and lonely, ready, at any moment, to rage at the world, or cry soul-searing tears.

It's easy to sit in judgment on our parents and wish they had done better. But if we spend too much time worrying about how our parents raised us, we can completely miss the fact that, as adults, *we are now raising ourselves.* When we leave home or reach the magic number that makes us "adults" in our culture, *we become our own parents.* Where our parents left off, our own parenting begins. This is a mind-blowing idea, which carries with it both thrilling levels of opportunity and staggering amounts of responsibility.

Once we grasp the idea that we are our own parents, we quickly realize that we face the same challenges our parents faced:

Inherited flaws,
Naive inexperience,
Limited resources,
Imperfect options,
And the inbuilt human desire to be free rather than responsible!

We also face another hurdle our parents did not face. *They knew they were parents, but we do not.* So we miss many vital opportunities to shape who we become. Or we toss our power to the most influential bidder, whether they are friend or foe, standing right beside us, or on our screens.

In our eager desire to fling aside the limits of childhood, we spin off into the night, burning rubber. Or we squander our pent-up energy on aimless entertainment, late nights, and unlimited junk food. Despite this, rather than because of it, most of us manage to grow up okay anyway. But we may suffer more setbacks than we need to and live an erratic life.

We may also live by a double standard without any idea we are doing it. For instance, we may tell our parents what they should and should not have done for us, point critical fingers at previous generations, then live with thoughtless self-absorption ourselves.

We may brim with self-righteous idealism and march for social justice, then trample on the rights of the people working to put a roof over our own heads. We may blithely drag beached whales back to their watery home and feel like environmental heroes, then rush home late at night to bang doors, rev engines, and disturb the sleep of friends and neighbors!

We expect our parents to give us unconditional love, nourishing food, and a safe place to live, to protect us from risky situations and give us a good education. We expect our parents to be totally devoted to us. Selfless.

But once we're in power, *how do we parent ourselves?*

Do we eat up all our vegetables?
Befriend only safe people?
Do our homework?
And put ourselves to bed on time?

Do we say *please* and *thank you*?
Share nicely and forgive quickly?
And when we speak to ourselves,
in triumph, or failure, do we use words
which nurture, encourage, and heal?

Can we honestly boast that we
are always patient and kind to
our growing selves? Brimming
with unconditional love?

That we are fully prepared
and committed to giving
ourselves a "happy adulthood"?

Not me!

While I was excited to be growing up, I was blind to my power. I was aware of an earnest desire to escape restraint but naively oblivious to my need to grasp the initiative and make life happen. I had learned to be obedient and a follower (with a touch of rebellion on the side), but many years would pass before I learned how to be a leader—in my own life or the lives of others.

I wonder how our lives would change if, on our coming-of-age birthday, we saw a big neon sign which read, "You are now your own parent," And in smaller letters underneath, "You are a single parent." Would we make different choices? As "new parents," would we realize what stunning power we had to shape how we grew up and who we became? And if we did, would we have the tools to use this remarkable opportunity?

These are not idle questions, for us or for our children.

Nor for our parents!

Because *if we parent ourselves poorly* or haphazardly, our parents have to remain on duty year after year. Providing. In effect, *still child minding us*. Advising. Picking us up and brushing off our debts. Losing precious sleep worrying about us (like they did when we were teething). Being forever responsible for us *while we play, and they continue to pay!*

In contrast, if we choose to parent ourselves well—with joy and purpose—our own parents can finally relax. Perhaps for the first time in twenty or thirty years, they can remember who they were before we were born: ordinary human beings. *Rather like us, really.*

Unfortunately, it often takes decades for us to realize that:

When we honor our parents and
free them to be human, we also
liberate ourselves from childhood
and our own self-centered immaturity.

And when we relax our grip on perfection,
everyone gets to breathe more easily.
we become kinder to our parents,
ourselves, and our own children.

This kinder, more realistic approach spills over into all our relationships—at work and at home.

Instead of calling on our parents because we are broke, we call on them because we enjoy their company. We stop whining and demanding attention and begin to listen. *We begin to hear*. We honor our parents with respectful curiosity and show them tender compassion.

We help to create an environment where our parents can at last feel safe around us. Instead of bracing themselves to listen to our resentment yet again or hear our peevish *if only*, they can start to trust us. And when they do, something magical happens. They begin to open up, to freely confess their flaws and regrets without prompting, to reward us with their stories and tell us their secret hopes and fears. They may even reveal their own unspoken dreams and present us with the sacred opportunity of helping to fulfill them.

In a safe and tender moment, we may even ask, "When I was born, what dreams did you have for my life?" For some of us, this is not a safe question to ask. We already sense we're not living up to their ideals, and we don't want to bruise the relationship further. Or they may be too sore and mixed up to answer kindly. But if we have a good relationship with our parents, we may hear very special truths in response to our question.

For instance, your mother may look wistfully into the distance, smile softly, and whisper, "I longed and prayed for you so much. When you arrived, I cried with joy and hugged you close. I've loved you since you were a just a bump. I guess I nagged you sometimes and told you to share your toys, but it was only because I wanted the best for you, wanted you to be happy and get along really well with others. I wanted to launch you into life well loved."

Or your father may pause, lean on a fence he's building, and say, "I wasn't sure about being a dad at first. It seemed such a responsible role. But when you arrived, I couldn't stop grinning. Even when I was up half the night, and you screamed in my ear, I kept a warm glow deep inside. I wonder sometimes if I was a good dad, if I was always there for you. I had such a grand vision of who you could become. I wanted you to stride into life, head held high, and be a good person. Whatever path you took, I wanted you to live with kindness, integrity, and purpose."

Sometimes we don't know *because we don't ask*. Or we don't ask because we're too distracted and busy, preoccupied with surviving now and figuring out who we are, and what we want.

But what if one of the first steps to understanding ourselves involves pausing long enough to understand our parents? The boys and girls and men and women they were before we were born, the struggles and dreams they had then, and who they are now?

And one more thing . . .

Whatever your background, *you're not destined to repeat family patterns unless you want to.* You're not locked into being clones of your grandparents or your "mother's daughter" or your "father's son" forever.

If you think your parents are your only ancestors, look again. Look across the water. Search under every spreading tree. You will discover the whole earth is full of your relatives. Everywhere your foot falls, you meet family. Scholars and scoundrels. Heroes and villains. People with stories to tell and wisdom to share.

Whether you travel by bicycle or pull out a book and flip through history's dusty pages, you'll find teachers everywhere. People of desert, field, and forest with yearning hearts and children they adore.

Of course, wherever you travel, you will take your own genes with you and your childhood. Other travelers will take their quirks and questions too. So the road ahead may not always be smooth or safe. But if you take your courage, instincts, and an open heart to guide you, most of the time, you will enjoy the journey.

Then, one day, full of gratitude and brimming with wisdom, you will turn toward home, put down your own roots, and, inspired by all that's good, beautiful, and true, you'll create your own imperfect but sturdy branch of Humanity's Tree

With great joy!

If you decide to sketch your own family tree one rainy afternoon, you may enjoy playing with the following questions:

Whose values and decisions have shaped my family tree the most? In what ways?

Have I made peace with my parents? All they are and all they are not? These questions are worth considering, for when I make peace with my parents, I begin to make peace with myself. With all I am and all I am not. For the grace and understanding I am willing to extend to them, I also extend to myself. And thus, I fulfill one of the three key things required for a meaningful life—peace with my past, purpose in the present, and hope for the future.

What decisions could I make, or what actions could I take in my life, or the lives of my children, to improve the beauty and strength of our family tree?

When I see myself as a member of "Humanity's Tree," how does this change how I view my neighbors or people from other cultures? Who—living or long dead—most inspires me? Why?

Am I a good parent to myself? How do I know?

In what ways am I training myself (and my children) to appreciate and use the freedom and responsibility that comes with living as a human being?

What if, originally,
we all had the same Source
and the same surname,
Love?[1]

LABELS

Whatever others have called you,
choose your own name.

One of the last memories I have of my mother is seeing her propped up in bed. Her wicker sewing basket is open in front of her, and rainbow spools of thread are scattered across the white sheets. The golden rays of the afternoon sun slant across the room and glint along her needle as she dips it in and out of the fabric.

I slide up onto the bed and snuggle up facing her, feeling the warmth of her legs coming through the quilt to warm my tummy.

Soothed yet curious, I linger there for a while, watching her face, watching her hands as she sews name tags on my new school uniform: the navy skirt, the V-neck sweater, and the blue shirt. She even picks up a pair of ankle socks and sews labels into their ribbed tops. The socks are gray, and I turn from them in scorn. My dad would call the color "serviceable," but I call it boring. Have the uniform people no imagination? Don't they know I long to wear pretty things?

Finally, my mother sighs and snips off the thread. She turns to me and smiles. All the labels are in place. Her task is finished. And she is free to return to the hospital.

Without me.

I am nearly nine years old, and I am about to say goodbye to my mother and father. Leave for boarding school in a town as far away as the moon. It's a huge step for a small, shy girl, and I think the clothes are more ready to take the leap than I am. But somewhere inside a sense of adventure is stirring.

Even today, I still cherish one of those white childhood name tags with my name neatly embroidered in red writing.

But not all the names we carry with us from childhood are worth cherishing. And not all the names other people call us are sewn into our clothes. Sometimes they are "sewn" onto our souls instead. And every time we answer to one of these names, another stitch of memory or habit anchors them more firmly in place. If a cloth label is sewn onto our shirt collar, we can unpick the stitches one by one, but it takes far more time and effort to unpick the labels people have "stitched" onto our souls.

Thankfully, most of us outgrow our childhood nicknames. Or we stuff them into the back of our minds, where memories of tattered teddy bears linger.

But even as adults, we may cherish a few good names and long to keep them forever because even on gray sock days, they remind us who we are.

The name I like best is tucked in an ancient story, and I have claimed it as my own. It's written in red writing too:

BELOVED[2]

For that's the name God calls me.
And God calls you.

I recently discovered a song about labels, which moves me deeply each time I hear it. The song is called "Remind Me Who I Am" by Jason Gray. It features men, women, and teenagers holding up cardboard signs. On the signs are scrawled derogatory names people have called them or put-downs they have used to describe themselves. These names tell stories of heartbreak and failure.[3]

But later in the song, these same people hold up different signs with a new name on them. Can you guess what the new name is?

HALL OF MIRRORS

The quality of the feedback
depends on the quality of the mirror.

When I was a teenager, I visited a country fair on a school trip.

Restless with excitement, my friends and I looked out of the bus windows, eager to catch a glimpse of the fairground. We passed fields where cows and sheep peacefully grazed and drove through green valleys where stone cottages huddled together in chatty groups.

Finally, we rounded a bend and glimpsed the top of a Ferris wheel. Excited cries filled the bus, and we scrambled to pull on our shoes and grab our bags. When the bus wheezed to a stop and the door whooshed open, we tumbled down the steps like a noisy waterfall of life.

Instantly, our senses were hit by the sights and sounds of the fairground. High above our heads, the Ferris wheel whirled and spun screams into the sunny air. And as we lined up to enter the gate, young children tumbled around us, already begging their parents for rides. Everywhere we looked, there was bustle and buzz. As we sniffed hot chips sizzling and eyed stands sparkling with sugary snacks, it seemed as if the whole world was ours to explore!

Plunging into the stream of people, my friends and I wove our way down grassy aisles, trying to see everything at once. Easily pleased, we laughed when clowns offered us bunches of helium balloons, bright and buoyant with joy. And we squeezed past stands overflowing with huge, bug-eyed stuffed toys.

One of my friends spied a large tent with a sign swinging in the sunshine that read, "Hall of Mirrors," and we skidded to a stop. We looked at each other, then dug into the pockets of our jeans for coins. When the fair attendant flipped back the canvas door, we entered the hall of mirrors one by one.

As our eyes adjusted to the dim light, we saw mirrors of all shapes and sizes propped up along each side of the tent, glinting in the light of a few dusty light bulbs. Some of the mirrors were concave. Some were convex, and some were so full of ripples that it looked as if glassy water was pouring down the wall of the tent.

I stepped in front of the first mirror to look at my reflection and saw a tiny doll staring back at me. She was dressed in my clothes, but she was no higher than my knees. When I moved to the next mirror, the doll disappeared and in her place, I saw a slender tree-like figure with her head as high as the sky.

As I wandered down the tent, my image leaped from mirror to mirror beside me. One moment I was round, the next, tall. In some mirrors, I was twisted beyond all recognition, and in every mirror, I appeared to be a different person.

A distorted caricature of *me*.

The other girls and I did a circuit of the mirrors, laughing at ourselves and at each other. Then we flipped open the canvas flap and stumbled out into the sunshine, bubbling with giggles. Hungry for food and fun.

I haven't been to a hall of mirrors since, and yet, in a way, *I still live there as a permanent resident*. And so do you. For in effect, we live our whole lives in a hall of mirrors. This is true, whether we live in a mansion or a motel room, a palace or a tent.

In our personal *hall of mirrors*, our image is not reflected back to us by silvered sheets of glass but by *living mirrors*. People with opinions. Family members and classmates who reflect back to us an impression of *who they think we are*.

Some living mirrors tell us in verbal and non-verbal ways that we are small and insignificant, of little value because we are the wrong color, shape, or size. Other living mirrors tell us we are heroes—wonderful and precious.

We spend hours trying to make sense of the feedback we receive from all these living mirrors, especially when we are teenagers. We agonize over each comment a boy makes or a girl in the next class. We walk with friends and discuss word for word what our parents said to us the night before. Day and night, we silently wonder, *who is telling the truth about who I am?*

When we begin a new relationship or start a new job, we are desperate to "make a good impression," so we smile into every mirror we see, hoping it will grin back.

The camera is a kind of mirror too. Depending on the light and the angle, or the skill and motives of the photographer, a camera can be cruel or kind. When we are in a group photograph, who do we look for first? Ourselves! Why? Is it because we don't know what we look like? No? So what are we looking for?

When I was about seven, a famous children's author attended my father's book sellers' convention. The author graciously deigned to have his photograph taken, and all of us children were herded in, bubbling with excitement. As we surrounded him, some of us were shooed to the back of the frame, but one girl, who had long golden curls, was lifted from the melee and placed on his lap. Used to such attention, she glowed like a princess. The rest of us, with brown skin, red hair and freckles also took our usual places in her shadow. Then, at the photographer's command, we obediently pasted on smiles.

(Of course, it would have been chaos if twenty children had tried to clamber on his lap. Someone had to be chosen. But children are not fools! They notice patterns. They see when the adults around them, and others with power and influence, routinely chose certain children. Or they don't! They notice when adults habitually befriend certain people, and shun others.)

Why do we take all these fleeting "reflections" of childhood and adulthood so seriously? Because we use each word and action to help us *build our identity. Our sense of self, and our sense of worth.* For better or worse, we use every scrap of feedback we receive from the living mirrors around us to create a mental picture of three key things:

Who we are
What we can do, and
Where we belong

We use the reflections of others to help us know ourselves, and to decide in our own minds whether we are beautiful or smart. Whether others love and respect us, or they do not.

This is a very risky activity! A dangerous plan!

Why? Because, just as a cracked or twisted mirror shows us a distorted image, so frustrated or angry people *will give us distorted feedback*. And, unfortunately, we often have no idea that it's happening, especially when we are children! So we take all their feedback seriously. We believe their "mirror" is telling us the truth, and assume we are at fault, even if we are not. For instance, a parent may say to a young child who is helping them in the garden, "How can you be so stupid? Those are not weeds. They are the new tomato seedlings I just planted!" In this case, the child's act may have been immature, and displeased the parent, but it does not follow that the child was therefore "stupid".

Whether we are nine or ninety, if we take each word and action of others personally, our self-image will bounce all over the place, *depending on the moods of the people around us*. If a person says, in the heat of an argument, "You're useless," we hardly pause to consider what kind of "mirror" they are or whether we should avoid them entirely. Instead, *we take their comment to heart and wonder what kind of person we are*.

Unless we already know who we are.

If we understand how feedback works, it can make all the difference in how we weigh up others' comments. But if we base our whole self-image on what people say, our self-image will become as distorted, chaotic, and changeable as my physical image was in that fairground tent.

But I had two advantages then.

Firstly, when I entered that hall of mirrors, I already knew what I looked like. I had looked in a perfect mirror day after day at home, and I had a clear idea of who I was.

Secondly, I knew that the fairground mirrors had been purposely designed to give me false feedback, to distort how I saw myself. Because of these two key factors, I could both enter and leave the tent *laughing*.

But laughter does not come as easily in real life,
Especially if we don't have a clear,
loving mirror at home so we can view and embrace
our real selves at the start of each new day.

As you play with the whole idea of mirrors and feedback, you may suddenly realize with deep emotion that you have *believed distorted feedback all your life and built your identity on reflections from broken mirrors*.

What then?

Then, come and rest for a while. Step into the sunshine and sit yourself down where gentle breezes blow and birds sing. Give yourself permission to let your emotions settle *because this is a big deal*.

Let the days and nights of your heart drift by until you heal, until you can begin to look upon yourself and your history through the eyes of compassion. Compassion for yourself—and for all those who, with their broken hearts and imperfect words, misled you.

If, after reading the notes above, you choose to wander back through your own mirror history, you may like to consider the following questions:

When you were a child, what was it like to be waist-high, looking up at all the adults? What feedback did you receive from the living mirrors around you then? From your parents, siblings, and classmates? What verbal and non-verbal messages did they send you?

Did some children ask you out to play, but others laugh and run away? Did some relatives hug you and give you gifts? Or did some ignore you and shower presents and praise on your prettier sister or smarter brother?

Were some of the adults around you so intent on polishing their own images that they forgot to help you create yours?

Whatever feedback you received as a child, doting or demeaning, you are now an adult and can be a little more objective. You can understand more fully the biases of those who spoke to you and adjust your self-image accordingly (though it may take a while and some friendly help before you can achieve this).

But gradually, when the mirror clears, I hope you will see three vital things:

How precious you really are
How capable you can become, and
Where you truly belong

Because your story is not finished yet.

There's more feedback on the way! Some of it will be good, and some of it will be bad, so you need to be ready. Tomorrow you may be rejected for a job, or you may be hired and given a raise. A person you love may walk away, or kneel at your feet and propose . . .

Some of the feedback you receive today and tomorrow will hurt you. Some of it will help you comb your hair and stand up straight, tall and strong, ready to face the world.

But whatever feedback you receive, please remember this: that even if you need to make a few changes, *your core value remains the same.*

This Mirror
has been donated by God in
honor of his son Jesus

By and by, as the years pass, you will gradually discover the roles are being reversed. You will realize that *others are seeking your feedback, and you have become their mirror!* Now, with a glance or a word, you can harm others or heal them. Lie to them, or tell the truth. In a thousand wordless ways, your family, friends, and colleagues will ask you, "Am I okay?" And your partner and children will ask you, "Am I worthy of love?"

How will you answer?

When you are their mirror, how will you use your power?

Will you tell them a twisted story, one that's distorted by personal pain? Or will you tell them a story full of truth and kindness, springing from your own healed heart? Will you use each sacred opportunity to build up another's spirit and show them their potential? Or, full of spite, will you reflect only their flaws and cut them down to size?

Ultimately, will you use your awesome mirror-power to belittle or bless?

FANTASY

Never let the noise of others' adventures
drown out the call of your own.

The school bell rang at the end of lunchtime, but not in my world. In my imagination, I was listening to the violins playing. I was dancing in white satin slippers edged with gold, waltzing around a castle ballroom, my crimson velvet gown swirling around me. I was the princess cradled in the arms of Prince Charming.

I was the one he adored. I alone held his gaze and heard his earnest whisper, "How beautiful you are, my love. Your eyes sparkle like stars." Except they didn't because I was not attending a ball. I was sitting alone on a wooden bench in the dim girl's locker room, wearing flat black lace-up shoes, and I was late for my history class.

Bother.

As a child, I loved curling up by the fire to read. When I lived in a book, I was never alone or sad. I was surrounded by friends. Safe. The heroine made all the decisions, and the hero took all the risks. He fought the flaming dragons. She hiked across blue-white glaciers to conquer Everest. He valiantly sailed across the Seven Seas on a reed raft and was soaked to the skin by the towering waves.

But I stayed in my chair with my sock-clad feet tucked under me, warm and dry.

In story land, I took no risks. I made no tough decisions. I faced no consequences. All I had to do was dream. And dreaming is important. It's the birthplace of every invention and the starting point for every exploit.

Stories tell us who we are. They help us understand others and form windows through which we can glimpse another person's life and they invite us to be guests in another culture without the cost of the airfare.

Good stories help us remember our values and forget our sorrows. They heal us and soothe us. They inspire us and help us make sense of life. They gently challenge each rigid bias. On weary days, good stories give us a break from drudgery and time to catch our breath and rest.

And this is healthy. *But if we want to truly live, we cannot live in stories all the time.*

Because, if our view of reality becomes too distorted by fantasy, we soon become detached from reality, bored by it. Irritated by the plodding nature of our situation at home or at work. We expect to solve our problems in a page or two or have all our questions answered by the end of the movie. We expect drama and romance to be served up with unlimited popcorn. *Then we become puzzled, or resentful when it's not!*

But even worse, *if we live too long in someone else's story, we forget to live our own.*

So, there comes a point where, if we want to live satisfying lives, we need to close the book, turn off our cell phone or computer, and re-enter reality. Why? Because it's fun, scary, thrilling, and at times, very tough.

Just the kind of world where
real-life heroes are created!

If you love to live in your imagination, you may have fun exploring the following questions.

What hero, living or dead, most inspires you? How did this person learn to be brave? What real-life challenges did they have to face or work through?

When you are tempted to be passive and let others shape your life, what helps you regain your vision? Your personal purpose and momentum?

How can you use the talents and skills you already possess in more bold, creative, and healing ways? How can you encourage family members, friends, or colleagues who are discouraged or vulnerable to live life to the full?

GREAT TIMING

According to calendars and clocks, we live our lives in the following sequence:

Yesterday
Today
Tomorrow

But our emotions follow a different schedule:

Yesterday
Tomorrow
Today

How we feel *today* is based on what we remember from *yesterday* and how we *imagine tomorrow* will turn out. This means that, even before our toes touch the floor in the morning, most of us have already created a script for the day and adjusted our mood accordingly.

When we do this, we rarely notice that *more than half the evidence isn't even available yet!*

If yesterday went badly, we drag ourselves out of bed, sure today will be equally doomed. If yesterday went well, we bounce out of bed, convinced the sky's the limit and tomorrow will be even better. Because most of this "reasoning" happens subconsciously, we can easily miss the fact that *we have the power to manage the whole process.*

We choose which memories to store from yesterday and how we interpret them. Then we choose which memories to select to help us predict tomorrow's outcomes.

In light of this, I have two questions for you:

How much of today's script did you mentally write in advance?

And, how's it playing out so far?

In the following seven topics, I explore several aspects of personal storytelling and role-playing. I touch briefly on the stories we tell ourselves and our children, the stories we hear, and the stories we come to believe.

Why are there so many topics on a similar theme? You'll see!

THE STORYTELLER

Little listeners
have big ears.
Mom

Since the day I was born, I have been immersed in a sea of stories.

My mother and father both read to me when I was young, and wonder of wonders, my father also sold books! Each time a new children's book was published, he smiled and handed it to me. Thrilled to be the first to read it, I grabbed it with both hands and ran to my room. Then, lying on my bed, I boarded a magic carpet in my imagination and flew here and there, visiting the children of the world.

At mealtimes, my parents and siblings also told stories around the kitchen table. No one called them *stories,* but that's what they were, brief biographical sketches about school and work, neighbors and stray dogs.

As the conversations ebbed and flowed above my head, I began to form a picture of reality. The stories helped me know who I was and who I was not. What *to expect from life,* and what was *normal.* They also told me who was safe and worthy of admiration and who was not. As I buttered my bread, my family unconsciously created heroes and villains, saints and rogues all around me—and that was just out of neighbors and relatives!

When we become adults, I think we forget how curious children are, how curious we were. How much information we absorbed from adult conversations as we listened to our parents and carers plot and plan, worry themselves silly, or laugh at life's ups and downs. Through our wide eyes and big ears, we soaked up ideas like sponges.

Even when we were very young, we quickly picked up on an adult's tone of voice. We knew when someone admired a friend or mocked a neighbor. We instinctively understood there were different kinds of laughter, some cruel and some kind. We noticed blatant or whispered judgments. We picked up on who was *an insider* and who was *an outsider.*

As a result of all our listening and watching, we soon copied our parents' attitudes and behaviors. We also learned how to copy the people around us and tailor our words and behavior to win their approval. We learned who to avoid, what to be ashamed of, and who to seek out or impress. For better or worse, most of us became *imitators of our parents. Children who were determined to belong, be praised, rewarded, and liked.*

When we became adults, many of us gradually forgot the power of stories, particularly in our families. When we shrug off the impact of our words or say to ourselves, *It's only the children listening; they won't notice what we say,* I think we make two significant mistakes.

Firstly, we underestimate how receptive children are. Our own children or our nieces, nephews, or students. And secondly, we miss a wonderful opportunity to tell significant personal and family stories, ones that have the potential to teach, inspire, and bless our children.

Stories about who we are and what we stand for as a family.
Stories about how we wrestled with difficult problems and the reasoning we employed to arrive at value-based decisions. How we prayed our way through each challenge and rediscovered the joy of life again.
Stories about how we learned to forgive ourselves or others.
Stories about how we felt when we failed and how we summoned up the humility and courage to ask for help and begin again.

When we tell stories about our experiences, in age-appropriate ways, we give our children valuable tools they can use in their own lives. Our stories also show them what we believe and what's important.

We also de-mystify failure and give them the language they need to express their own emotions. We show them that mistakes and loss are as much a part of life as purpose and joy. We teach them about setbacks and recovery, grief, and healing. By the very fact that we are still alive and able to function after all we have been through, we role model vital qualities like faith, hope, and resilience to our children.

Because we can surround our children with stories wherever we go, at the table, on long car journeys, and just before bed. *Telling stories also saves us from making long moral speeches!*

In addition to conveying information and values, our stories reveal our moods and motivation. By the tone of our voice and what we focus on, we say whether we see life as basically fair or unfair. We cast ourselves in the role of passive victims or heroes. We share despair, or hope and a sense of creative optimism.

When we tell our stories, even ordinary everyday stories, we usually include five things:

The event and a description of who was there and what happened,
Our emotions then,
Our emotions now,
What we learned from it, and
What we plan to do in the future.

For instance, after returning from a camping trip, one woman may say to her neighbor, "We had such bad luck on our vacation, just like always. One day it rained, and we moped around inside. I was miserable, and so were the kids. After that, we seemed to spend the whole week wading through mud and washing clothes by hand. It was appalling, and I'm exhausted. I'm never going there again, and I'm selling our tent today!"

Another woman may tell her friend about the same trip and say, "It only rained one day, and we spent it relaxing, reading, and laughing. The rest of the time, it was sunny. We had a wonderful week away, and we all loved it. It was really worth packing the extra snacks and board games! I've already booked the same spot for our summer vacation next year!"

As the years pass, our children may lose interest in some of our old stories and moan, "Oh Mom, not that one again." or "Oh Dad, you've told us that story a million times!" *But while they're little, they'll listen!* Even teenagers can listen while they look the other way!

Whatever a child's age, good family stories have the capacity to give a child an abiding sense of *significance, identity*, and *belonging and these* are enduring treasures in any language.

MY STORY

I shape the story,
then the story shapes me.

Almost as soon as we learn to speak, we learn to tell stories.

At first, we tell simple stories about pets, about food that is yummy or yucky. We tell Mom about the actions of a brother or sister and insist with great passion, "He hit me first!"

Like other children, my audience grew wider when I ventured out into the world of school. At morning break, I whispered stories to my friends about my family. Then, when I arrived home, I told my parents about the students and the teachers at school.

Each time I told a story, whether it was about my pet goldfish, my dog, or my summer holiday, I unconsciously adapted the length and content of my story to suit my audience. I began to use stories to share my sorrows, subtly boast about my achievements, and reveal hints about my primal desire to be accepted.

Every time I told a story, I changed someone's life just a little. Even when I was a young child and apparently powerless, with the lift of an eyebrow, a shrug, or a smirk, I could ruin or build a friend's reputation. And I still can. So can you. Where our relationships are concerned, our words and our stories hold the power to unite or divide, hurt, or heal.

Each story I heard or told also shaped what I believed, and this began to change my life more than I realized.

As I grew up and tried to make sense of life, I strung my stories together to form life narratives. Soon they developed into descriptions of who I was. They became, not just my perspective, but The Truth as I Saw It. My truth. Once this happened, with youthful bravado and naive passion, I defended these narratives as one defends a citadel of the self, for that is what my stories had created. These stories had become so powerful, so dominant, that now I did not just own my stories; *my stories owned me*. For instance, a school student may come to believe that they are not sporty, then use this story to justify being sedentary for the rest of their lives.

Though I was unaware of it at the time, in addition to telling stories to others, I also told myself personal, private, stories.

I told myself who liked me and who did not, sometimes with very little evidence. I fabricated prophecies, and, based on these, I decided in advance whether I was likely to succeed or fail. As I grew up, *these stories profoundly affected my motivation and mood*. Yet most of the time, *I had no idea I was creating my own propaganda. That my Self was listening to the story I was telling.*

Now, when I consider our personal storytelling, I am stunned by the impact our silent, internal stories have on our lives, on our health, relationships, and careers. On the path we take through life—both physically and spiritually. When I pause to examine the stories I tell myself, I notice a common pattern in how I create them, a cascade of cause and effect, which goes something like this.

Foundation: I like to think that I'm an independent, logical thinker, but in reality, each story I create is heavily influenced by my family background and the opinions and beliefs that have swirled around me since childhood. Before I'm even conscious there is such a thing as a *personal identity*, I have already begun to form one. And before I'm aware of the wider world or have boarded a plane, I have already begun to form a *worldview*. All these factors predispose me to interpret emotions and events in a certain way, and therefore, I naturally gravitate to certain sources of information and create certain types of stories.

Evidence: Every moment of the day, I am surrounded by data that offers me *intelligence* on how life works and who I am. From all this data, *I choose* what to store and what to discard. This process is essential to create order out of life's chaos, but I can easily slide into being biased. Depending on the evidence I choose, I can feel wronged or blessed, angry or grateful.

Emphasis: Once I form a theory, I naturally look for evidence to back up my point of view. This is partly because I honestly want to arrive at truth and partly because, even in the early stages of idea formation, I want to be right, not wrong. After a while, I become increasingly selective in the information I gather. I place more weight on some *facts* than on others. I trust some sources more than others.

Ownership: Because I have invested so much emotional energy into creating my story, as mentioned above, I begin to *own* it. I adopt it as personal truth. Once I have done this, I tend to reject any further evidence and close the door on any new information. I may even believe that *anyone who challenges my story is attacking me personally* and slide into viewing them as *the enemy*, a person out to get me and threaten all I am and all I stand for. If I allow this to happen, my reasoning power wanes, leaving a leadership vacuum. Then my raw survival instincts leap to fill the gap in command and I become reactive and quickly slip into flight, fight, or freeze mode.

Emotions: Throughout the story-building process, my emotions are engaged. Therefore, as I build my internal storyline and my script takes shape, my emotions become increasingly intense. Depending on what I'm telling myself, my fears deepen, or my hopes soar.

Effects: My internal dialogue affects my mood and the tone of my voice. It affects all my body language, including my posture and the way I sit, stand, and walk. My ability to work, sleep and digest food. My sense of loneliness or connection.

Environment: Soon I create a physical and emotional *force field* around myself. Once this happens, everyone I meet soon knows it. They sense whether I am safe and worth knowing or better left alone. Even in the little things of life, I'm a person of influence, and my moods matter both to myself and to others.

Tribe: As my worldview begins to take shape, I gradually gravitate toward people who think like me. The more a group of like-minded people forms around me (or I join them), the more confident, safe, and smart I feel. Initially, this is exhilarating. I feel wonderful because my growing tribe satisfies two powerful personal drives: my need to be right and my desire to belong. The pull of these two drives is so strong that once I've joined a tribe, I will do almost anything to stay there. I will give my time, energy, and money to my group or shared cause. I may actively suppress personal volition and reasonable doubts in order to win approval from other tribe members.

When the tribe is healthy and motivated by love, kindness, and service, joining a tribe can be a very positive, healing experience, a lifelong source of joy, meaning, and purpose.

However, if the tribe is toxic, it will gradually erode my sense of self, my conscience, and my autonomy. I will start to hand over my power to the dominant people within the tribe, making them even more powerful. By pleasing and appeasing, I may also tacitly enable bullies. At first, if I am rewarded for making small compromises to fit in, I will make larger ones. I will begin to behave in ways that go against other values I hold dear. For instance, I'm likely to become intolerant, even hostile, toward outsiders and catch myself using words and phrases about them that would have appalled my pre-tribe self.

Desperate to belong, I may voluntarily silence internal warnings or gloss over the glaring mistakes of bullies. Along with this, I may become even more strident in my opinions in an effort to convince myself I'm on the right track. I may shut down and reject even close family members and friends. When this happens, *the tribe that promised belonging no longer provides a refuge but a place of imprisonment.*

Actions: Once I have *owned* my beliefs, my emotions have been stirred, and I have the backing of a tribe, *all* my decisions and actions will be affected, either for good or ill. I may even change jobs or move house to make my lifestyle more closely match my story.

All this power! Power to heal or destroy. Power to shape my identity, relationships, and personal beliefs. Because of *the story I chose to tell myself* or the story *I choose to believe.*

But what if I choose to reshape my story? Tell a different tale? What if I realize with stunning clarity one moonlit night something profound? While staring into the starry sky and the vast silence of space, I know for sure at least one of two things:

The stories I have been told are flawed?
I see that, at best, they are mere fabrications, or at worst, they are riddled with lies, prejudice, and hate. That *they are shaping me into someone I do not want to become.* Or under their influence, I have played a certain role I did not need to play and lived in unnecessary misery or pain for years.

The stories of love and faith from my early years, which I have neglected, are deeply significant?
I see with fresh eyes that, even if I have overlooked my stories for a while, they are of paramount importance to me. They are based on enduring values, which have the potential to shape and transform me. They give my life fresh purpose and fill me with joy. They make me whole and then supply the motivation and means to bless others.

What then?

Then I arrive at a mental fork in life's road, where two paths diverge.

The first path looks wide and smooth and I naturally gravitate towards it. The trail feels familiar and I readily drift into telling all my old stories, whether they are true or false. As I saunter along, I relax in the knowledge that I can come just as I am, and remain as I am, unchallenged and unchanged. I can believe whatever I like and trust whomever I like. Even if the road is sometimes painful, the pain is familiar.

But gradually, the ease of this path and my apparent freedom betrays my best good. Instead of blessing me, and helping me grow, this path leads me to an empty ravine of cynicism and nihilism. A desolate place where nothing matters any more. Where questions are stifled, logic is banished and conscience is smothered. Where my own stories trap, control and dominate me and my dreams curl up and die.

If I take the second path instead, I immediately embark on an uphill journey of reflection and transformation. At times, as I clamber along this path, I resent the steep ascent, and often pause to catch my breath. Here the fresh winds of change blow, and at every turn I encounter glimpses of truth which invite me to be honest with myself and with others. Each one challenges me to explore who I am, what I believe and where I am going.

On this path, I am invited to climb ever higher. This not only challenges my mental muscles, it also means that I will leave one or more members of my old tribe behind. So, even as I look ahead with eager anticipation, my heart grieves their loss.

I also wrestle with questions like the ones below.

Am I willing, whatever the cost, to place authenticity above habit and ego? Am I compassionate enough to be kind to myself in spite of my flaws? Can I forgive myself for my past errors and also forgive the people who duped me? And, whatever my level of investment in the old ways, can I trust God, life, and myself enough to begin again, even now? Grasp the initiative and make a fresh start?

Every day, questions like this continue to challenge me and reshape the stories I tell. But step by step I am giving this new path a go, especially with reference to my childhood.

For years I told myself and others stories that reflected the sorrows of my childhood, the losses, and the lonely days. By the tone of my voice and the tone of my stories, I said, in effect, *please pity me as I pity myself.* When I began to realize what I was doing, I was shocked. I was ashamed of my *poor me* stance when many other people had fared far worse than me.

After pausing to let my emotions settle, I saw two options before me, two potential scripts.

I could cling to the old patterns and continue to dwell on my mother's sickness. I could wallow in the fact that she died two days before my eleventh birthday and picture my whole childhood bathed in gloom. I could feel sorry for myself and resent my peers.

But I saw that if I did this, I would slide into feeling owed for the rest of my life.

Or I could choose to change the script and remember happier times, focus on splashing in the Cornish Sea with my cousins and eating sand-flavored egg and cheese sandwiches on the beach. I could remember the good times in boarding school, like having secret flashlight midnight feasts with my friends and giggling over old movies.

Then, instead of feeling owed, I could increasingly feel grateful for my happy childhood.

Later, I realized I could write a third script, (or take a middle path) one which embraced the two above. *I could honor the fact I had a mixed childhood, because, like* most people on earth, I experienced joy and sorrow. I encountered bullies and made friends. I trembled in the whispering dark and wondered what was hiding under my bed. I bent over endless homework and also ran barefoot in the golden sunshine.

When I take the time to adopt the third option and honor the rich tapestry of my childhood, three things happen:

I feel grateful for most of the experiences in my life because some have taught me about love, and some have taught me about courage and compassion.
I begin to recognize God's providence and acknowledge his divine healing.
I see myself as an active player in humanity's story and more deeply connected to others. To you and your story.

Because my inner stories have such power to shape my identity and worldview, I am trying an experiment: when I feel a narrative forming and my emotions stirring, I am trying to pause and ask myself, *What story am I telling myself now?* The answer often surprises me. Once in a while, when enough logic is coursing through my veins, I even choose to change my inner script!

Being able to monitor and choose which stories we tell ourselves and which stories we tell other people matters because our life is shaped by our stories. Though we may remember some facts clearly, we remember most things in the form of stories. Therefore, for most practical purposes, we create our own truth as we go along, often with only a slight nod toward *real truth!*

Whoever we are, the stories we tell ourselves today create the history we remember, the life we live, and the legacy we share.

RUNNING A STORY AUDIT

Where your personal stories are concerned,
whatever others believe or say,
you are your own auditor.

When I saw myself as a storyteller, my whole view of reality shifted. I realized how much power I had to shape my perceptions, mood, and destiny. When I ran an audit on my most cherished stories, I realized that some no longer served me, not because they were untrue but because they were biased. And any bias matters because our stories are more than narratives; they are building blocks of our personal identity. And as we change our stories, we change our view of who we are. We also change our beliefs about the past, the present, and the future.

This affects all our relationships.

If you feel like exploring your own storytelling style, check out some of the sample scripts I have written below. Can you hear yourself speaking?

Wishful thinking stories: "If only I was . . ." "If only I had . . ."

Limiting stories: "I'm too old, too young, too unskilled, too time-poor to try . . ."

Empowering stories: "If I break that goal down into smaller steps, I'm sure I can achieve it."

Excuse stories: "I would have been on time, but the traffic was bad this morning." "The shirt was on sale, so I saved a heap of money buying it!"

Prophecy stories: "I already know I'll fail, so why bother trying?"

Medical stories: "In the doctor's opinion, I only have . . . to live."

Mind-reading stories: "I already know what you're thinking, but you're wrong!"

Purpose stories: "I was born to . . ."

Amusing stories: "I still laugh when I remember . . ."

Stubborn identity stories: "This is just the way I am! Like it or leave it!"

Habit stories: "At times like this, I always need a . . ."

Commitment stories: "I'll stay loyal in love because this is what I promised to do. This is who I choose to be."

Caring stories: "Even though it's tough and messy, and there's no guarantee of success, I'll do what I can to help."

Comparison stories: "Of course, if I had received your start in life, I would have achieved as much as you."

Self-pity stories: "No one knows how much I suffer."

Hope-filled stories: "I've only just begun, but I'm excited to be . . ."

Fantasy stories: "If I wait here long enough, a knight in shining armor will come galloping up and . . ."

Hero stories: "I'll step forward and give it a go. I'll take the initiative."

Love stories: "I still remember the day when . . ."

As you consider the stories you tell, you may begin to realize that, in a very real sense, *you are your own reporter. You are your own internal media source*, and one of your stories may yet change the course of a war, a romance, or a child's life. So what is your dominant story, and how do you tell it?

How do you remember and tell the world that you are deeply loved?

That you are brave enough to forgive?

That your life is an adventure?

PAINTING INTO A CORNER

Even if we've painted ourselves into a corner,
we can still choose to walk out of the room.

I've never painted a floor. But I've walked on painted floors, so I know someone, somewhere, has painted one.

Today I will paint the floor of my room in my imagination. I'd love to have your company, so come on over. In your mind's eye, you can picture it, can't you? See me kneeling before you, stirring the pot of paint. When you look more closely, you notice the label says Sky Blue. You smile and privately wonder why I would paint my floor to look like the sky, but you're too polite to say anything.

Knowing the job could take a while, you grab a stool and sit down by the door, ready for a friendly chat. I dip my brush into the paint, and the bristles come up dripping with glorious color. I wipe the brush on the edge of the tin and make my first careful line along the wall. We are so deep in conversation that neither of us notices that I have started painting by the door close to you. Splosh, splash. I paint the floor with great sweeps of enthusiasm.

Pleased with my progress across the room, I gradually back away from you. Suddenly, you notice what I am doing, and you pause mid-sentence. I hardly notice and dip and splash on, filling your silence with my own chatter. Oblivious.

Now you face a dilemma. You can see me painting myself into a corner, but I am so happy with my progress, so certain of my success. Silently, you wonder, *Do I tell her now? Or do I let her wait and find out her mistake for herself?*

While you are deciding what to do and suppressing a few giggles, I reach the far side of the room and back into the corner, still kneeling. Almost done.

Almost done for!

As my feet hit the far wall, I realize my problem and look up. I see the expression on your face, and I watch your giggles burst into full-blown mirth. I watch you rock with laughter until you almost topple off the stool. I try to see the funny side of my situation, but inside, I am fuming, humiliated, and caught in the act of my own red-faced mistake. I can't deny my error of judgment, for it's glaringly obvious.

I look at you smugly sitting there outside the door, and I think how much *I hate being laughed at.* Awash in humiliation, I try not *to hate you as you witness my shame.* Though I would *love to blame you somehow* to shift the focus from myself.

But no amount of blame or emotion will help me now, so I gather my wits, summon my shredded common sense, and assess the situation. I try to calmly make the best of it.

Conscious of the sticky sea of blue all around me, I carefully rise from my knees and ease to my feet. I look over my lovely, shiny, perfectly painted floor, my pride and joy that now mocks me. I look down at the tiny corner of brown floorboards around my shoes. What can I do? Stand in the corner all day like a fool? Wait, hungry and thirsty, until the paint dries? Leap across the floor, hoping I won't slip, leaving my footprints for all to see? Climb out of the nearest window and make a run for it, leaving someone else to clear up the mess?

Oh my!

Thankfully, this time, I've only painted an imaginary floor, so I can lay down my brush with ease. But re-grouping from my other mistakes has not proved so easy.

Under pressure, how often have I painted myself into a verbal corner? Trapped myself with my own words and stories? Especially when I've been distracted by fear or by the chatter of others? How often have I allowed my inner world to become chaotic because my outer world was in chaos? How often have I lost sight of logic when swamped with loss and grief? Banished common sense when frustrated by minor inconveniences?

Too often. In doing all this, how often have I unwittingly painted myself into:

Emotional corners?
Ego-centric corners?
Opinionated corners?
Corners from which it's hard to escape without losing face?
Without feeling humiliated or suffering the scorn of others?

And how often have I responded to my self-created situation by:

Blaming someone else?
Pretending nothing's the matter?
Boldly announcing that my corner is the only logical place to be, and everyone else is wrong?

In the short term, it hurts to admit, "I was wrong." But, in the long term, it hurts everyone concerned if we stay wrong!

While we can instantly feel the discomfort of being trapped in a corner, it may take a lifetime of experience to see potential corners in advance and avoid the trap. Or to see that, by our demands, accusations, or actions *we have habitually trapped others in corners ourselves!*

Dear God,

When I'm about to paint myself or others into a corner,
please help me see this sooner rather than later.

Give me the insight to see when I'm wrong
and the courage and humility to admit it.

Help me to accept your forgiveness and

forgive others for witnessing my mistakes!

Teach me not to measure truth according
to my own level of emotional investment,

But be ready to make a U-turn, when required
to find a more honest and healing response.

And wherever my feet fall, may I live from
love, not fear, to bless and be blessed.

In your name, Amen.

THE GARDEN PATH

If you are *led down the garden path,*
you may encounter thorns or roses,
depending on who you follow.

If, at any time, you realize you are
on the wrong path, whoever is urging
you on, stop walking!

When I was a child playing with my dolls on the floor, I enjoyed listening to the mothers chatting in the world of women above my head. Sometimes tasty bits of gossip floated down around me to tickle my imagination. A typical scene went something like this . . .

As I folded a handkerchief and pinned it around my doll for a dress, a woman said sagely, "Oh, she was just being led down the garden path."

I looked out of the rain-spattered window but saw no path. Puzzled, I listened in. Oblivious to my flapping ears, the mothers discussed in solemn tones how another woman had been duped by a smooth-talking man. Their knitting needles lay still to make way for their wagging tongues as they whispered about how the woman had been led astray by a charmer. Finally, when their gossip tanks were empty, they shook their heads sadly and sighed. Then they picked up their needles and knitted and purled their way to the next topic.

Their voices have faded into history now, but their stories linger on because there are just as many charmers around today. Though, sadly, few carry roses and chocolates.

Instead, they carry ideas.

Seductive ideas. Soothing ideas. Ideas wrapped in the tinsel glitter of false hope or laced with the thrill of fear.

To lure us in; all an idea peddler has to do is offer us something we long for, something we don't yet have, and that's relatively easy because many of us are dissatisfied with life. We are wide-eyed with longing and square-eyed with screen scrolling.

Like lone travelers in a barren land, we thirst for love. Like war-torn refugees with shredded nerves, we pursue peace and safety. Like aimless wanderers wading through endless swamps of information, we hope to arrive at certainty. We long to climb the rocky path to purpose without moving from our easy chairs. We want truth without study, faith, without real connection or risk, and enduring love without commitment.

Knowing this, the idea peddlers gather. They linger by the roadside of life, either physically or in a virtual world. They loiter like mental pickpockets on the edge of our consciousness, eager to attract our attention, ready to plunder our purses, twist our values, and corrupt our reason.

In our headlong flight from uncertainty toward certainty, we hardly notice. Travel stained and weary with wondering, we want clarity. Fed up with facing endless storm clouds of change, we hardly care. At the end of the day, all we want is a refuge, a place that *stays still* long enough for us to lay down our throbbing heads and rest. And when someone offers us this, even if they are a stranger, we hand over the bulk of our intelligence and dig into our pockets for the last coins of our independence. Then we meekly stumble after the one who has promised us a safe haven, the one who holds out before us the mirage of certainty, belonging, and safety.

Lured by the smooth-talking peddler and their well-rehearsed rhetoric, we easily forget that they are spinning tales *for their own benefit* to boost their own ego or line their own pockets. And we rarely pause long enough to see they are leading us through a gate that's only painted with roses to a prickly bed of thorns, to their lair.

What on earth can we do?

For a start, we can breathe. We can step away from the rushing crowd that threatens to carry us headlong into mass hysteria. Ease up on the desperation which makes us vulnerable, and be still. We can take time to look and listen and watch. We can remember universal values that unite us as human beings rather than fears, which threaten to divide us.

We can head into the hills or to the nearest park and just sit. Ponder deep questions like, *Who am I willing to loan my mind to? What price am I prepared to pay for takeaway certainty?* And *what kind of person do I really want to become?*

I care deeply about these vital questions.

I care, too, about the story exchange that is going on all around me, the stories I tell myself and others, *especially during times of crisis,* and the stories others are telling me. I know how easy it is to give in to overwhelm, to fall into the habit of sharing ramped-up stories soaked with fear, then coming back, like an addict, for just one more story laced with drama.

I've seen how stories told and spread in times of crisis can destroy families, undermine careers, and separate friends. How they can lead people into forming polarized, panic-based mobs on streets where once they walked together and celebrated community.

At a time in earth's history when multiple voices are urging us, "Follow me," I want to actively choose a path of peace. Share stories that lead to harmony.

What about you?

As you walk along the road of life, I pray
you will keep your wits about you
and not be preyed upon by scoundrels.

That you will find creative ways to live calmly
in the face of uncertainty and be willing to

endure some temporary dissonance as you
wrestle with questions and search for truth.

That you will refuse to hold your opinions in
a strangle hold, lest they escape, but instead,
choose to hold them lightly so they can breathe.

I pray you will *volunteer to become humble*
rather than have humility forced upon you.

That you will keep a calm, loving, and teachable heart,
a heart which recognizes day by day that the person
walking beside you or living across the sea
took a similar path to their opinions as you did to yours.

Then, filled with luminous humanity and
gracious compassion, you will understand that
our world will be a safer place when all of us
seek truth together in an atmosphere of
kindness and love.[4]

ROLES

The roles you play before the world
are the visible markers of the
invisible stories you are telling yourself.

How many roles do you play?

If you consider the roles you play in every aspect of your life, including your
family, workplace, and neighborhood, you may need all your fingers and toes
to count them. Each one of these roles, whether you like playing them or not,
expresses an aspect of who you are, who others think you are, or who you
want to be.

In addition to your more obvious roles, you may unconsciously be playing several hidden roles, roles that affect all you think and do despite the fact that
you rarely name or even notice them.

For instance, if you love being with people, you may play the role of a rescuer or become a party person or social butterfly. If your life has been tough, you may slip into playing the role of a victim. If family and friends are demanding or money is tight, you may give up your own rights and legitimate needs to play the role of a martyr. And if you've recently been betrayed, you may be reading the script of an avenger and wondering if you want to play the part.

But before you drift into any role—as a hero, a rascal, or a savior—remember, others may influence the setting, but ultimately:

You are the scriptwriter and the director.
You have the leading role in your own life.

This is true for the roles
you play in front of the world and
even more true for the roles you play
to an audience of one
in the private theater of your heart.

TYPECAST?

To keep walking life's red carpet,
you may need to learn new scripts.
Repeatedly.

If you are a movie star and play a certain type of role for a long time, you may become *typecast* as an actor. When this happens, directors find it hard to picture you acting in any other role. For instance, if they have always seen you wearing a long skirt and a beribboned sunbonnet. Or if they picture you twirling a lace parasol in your gloved hand, they are unlikely to give you a role as an Olympic runner.

You and I can drift into being typecast in life too. Others may see us as *the one who always copes, the person who makes everyone laugh* at family picnics, or *the self-sacrificing soul* who is so busy washing dishes, they miss out on dessert.

If you play any role repeatedly, it tends to take over your identity, casting other aspects of your personality into shadow, where they wither for lack of light.

But life has a way of unsettling the status quo and casting us in new roles, whether we like it or not. Sometimes the role seems to choose us when we are least prepared, knocking us off our feet. At other times, we audition for the new role ourselves.

Whether we choose the role, or it is pressed upon us, we can have very mixed emotions about the changes it demands.

For instance, a few years ago, I resigned from my government job in Canberra to marry my second husband and move to another part of Australia. I was thrilled to be getting married but not so thrilled with the termination letter I received. In part, it read, "This is to confirm that you are no longer required . . ." As I scanned down the page, I saw no mention of thanks, no best wishes. Even though I had chosen to leave, every line reeked of rejection. Suddenly,

I was unemployed, and I felt like a nobody, without claim to place or status. I couldn't even walk through the door marked "Staff" anymore because my pass had been canceled.

A few weeks later, my husband was transferred to another city, and we moved house. When we met folks there, they often turned to me and asked, "What do you do?" As this is code for deeper questions like, "How high are you on the social ladder?" and "Are you worth getting to know?" I fumbled for an answer. Usually, I said something like, "I used to work for a government department that managed adult literacy programs" or "I used to be a high school teacher." Everything I said was in the past tense. Why? Because I still hadn't figured out who I was *now*.

Whenever we change roles, we face a similar dilemma. We know we are on a new path, but we are not sure yet of who we are or where we are going.

If we are living or working closely with others, as we change, their world changes too. When this happens, some people may become angry, and others may applaud. This usually depends on whether they stand to gain or lose from the changes we are making!

As human beings, we like things to be predictable (with a few surprises sprinkled in to keep things interesting). And we balk at fundamental changes, especially if we sense three things: the changes have been imposed upon us, they are not to our advantage, and we are *losing control of our lives*.

If you are facing big changes at the moment, please be kind to yourself. It's no fun to feel unsettled and lost. As you *find your feet* in a new role, you may even feel incompetent.

Why? *Because you are*. Naturally.

As a beginner, you will *naturally* tag behind someone who has practiced the role for years, whatever their role may be, whether they are a pianist or a pro golfer, a farmer, an accountant. Whether they are a new mother, or father. If, through accident or illness, you suddenly find yourself in hospital, you often feel unsettled there too. Not only worried about the outcome, but also what is expected of you. As you sink back on the starched pillows with your heart full of fears, you may feel like a hospital novice compared to the other patients.

Whenever you make a new start, in contrast to the *old timers*, you will feel like an idiot who doesn't know which way is up. If this happens, please don't despair.

Give yourself time to adapt because being *competent at life* often involves feeling temporarily incompetent in a new role. And beginner's nerves may not be a sign of imminent catastrophe but of new growth. Gradually, you will learn the rules of survival in your new setting, whether your setting is a high-rise office or the freshly painted nursery where your newborn is screaming.

Most of the time, more experienced folks will rally around you, glad to pass on their wisdom. And even if they don't, you will soon figure things out for yourself. You will adapt some of your old skills to the new situation and manage just fine.

Whatever you do, please give yourself time and space to *have a go, to try*. You don't have to rush into taking the initiative, even if you are usually a leader. You can look, listen and learn. You can check things out first, before you leap.

As you explore your new role, all sorts of creative instincts that have lain dormant for years may come to light. So here's to you. Whatever role you play, I hope you have a quiet confidence that tells you, *I'm okay*. I also hope you'll have the opportunity to walk life's red carpet once more.

In your new role,
and with a smile!

TEACHING OTHERS THE ROPES

"It's easy,
Any dummy can do it!"

So now you are a teacher. You know your way around the factory or the nursery or the shipping yard.

You're a pro. Good for you. You've come a long way.

But the new guys haven't learned this. Yet. They are still standing, sweating, at the starting line, so please go easy on them. *And watch your language!*

If you tell someone, "It's easy" or "Any fool can do it," you may think, *I'm encouraging them to try, to have a go*. But what if they fail? Uh-oh! Now they really feel dumb!

It may be kinder in the long run to say, "It's not easy at first, but you'll soon pick up the skill with a bit of practice." When you say this, you help them in two ways: you show them you understand it's tough trying something new, and you set them on the path toward competence.

If you are a leader of any kind, you may like to consider the following questions:

What kind of teacher are you at home or at work?

Have years of work and life experience turned you into a fossilized know-it-all? Convinced your way is the only way and critical of any other route? Or are you still humble, teachable, and generous-spirited? Still curious? Delighting in your own wonder-filled journey?

When your partner or child asks for help to learn a new skill, are you glad to give them a hand?

Throughout the learning process, do you respect them and make them feel safe? Give them confidence to risk trying something new? Do you patiently listen to their concerns and actively encourage them? (Or are you impatient and itching to get on with something more important?) Do you using caring words, but silently scream through your sighs and body language, *How can you be so dumb?*

At work, do you hold others accountable for their tasks but also give them space to learn and grow? The chance to develop new ideas and show initiative?

If you were new on the job,
would you like to learn from you?

THE COMPOSITE BUG

A composite bug can
neither walk nor fly.

When a caterpillar looks around the garden, I wonder if he notices the other bugs. Does he look up in envy as others fly past in a blur of wings? Or wish he could play leapfrog over twigs and leaves? Does he look at his reflection in a dewdrop and picture himself wearing the beetle's red coat?

Who knows?

But what if the caterpillar awoke one morning to find all his dreams had come true? That, overnight, he had acquired all the qualities of the garden creatures he so admired? The waist of the ant, the buzz of the bee, and the taut and terrifically muscular legs of the frog. What then?

Could he walk, or swim, or fly? No! All his dreams would have come true, but his life would be a nightmare.

We may not live in a garden or envy beetles and bugs, but we may dream away our days, envying each other. As I have!

When I was a young mother, I cared deeply for my children and wanted to do a good job of raising them. Hoping for a few tips, I started to compare myself to other mothers. I noticed some mothers were playful, others were great at baking cakes. Some mothers jogged each morning and played sports with their children after school. One mother was so organized I thought she could run a country in her spare time.

Without realizing it, I began to make a mental list of everyone's qualities. Soon this list became my own unspoken checklist. Subconsciously, I decided that if I could tick off each item every day, I could finally relax. I would be immune from criticism. And best of all, my children would have a perfect mother!

But it didn't work out that way. Whenever I focused on one quality, I forgot to polish another. Bother! Finally, I realized that such an approach was bound to fail because *I simply could not express all the good qualities of everyone I knew!*

Not one of the other mothers had *all* the qualities I so admired. Therefore, my composite list was not only absurd; it was cruel. I was placing a burden on my own back that no human being has ever been able to shoulder.

Though we may admire others and pick up a few tips from them about how to manage life, there's no way we can instantly display all their good qualities ourselves. If we pick up too many *shoulds* and *oughts* from others, we will stagger under their weight. In our frustration, we may even be tempted to take up arms against ourselves, to see ourselves as our own worst enemy.

What a waste of energy!

When all the while, our own best self is waiting in the wings, ready to take center stage and bless the world.

RESENTMENT

There are many paths to loneliness.
One of them is resentment.

Growing up, I squandered a lot of emotional energy, believing that my best friend's success meant my own failure. I had no idea that my jealousy was creating a gulf between us or undermining my own talents, the opposite of what I really wanted.

I also had no idea that my growing resentment was a twisted form of unexpressed loneliness, loss, and grief.

In this crazy, mixed-up world, there will always be opportunity to feel *less than*, to be hurt or rejected. To feel unlucky and envy people who seem to have an easy life. But if we let jealousy harden into resentment, we are destined for heartache.

For resentment is a cruel and deceitful master.

First, resentment convinces us that because of all we have lost and suffered, we are owed. Then he urges us to seek justice. If we listen to his diabolical whispers long enough, we start to approach everyone in the role of a *taker*, not as a *giver*.

We come to every relationship with empty, begging hands.

And the heart of a thief.

Resentment doesn't start by urging us to steal cars. Instead, he encourages us to steal the limelight, to sulk and mope and rob others of emotional energy. He goads us on in every game and each debate. He convinces us we must win at all costs. We must fight for our rights, even if we trample others beneath our stomping feet in the process.

Resentment makes us hijack others' conversations to tell our own tales of woe. He urges us to keep records of wrongs to display like trophies.

For instance, when I was in my early twenties and newly married, another family invited us to dinner. I was looking forward to catching up with them and eager to chat. As we stepped through the door, the couple greeted us with warm smiles, but before we could say a word, the husband herded us past his wife and led us into his study. As we passed, I heard her sigh and turn away.

Once we were cornered there, he showed us drawer after drawer of bitter letters, each one reflecting some supposed slight he had received. In his filing cabinet, he had catalogued and carefully stored a paper trail of evidence that he hoarded like treasure, proof he was a wronged man.

Eventually, we escaped his tirade and sat down to the cold dinner with our ears ringing and our stomachs in knots. In his blind quest to win, this man did not notice he was on the brink of derailing his career and losing his friends or that he was alienating his wife and children and role modeling revenge.

But sadly, he is not alone.

I also witnessed this kind of resentment on a national scale when I lived in a country where a civil war simmered. I noticed how neighbors routinely gath-ered evidence against each other, how they hoarded and shared it. I watched wronged people band together, using their common grievances as social glue. Then, to prove the passion of their cause, I saw how they egged each other on to greater strife, and to "justified" acts of violence.

I heard people weep bitter tears when bombs were rolled under their cars or flung through their own front windows, shattering glass and lives. Thankfully, most of us do not live in a war zone.

But in many families, there are one or two people who feel owed. And most peaceful societies have one or more groups who wage silent war. Groups of people who try to win by beating a social system or living at others' expense in a bid to claw back what they feel they have lost. Individuals who slide through life hoping for a free ride on others' coat tails.

In every war, each side hopes to win ground, either physically or emotionally. But when jealousy and resentment come out to play, no one wins, neither those who are robbed nor those who, by their cunning, seize some passing gain.

Why? Because war, by its very nature, erodes truth and dehumanizes us.

It turns the *haves* from people into prey. Into *them*, the nameless resources that are open to indiscriminate plunder.

It turns the *have-nots* into physical or social thieves. People who are so imprisoned by stories of their past that they forget to build a present. People who are so busy scheming they forget to learn, grow, and use their own wonderful talents for good.

Surely there's a better way for us to release our pain.
To make peace with injustice and loss.

To love ourselves and others,
and heal.

OUR CLUB OF CHOICE?

At first,
we clung together in our pain and
clubbed together in our resentment,
and we called ourselves "The Victims".

But as we healed,
we saw there were no exclusive clubs
on earth, only our shared humanity,
and we dared to call each other "Friends".

The Apple Law

If you want to reduce
the suffering in the world,
begin by caring for yourself.

Beside my kitchen window, there is a small patch of flowers. I enjoy these flowers and the butterflies that dance above them in summer.

Each spring, after I have planted the seedlings, I faithfully water them. I watch for the first buds to appear, and I celebrate each new flower . . . at least in the beginning. But sometimes I become distracted by other interests, and I forget my plants. Then the soil dries out, the weeds grow, and the flowers wilt. Some plants even drop their leaves, and if I want to save them, I have to scramble for the watering can.

All plants are naturally designed to respond to the law of cause and effect, where input affects output. For better or worse, so are we.

Unfortunately, unlike plants, we tend to have a rebellious streak. We believe, somewhere deep within, that freedom lies in being able to live above natural law, even beyond it. So we stay up until the wee hours and expect to wake up bright-eyed and bushy-tailed in the morning. We work late, day after day, then blame someone else for sneaking off with the family's laughter.

Most of the time, the absurdity of our approach quite escapes us.

We teach our children that draping a red cape round their shoulders does not make them invincible. And raising an umbrella does not help them beat gravity or stop them from hitting the ground if they leap from the branch of a tree.

But as adults, in effect, we leap from trees in slow motion daily and naively expect we will fly!

We take life's corners too fast. We squander money on sunny days and hope the rainy days never come. We nibble mindlessly on salty snacks until one day, we hit the ground with a heart-stopping thud and are driven to the emergency room, sirens screaming.

Life is full of uncertainty and the impact of other peoples' actions, so not all our consequences reflect our own choices. But many do. So, whenever we can, let's make our consequences truly splendid, a glorious blooming of all the seeds of love and wisdom we have sown.

And a harvest to celebrate.

The law of cause and effect is an old law, first recorded in the book of beginnings, called Genesis.[5] But I think of it as *the apple law* because it was role modeled for me by my grandmother.

One day, when I was only a child, she ate an apple and pulled a plump pip from the core in her hand. On a whim, she walked outside and pressed the pip into some soft soil in a corner of her cottage garden. Then she waited. By and by, the seed sprouted, and as I grew taller, the apple tree grew taller too. By the time I was an adult, the tree was taller than me. It was a beautiful leafy tree full of shiny green apples, great for munching and making pies!

SELF NURTURE

When you care for a Living Being,
you say their *being* matters.

As a young child, I enjoyed being fussed over. When I was sick, my Mommy made a bed for me on the floor beside the fire and tucked the soft blankets under my chin. As I snuggled deeper into her feather bed, I knew without a doubt that she loved me—even with my red eyes and runny nose.

But life is not all hot water bottles and fluffy slippers. Sometimes life is lonely and tough. There are days when we feel lost or vulnerable, and no one is around to care for us. No one hears our wails, wipes our tears, or puts on the kettle. When this happens, we can feel a gut-wrenching sense of isolation. As if we are in this life all alone. When this happens, what can we do?

For a start, we can recognize that such feelings are normal and that to feel, in itself, is human. We can remember that even the brightest and toughest people know times when they are weak, lonely, and sad, bereft of hope, and low on motivation.

On gray days like this, even tiny steps toward self-nurture make a difference. Actively choosing to care for ourselves as if we are caring for a beloved friend helps us create a double miracle. Why? Because we simultaneously take on two positive roles. We become both the person who extends a hand of kindness and the person who receives its grace.

There are so many simple ways to nurture ourselves.

We can place a chair in a sunny window, then take the time to relax and let the sun's healing warmth seep into our bones. We can wander among green trees admiring a leaf here and there, or linger by a shimmering lake. Even if we live in a concrete jungle, we can water a single potted plant or grow bulbs on our balcony.

I know from personal experience the difference nurturing ourselves makes.

Sadly, my mother was dismal at nurturing herself. Busy caring for others and *feeling their feelings*, she barely made time for her own health or her own feelings until it was too late.

In contrast, I noticed one of my aunts had a more healthy, sustainable approach. Alice was a busy professional woman with many friends, but she lived alone. Experience had taught her that "the blues" could creep in and darken her life if she let them. So, instead of passively waiting to feel down, she developed a few regular rituals of self-care and nurture in advance. For instance, on Saturdays, rather than working from dawn to dark, she regularly took the day off for rest and renewal.

As the sun rose, she wandered into the kitchen in her dressing gown and pulled out a pretty tray. While the kettle boiled and the bread browned, she laid out her best china and cutlery. On sunny mornings, she sometimes slipped into the garden to pick a few dewy flowers. Then she filled the tray with hot buttered toast and fruit or juice. Once the egg had boiled, she slipped it into an egg cup. Then she tucked a tiny woolly hat or "egg cozy" over it to keep it warm. When the tray was ready, she returned to her room and slipped back under the still-warm covers.

When I visited her, I watched her go through this ritual most weeks. There was no air of self-pity or laziness in it. Instead, there was a quiet rhythm of grace. When she stretched her toes out under the sheets and leaned back on the soft pillows, she seemed to be savoring life, her own life. And as she relished each sip of grape juice and bite of bread, her whole being radiated contentment.

Gratitude for life.

Like my aunt, I've found that taking Saturdays off gives me a wonderful boost. It's as if time itself changes on that day. It relaxes and breathes again, and so do I. Released from the pressures of making a living, I have time to actually live, time for myself and for those I love. Time for gratitude to God to seep into my heart and soothe my soul.

We can trace the idea for such an inspiring and healing *holy day* way back into ancient times, to when life and community first began. In one record, it states that everyone alive was designed to have a day off work each week. A day of rest to re-group and find physical and spiritual renewal. A day to honor the Life Giver and celebrate every breath.[6]

I see this "time gift" as an amazing blessing. It's available to anyone, whatever their income, age or culture. It's an example of self-nurture in its most generous form, because *it's not just about self-care for me alone, it's about self-care for us*. You and me. It's *God promoting equality, long before our generation made equality* fashionable.

When I explored the original record, I saw the plan takes equality a step further than most of us do, because it states that working animals can have the day off too.

Imagine what this would look like on an old-style farm.

Can you picture the farmers unhitching their weary oxen from the plough, rubbing their backs and pouring out extra feed? Can you see the cowboys lifting the saddles from their horses and, with a pat on their rump, shooing them out to pasture? See the children climbing the fence to sit on the top rail giggling as the horses roll in the grass and kick their legs in the air for the pure joy of being free? Can you imagine the donkeys finding an extra day's supply of hay in their stall and, relieved of all burdens, nibbling in peace or snoozing in the sun along with the sheep and cattle? Can you see the farm dogs stretched out in the shade with their noses resting on their paws?

What a wonderful gift God designed
when he made the sabbath a holy day.
A day of healing and liberation for all creation!

Nurturing Others

When I care for you
with love and creativity,
I bless myself as well.

When we live alone, nurturing ourselves is both vital and healing, but often, we live with other people. At times, this is a real challenge, but it can also be fun, especially if we get to pamper them once in a while.

Several years ago, I stayed with a vibrant lady called Gill. Originally, Gill was my mother's niece, but my mother had adopted her before I was born. So, even though she was my cousin by birth, I had always known her as my sister.

Gill had carved out a successful life for herself and her family. She was full of bounce and energy and a marvelous cook. Whenever guests came, she designed splendid meals for them.

But in quiet moments, I noticed her eyes had a lingering sadness. And as she shared her story with me, I began to understand why. When Gill was young, her parents were unable to care for her, so she was placed in an orphanage. Later, she moved from one foster home to another until she was finally adopted by our well-meaning but very imperfect family.

Her story moved me to tears.

As an adult, she cared for others with lavish hospitality, but when she was young, who had cared for her? The more I got to know her, the more unfair this seemed. I wanted to do something, however small, to make her feel nurtured, to give her some of the love she had missed as a child.

But what could I do?

Eventually, I decided to give her three small gifts, one to honor each stage of her life from childhood to adulthood. I had fun exploring the shops and wrapping the gifts. A few days later, I visited her again, the gifts hidden in my bag.

We wandered into the kitchen, and she poured me some peppermint tea, then we settled on the lounge to chat. When Gill had taken a sip of her coffee, I told her I had a surprise for her. As I slid the first gift from my bag, she put down her mug.

I handed her the small package wrapped in childish paper, and she took it with a puzzled smile. When the wrapping fell away, a small teddy bear with his arms full of chocolates peeped out at her. She picked him up to stroke his fur, and I leaned over to whisper, "This is for you as a child, for all the toys and treats you didn't get."

Then I handed her the second gift. Hiding in the folds of glitzy teenage paper were some items she was denied then, including chewing gum and mini joke books. As she opened the books and flicked through the pages, she began to open up about herself. Stories of her childhood and teenage years spilled out of her soul and poured over us both.

Finally, I slipped the third package onto her lap. As she untied the ribbon, the soft folds of a silky grown-up nightdress flowed into her hands like a shining lilac waterfall.

Even as she reached out to hug me close, I knew that all the teddy bears and chocolates in the world could not erase her scars nor give my wonderful older sister the happy childhood she deserved. They could not heal the years of loneliness she had endured before I was born.

But there on the lounge, while our discarded drinks grew cold and our tears, stories, and laughter mingled, I saw that even in today's busy, complex world, one teddy bear can still make a difference.

And a little kindness and chocolate can still say,

"I love you." So two people can be blessed.

Since that special day, I've learned a little more about nurture. And I realize that when we reach out in love to care for someone, we have no sense of being superior, no sense of condescending to their lower status. Instead, our desire to nurture them springs from a recognition of *our common humanity*, our common *value*. And in honor of this, we long to share the good things of life with them—not out of duty but out of empathy and joy.

And as we do, *we create "us" moments,* times of bonding that increase our individual and shared worth, whether we are the one who gives, or the one who receives.

CURIOSITY

You don't need beach balls
and birthday parties to remain
curious; just the eyes of a child
and the mind of an explorer.

The courage to outwit cynicism
long enough to see that wisdom
still waits to be found, and wonder
still longs to be invited out to play.

L Plates

When you remember how much
fun you have learning new things,
every day is an adventure.

In England and Australia, student drivers display badges on the front and back
of their cars showing the letter L for Learner. These badges are called L Plates.

The learners keep these badges on until they have passed their driving test. Then they tear them off with a joyful flourish!

We recognize that new drivers are learners, but we often forget that *we are all learners on the road of life*. Perhaps, if we were all given L Plates at birth, we would remember to be kinder to each other and to ourselves. We would pay more attention to the beauty of life's rolling hills and, like country folk, wave at oncoming drivers. We would be more patient and forgiving and less inclined to bump others off the road.

We would realize that when we sneer at other travelers, we are actually despising our own humanity. We would be less afraid of admitting we are lost and more willing to ask for directions. Maybe if we wore L Plates, we would pace ourselves more and enjoy the scenery. Relish the rugged rock-strewn ascents that challenge us, and the lush green valleys, where sparkling streams meander to the sea. We would be able to set our course for the far horizon but still roll down our windows to breathe in the glorious mystery all around us.

Maybe if we wore L Plates, we would remember that it takes practice to make good choices, experience to create lasting relationships, and wisdom to nurture the life of the spirit. We would remember that life invites us on the greatest road trip of all, and calls us to explore the most scenic journey on earth: the route from fear to love.

When we are learners, we never have to worry about coming away from an event or relationship empty handed. Oh, we can fail to meet a goal, or come away sore and broken-hearted. We can miss out on something we really, really wanted, but we don't have to miss out on the lesson!

Though the course may cost us a great deal. For no course is free.

Some courses cost us money, but most charge us far higher fees, for they require us to pay attention, and pay a deposit of minutes, hours or years. Pay with our blood, sweat and tears.

Each life-course invites us to change. We can accept this challenge or choose to walk away. Some courses invite us to hand over a grudge or a prejudice. Relinquish a worn-out habit or a release a practice that's harming our health.

Because change can be painful, we anticipate it with as much trepidation as having a Band-Aid ripped from our skin. So we resist. We bluff and bluster and pretend everything is fine as it is, *that we are fine*. But at last, a tipping point comes, and the benefits of change and growth begin to outweigh the benefits of stagnation. Then, excitement begins to nudge aside habit, and anticipation begins to dismiss fear.

Throughout the learning process, questions linger in the wings, hoping to take centre stage in your mind; *How much do you want this outcome? What effort are you willing to put in to achieve your goal? Are you willing to put up with some short term pain for great long term gain?*

Only you can decide the answer to these questions. Other people may lead, nudge or bully you into changing, but you have the last word. The casting vote.

What price do you put on adventure? How do you measure the thrill of opening your arms wide to life and love? The joy of embracing, in all their messy splendor, the glorious lessons of our shared humanity?

If we are learners, who then are our teachers?

Often our greatest teachers have no name, *for they are life experiences*.

But I've also encountered human teachers everywhere I go, people who have mastered at least one good skill that I'm yet to learn. People of joy, understanding and insight. People who have natural talent and are *in tune with life*.

For instance, a few years ago, I traveled home to England to see my family. One sunny afternoon, we went for a walk near their small village. About a dozen of us set out, including a gaggle of kids and several folks who were over seventy.

We began our walk high on the windblown edge of the Cornish Moors and wandered down a narrow path into the more sheltered valley. As we ambled down the hill, we passed under leafy trees and beside flowering yellow gorse, chatting as we went. Suddenly, we noticed a group of wild ponies trotting toward us on the path fresh off the nearby moor. Uncertain how they would react, we instinctively stood aside. But my cousin was so in tune with the natural world of his childhood that he stayed on the path and stood very still.

While the rest of us pressed back into the bushes in silence, he began to talk softly to the ponies, and they ambled to a stop right in front of him. Within minutes, he was gently stroking the mane of the first pony, whispering words of ease and calm. Unafraid. For several minutes, we watched in awe as the man and the wild pony enjoyed each other's company. Then my cousin stood aside, and the ponies trotted off up the track. They came so close to me that I could hear the soft whoosh of their breath as they passed.

Back here in Australia, I've noticed there are lots of role models and potential teachers too. A boy on the next farm is so agile he can scurry up a tree in the time it takes me to gasp. Last time I saw him, I drove home full of wonder, muttering to myself, *how can I brush up on my own fitness?*

The women here amaze me too. Many of my neighbors can herd sheep into pens in the morning and bake sponge cakes that rise to golden perfection in the afternoon. Nothing seems to faze them, and they continually inspire me with their resilience and cheery good humor.

Wherever we live, you and I
have a lifetime of good teachers
just waiting to be discovered!

MY PLACE

Even if my island is small,
when you respect my borders,
you respect me.

I lived in a dormitory room for about five years, from when I was nine years old until I was fourteen.

At the beginning of each school year, I urged my father to drop me off a few hours early. Hurrying up the stairs, I would rush to the room that had been assigned to me. With every step, I fervently hoped I would be the first girl there and I could claim my territory. I wanted the most roomy storage, but most of all *the best bed*.

I did not care about the mattress or the blankets; I cared about the position. I wanted the one with the brightest lighting, the one near the window. And most of all, I wanted a top bunk. *My top bunk. My own space.*

The place where I could be myself. Where I could squish my pillow into any shape I chose. Arrange my soft toys in a friendly group. Snuggle up on a wet afternoon to read a book or look down on the comings and goings in the room below.

In a world where everything else was shared, and we competed for food, attention, and space, my bed was mine. My refuge. *The place where I belonged.*

I knew it, and everybody else knew it,
and that mattered.

SELF-CONFIDENCE

The route to self-confidence
is an open secret,
one we all intuitively know.

Wouldn't it be great if we could pick up a pack of self-confidence along with our weekly shopping? Give our confidence a boost by sticking on a label that reads "I'm awesome!" Or slip our feet into a pair of high-heeled shoes to help us stand tall in our own eyes?

But that's not how life works.

Many of us struggle with a lack of self-confidence for most of our lives. If we meet someone who seems to have a lavish amount of it, we may withdraw, bluster our way through the relationship, or look sideways at them, intrigued.

When I worked at a career information center, I became curious about some of the students I met. Several times, when I visited schools to conduct mock job interviews, I noticed that one or two students in each school were exceptional. They stood head and shoulders above the rest. (If the interviews had been real, I would have employed these students on the spot.) Because these students smiled readily, shook hands firmly, and spoke up easily, I sensed they were trustworthy and ready to work.

As I interviewed them further, I discovered that most of them came from rural backgrounds. They were used to working with their hands and helping their parents in a family business or on a farm. They routinely fed animals and instinctively shut gates when they left a field. They also contributed to their community as members of local sporting or faith communities or as volunteer firefighters. These students already knew how to work in a team and find creative ways to solve real problems.

The natural confidence of these young people was not a mystery. It came from years of learning on the job. From repeated and varied experiences inside and outside the home, where they developed physical and emotional muscles; years of being given a chance to try, fail, and try again—until they succeeded.

Each time they took the initiative and solved a problem, these young people increasingly came to believe two vital things: "Whatever happens in life, I can cope" and "I have something of value to offer others."

More recently, when I moved to a rural community, I saw firsthand how these young people gained such natural confidence.

A local family kept chickens, and they were teaching their toddler to collect the eggs. He was about two years old, and as he stood on tiptoe to look into the nesting box, he eagerly reached up his hand for an egg. His mother placed one gently in his hands and told him softly, "Be careful." And he was.

With great concentration, he cupped the egg in his hands and watched it intently in case it escaped. But as he toddled after Mom, he became distracted. He saw Mom was a few paces ahead, and forgetting the egg, he hurried to catch up. On that sunny morning, he not only discovered that eggs break, he also discovered that yellow gooey stuff is hard to pick off your bare toes!

But the next day, there he was with Mom again, reaching up his chubby fingers for an egg. And again, his mother gave him one to carry. A few days later, she found him an old straw basket, so he could carry two or three eggs. At last, one bright morning, he managed to carry all the eggs to the kitchen safely. Delighted, he hugged the knowledge of his great accomplishment to his heart all day long until Dad came home. Then, with a gleam of triumph in his eyes, he climbed onto Dad's lap, pulled down Dad's dusty head, and whispered in his ear, "I collected all the eggs by myself today."

That summer evening, perched on Dad's patched knees, his self-confidence was born.

When you were growing up, there may have been no stray lambs in your life to bottle feed or calves to teach you responsibility. You may not have enjoyed the support of a loving family. But the good thing about self-confidence is that it can be born at any age, and *it can be reborn a thousand times*. Every time you live your values, realize you have the capacity to lend a hand or give and receive love your confidence grows stronger.

None of us feel confident all of the time because we have different strengths and weaknesses. Where I fail, you may cope brilliantly. And where I feel strong, you may quake in your boots. But gradually, as we repeatedly do small things until we succeed, a *can-do attitude* settles into our bones. And when this happens, we will naturally stand a little taller and hold our heads a little higher, even without buying shiny new shoes!

CONFIDENT TOGETHER

In "us" there lies
great strength.

It's true that competence makes us feel confident and live beyond our fears. But competence can also give us less obvious gifts, especially in a community that we are born into, join, or create ourselves.

In a healthy community, *we get noticed and known*. We are surrounded by people who see and acknowledge our life milestones. They celebrate with us in times of joy and support us in times of loss or crisis. And in a world where loneliness and isolation are common, this is precious indeed.

When we are part of a community, we also become more resilient and flexible. *We grow a larger comfort zone filled with a variety of skills.*

For instance, in daily life, two of my friends have very different roles. One caters for weddings and serves beautiful food with practiced ease. The other can guide a large flock of sheep through a labyrinth of gates and lanes without losing a single lamb.

Normally, if these friends swapped roles, they would flounder. The shepherd would stare at the crowd of hungry people in dismay. Paralyzed. And the talented chef would stand knee-deep in woolly ewes, hoping to be guided and rescued herself! But because they live in a community and often visit each other, they would feel comfortable in both settings, confident they could make a valuable contribution wherever they were.

Many of our families today are small and have a nucleus of only two or three people. Also, we often live a long way from our family of origin so we can't access the skills of our extended family. This leaves us with only a limited pool of skills to draw on, then pass on to our kids. *But in settings where the nuclear family struggles, the community really shines and* steps up to play a starring role. *Because people in a community share their skills, and this benefits both the individual and the group.*

When I consider *community*, three very different types spring to mind.

For a start, I am constantly amazed by the people in this rural community. Folks here live by the proverb that I heard as a child, which states, "Necessity is the mother of invention." This makes them very adaptable, flexible, and able to cope with a huge range of demands. On a typical day, a farmer may jump on his tractor and roar off down the track. But, if he is busy with the cattle, his wife may drive the tractor instead. Many of the parents and grandparents here drive school buses. Children and teenagers pitch in to help with the sheep or take meals out to the workers during seeding and harvest. They see what their parents do for a living and know their contribution matters. In summer, when the whole land shimmers in the heat, and the hay is tinder dry, everyone stops what they are doing to rush to the rescue of a neighbor when a bushfire roars through.

Such support is not only vital for physical survival, but also for mental and social survival. But we don't have to live in a rural area to be part of a community. We can build healthy communities almost anywhere.

The second community which helped me was located near our city hospital. It was run by the Cancer Council to provide rural cancer patients and their families with accommodation during treatment. The staff at this facility worked very hard to create a cheerful and hopeful community, to make every interaction positive. They employed a counselor with a kind heart and ready, listening ears and they surrounded all the buildings with beautifully landscaped gardens. Their whole aim was to serve us, to help us regroup, relax, and heal, and their kindness was almost palpable. Volunteers also came several times a week to run morning teas and help patients meet each other and swap stories.

When I heated my soup in the shared kitchen, I met residents from many parts of Australia, each one bound by the common desire to get well. Everywhere I went, there was an air of acceptance. Did a woman show up in the common room at noon still in her dressing gown? So what? Who knew what she was enduring or how she had slept the night before. Did a man prop his crutches by his chair as he spread out pieces of a jigsaw puzzle for us to do together? Good for him for making the effort to join us.

Many residents freely shared tips on managing treatments or living with the emotional rollercoaster of a life-threatening diagnosis. One woman showed me how to extract juice from fruit and vegetables to boost my immunity. Another mentioned using a certain cream after radiation to reduce scarring. Encouraged by the kindness of staff and patients, we felt more equipped to cope with our own journey. Even on tough days, *community helped replenish our hope.*

I am also deeply grateful for the third type of community which has surrounded me since birth and very thankful that our sons had similar support in their earliest years.

As they took their first steps, our boys were cheered on by people of different colors and cultures in our local church. Teens played with them or guided their childish fingers over the buttons on the sound system, teaching them how to manage the microphones and music. Leaders encouraged them to stand up the front and read, announce events, or sing. At shared lunches, older women handed them the ladle and showed them how to serve the soup without dripping too much on the bench. Older men showed them how to mow the lawn and trim the bushes. They also had fun with other children and teenagers their age, playing games in the hall or camping. In Adventurers and Pathfinders, they learned how to pitch tents, cook over open fires, and use a compass to navigate paths through rough terrain.

The boys were also encouraged to gain skills beyond the walls of the church. For instance, they noticed people who slept on the streets and shared blankets with them. Or they helped pack food hampers for folks who were struggling. As the boys grew to be men, their desire to make a difference grew too, and they volunteer in various roles. Now they are teaching their own children to be kind.

Because their community gave them plenty of experience in relating to different kinds of people, our boys also found it easier to make new friends. For instance, one Christmas, our family decided to have an early celebration for folks who were away from their homes. We offered an open invitation at church, and a diverse crowd showed up. This included several overseas students and some older folks who lived alone.

As I was welcoming the guests, I happened to glance across the room, and I saw a sight which really touched me. Without any prompting, one of my sons was approaching an overseas student. With a shy smile, he looked up and said, "Great bag!" The student grinned, and for several minutes, they examined the homespun cloth bag together; the tall black African student, bending over the small blond boy, happily discussing the vibrant colors and intricate weaving of the bag.

Because of the power of community, these two people from different backgrounds were able to meet, share ideas, and celebrate Christmas together. Their meeting was not organized, as such. They were not introduced to each other. They were simply placed in an environment where they were free to forge their own unique connection.

One of my friends recently mentioned a similar story involving her daughter who was studying physiotherapy at university. As part of her training, she was sent out for work experience. When the students returned to class, they debriefed about the exercise. Several complained, "It was so hard to talk to strangers. I couldn't think of a thing to say, especially to the older folks." Then they turned to my friend's daughter and said, "But you seemed to manage okay." Surprised, she shrugged and said, "I didn't really think about it. Growing up at church, I've talked to people all my life."

Whether it's located in the city or country, each community will develop its own unique culture, but where members have a shared purpose and focus on helping each other, young and old can flourish. Kids who grow up in healthy multi-generational communities are surrounded by mentors. They learn how to listen, cooperate and negotiate. They feel secure and become team builders who have a wide repertoire of physical and social skills to draw on. This means that, whatever they face, they are more likely to cope, to be resilient and maintain a *can-do attitude*. They also tend to pass their skills on to the next generation.

I am so thankful for all the people who gave our sons skills I could not give them.

And for the communities that invited us to explore together

key qualities like resilience, faith and hope.
All wrapped up in the love of God.

FOOTPRINTS

What tracks are others leaving in
life's sand? Where do they lead?

When I was a young mother, I did not have a mother to guide me, so I looked around for another mentor, someone who could offer me tips on managing life and motherhood. In the end, I did not find just one mentor; I discovered many informal mentors.

Each time I got to know an older woman, I quietly asked myself, *What can I learn from who she is, and from the decisions she has made?*

I noticed some women had let their lives drift for years. When their children started school, many of these women had to scramble to find work to keep the family going. Others had to search for employment following a divorce because they had suddenly become single parents. In their desperation, they grasped for anything they could get. They took the lowest paying jobs with poor prospects and long hours, then struggled to cope.

I noticed other women were more aware of life's ups and downs, and they had looked ahead. Even if they started adult life with very little schooling, they had prepared for the future. They knew their children would soon need money for clothes and schoolbooks, so they began working on their own job readiness. Little by little. They took low-cost courses, or they brushed up on their skills through distance learning.

These women fared much better. They were able to pick up part-time or full-time work more quickly when, and if, they wanted it. They had a higher level of income and job satisfaction. Their children also benefitted from seeing Mom's attitude to education. She didn't yell from her seat in front of the television, "Do your homework!" She did her own homework and led by example.

We all have different values, and some of us choose to work for pay or volunteer, and some of us choose to stay at home full-time. So I think the key element here is not which route we choose, but that, within our situation, *we do what we can to maintain, or increase, our level of choice,* to prepare for the future so we have the capacity to care for ourselves and our families. This helps us feel that *we are in the driving seat of our own lives and gives us a quiet confidence.*

After watching older women for a while and witnessing their choices, I re-enrolled in university so I could finish my postgraduate teaching diploma. This meant studying part-time through distance learning, even though I still had a baby and a toddler at home. It also involved several months of work experience. This was not an easy decision, and life was not a picnic.

If you had peered in through my window on one of those dark evenings, you would not have seen a glamorous sight. Dressed in comfy track pants, I sat at the computer. With one hand, I jiggled my teething son on my knee, and with the other hand, I typed up my assignments.

Was I a perfect mother during those years? No. Did I get all A grades for my assignments? No. But my kids were fed, clothed, and loved, and I passed all my courses. And that was enough.

A few years later, when the baby that I had jiggled started school, I was able to gain a full-time teaching position. This gave me more confidence as a woman and as a mother. It also gave our family more financial security when my husband was diagnosed with a brain tumor, and our future became very uncertain.

When we look at people with self-confidence, we tend to see it in its finished form, and it can look very glamorous then. People with confidence seem untouchable and secure. But the road to self-sufficiency and confidence, in any field, is rarely glamorous. It's often scary, messy, and full of slippery patches, where we can easily slide into muddy potholes of self-doubt.

But let's resolve to keep learning and growing anyway, building valuable life and job skills.
Let's hold our heads high and *support each other* all we can. Encourage each other to learn—
not from last-minute desperation but for the sheer joy of exploring ideas today and building a more secure future for ourselves and our families tomorrow.

GROWTH

All living things grow through change,
including hermit crabs and humans.

The changes they choose themselves,
and the changes which choose them!

Section 3: The Cocoon

Part 1 Loss and Grief

Even caterpillars can be taken by surprise . . .

Dawn had come, and the waking sun sent her golden rays to skip along the eyelashes of the caterpillar. He roused from sleep and blinked. During the night, the sky had scattered dewdrops among the cabbages, and they sparkled like diamonds in the creases of leaves or glittered like crystals in the curling fronds of ferns.

Everywhere the caterpillar looked, the dewdrops glinted and quivered in the sunlit air. Some swayed gently to and fro, suspended from translucent filaments of silk.

Dazzled by the glory, the caterpillar took a moment to yawn and stretch. The stretch rippled down his back. One bump nudged the next bump until the message reached his tail, which awoke with a wiggle. Once his whole body was awake, the caterpillar started his breakfast. He took a sip of the nearest diamond, then nibbled the edge of a leaf. All was well. And yet, somehow it wasn't. His mind vaguely sensed his gut was sending him a message, but he couldn't tell what it was. All he knew was that even in this garden paradise, some unknown something was poised, ready to pounce; that change was coming . . .

If only he could figure out what it was.

FIRST RESPONSE

Your reaction to
life's surprises
is as normal for you
as mine is for me.

Young caterpillars do not attend school on Monday morning or sit through lessons on "How to create a cocoon." And they don't thumb through tattered textbooks looking for diagrams entitled, "How to spin silk in three easy steps." So, when a wiggly little caterpillar finds himself tightly trussed up in his self-made cocoon, I wonder how he feels. Does he stare wild-eyed at the shifting canopy of leaves, where sharp-beaked birds circle? Does he wiggle and giggle and try to untangle the sticky strands of silk one thread at a time? Does he bemoan his sticky predicament and dissolve in tears? Or does he simply accept nature's timetable, snuggle up in his silk sleeping bag, and drift off to sleep?

I don't know. But I do know that when you and I face unexpected change, we react in a host of different ways. We shrug and sigh and weep. We pretend nothing's happening and plunge into endless hours of work, fueled by desperate bravado. Or we slip and slither down the oiled slide of despair.

When things get tough, how do you react? Do you comfort yourself with chocolate? Go for a jog? Lose yourself in a romantic movie?

Whatever you do, your reaction feels justified because, for you, under the circumstances, it is.

Within our human tribe, for better or worse, normal has many faces!

Loss

All creation
seems to sense
that life was not
designed to die.

In a wire pen on our fledgling back lawn, we had two orphaned lambs.

They were too old to be comforted with bottles of warm milk, so each day, I crushed lupin seeds for them and stirred in some oats. As soon as I poured the grain into their square plastic bucket, the lambs came running. They dipped their heads into the bucket and began to speed-nibble. One of the lambs liked to put his front feet into the bucket too. This made less room for two noses.

When the lambs were full, they played. Sometimes they skipped around the pen or arched their backs and leapt high into the air on their tiny hooves. Later, they curled up together, fleece-to-fleece in the sun to snooze.

But one day, the boy lamb did not come running when I poured out the grain. All day he did not eat, drink, or chew his cud. And gradually, as the pale winter sun edged higher in the sky, he sank lower. The girl lamb tried to rouse him, touching his nose and nuzzling his neck. But he was too wrapped up in his own misery to respond.

The next morning, when I looked out of the bathroom window, I saw him stretched out in the dewy grass, lifeless and still. His little woolly body looked very cold and lonely.

When I reached the kitchen, I sadly looked out again, but this time, the lamb was not alone. The living lamb had woken up and come to curl beside him. Snug and close. For several hours, she lingered near him, placidly chewing her cud, keeping him company. Eventually, my husband lifted the side of the pen and gently edged him away.

Instantly, she leapt to her feet and began to cry. For hours, she walked up and down her pen, ears alert and eyes searching, baaing for her friend, the friend who could not return.

Her calls moved me deeply. They reminded me that *death is a robber*. Always. Whatever the person's age or circumstances, death steals something from us which is more precious than gold or silver. Death takes away our loved one, and sooner or later, it breaks all our relationships. It cuts across our conversations, leaving our words to hang unsaid in the void.

It steals our hugs and our hope and carries away our dreams.

And in response,
like all living things,
we grieve.[1]

THE UNKNOWN

We can grieve for things
we've never lost
and people we've
never known.

For a babe, unborn,
bright dreams, unformed,
deep love, untouched,
or health, unknown.

In the past, I believed *loss* happened when a relationship finished or a person died. But now I know we can grieve for events, experiences, and people *we've never known. Mourn for journeys of life and love we've never taken. Yearn for goals, wrapped in regret, which languish, even now, on the back shelf of our minds.*

For instance, growing up, you may have craved a parent's love but rarely received it.

Longed to marry, but remained single.
Yearned to cradle a child, but never hugged one of your own.
Dreamt of a great career, but cared for others first.
Sought a healthy body, but kept doctors busy instead.
Pursued food security, but carried home only famine's scraps.

Who knows? *Who knows?* Who have you told?

Have you even told yourself? Named the pain? Taken the time and space to pause and acknowledge your loss? *Have you given your silent grief the same status and honor an acute and public loss would receive?* These are important questions to ponder,

Lest your grief remains unshaped,
like a deep amorphous ache within,
corroding your soul. Leaving
your chronic pain, unmourned.
Your resilient courage, unseen.

Lest you waste your precious life
being a jailer of locked-up losses,
while sadness seeps out of you in a
thousand wordless ways that harm
you and those you love.

I don't know what you've lost, nor what you need to mourn, *but you do.*

You know *how significant your loss is to you*, how much missing out on a relationship or opportunity has shaped your life. Sadly, you may never be able to fill the void your loss has left, but *you can* choose to mark the significance of your loss. Honor it.

And as your emotions heal, you may even be able to turn the energy of your pain into tangible acts of compassion and kindness. Play with fresh ideas or use your talents to create practical solutions for yourself and others. For instance, you may be able to take other children under your wing physically or financially and give them the happy childhood you yourself lacked.

There's also something else you can do.

You can hold your head high and honor your own steady resilience, the tenacity and endurance it's taken for you to come this far. To make something of yourself in spite of your loss, to make a contribution to life, even with your wounds.

And you can celebrate,

with all your heart and soul,
that you are enough,
even in the face of not-enough.

REFUGE

When you are hit by sudden loss or tragedy,
your most

Sane
Smart and
Natural

Response may be to crawl under the covers, curl up in a ball, and sob.

It may also be your most healing. So go ahead and cry. Grab a box of tissues
and let the tears flow. If you dissolve in tears, you will neither melt nor rust.
God has made you washable on purpose!

Animals go away to lick their wounds when they are injured, and when we are
wounded by life's losses, we need to find a safe place to hide too. Somewhere
to shelter until we feel stronger, until we can begin to accept the unaccept-
able, grow a thicker skin, and feel less vulnerable.

Safe places come in all shapes and sizes.

Snug cushioned places by glowing log fires.
Peaceful forests where moon-frosted trees glisten above crystal snow.
Ocean bays where aqua waves lap arcs of golden sand.
And holy places, where candles glimmer and polished organ pipes reach
singing arms toward heaven.

Whatever retreat you choose, you are seeking the same thing: one day's supply of courage and one night's supply of comfort and hope.

NUMB

Numb is not painless,
nor does it shield my soul
from words that wound.

It's a chronic ache I create
in an attempt to protect
myself from acute pain.

A refuge where I hide
until I sense it's safe
to live and feel again.

In Shock

My mind is busy grieving today.
Please come back tomorrow.

The last thing I needed was for my brain to take leave. With my grief still fresh, I needed all the intelligence I could muster. I had decisions to make and work to do.

I was smart. I could focus.

So I sat at my desk in the big glass building and began to check a contract I had written a few days before. But something was wrong. I was no longer smart, and I could not concentrate. My eyes were still at work, but my brain had already slipped away and gone back home. The contract kept fading out of focus because all I wanted to do was crawl under my desk, curl up in a ball, and cry. Thankfully, I had enough sense to stay in my seat, but only just.

After a few fruitless attempts at focusing, I realized I could not reason my way out of grief, that pushing myself harder was not going to work. If I was going to get anything done, I had to honor my emotions and give my mind and body time to heal. So I took mini breaks whenever I could. I went to the kitchen for water or delivered a letter in person to my colleague on the next floor. Each day I focused on essential work and let the rest go.

At lunchtime, I left my desk to walk in the local park. As I wandered there, I paused on a whim to watch a new leaf unfurl or stopped to smell a climbing rose. I sat on a bench and let the warm sun bathe my back and watched a gentle breeze running playful fingers through the grass. Even when I was too emotionally fragile to talk with lots of people, I opened my heart to the beauty of nature and listened to the songs of birds.

Gradually, as I slept and cried,
wandered and dreamed,
I began to rise above
life's sadness,

And my mind, reassured,
felt it was safe to come
back to work again.

When I'm under extreme or chronic stress, I find it hard to think clearly or make decisions. Unfortunately, this adds a layer of frustration to my grief or shame, and I tend to mutter, *What's wrong with me?* This is not a helpful question!

It leads me down a winding path of memories, past all my flaws and failures to where old griefs still linger. So I'm trying a different approach.

Instead of shooting myself in the foot for stumbling on life's path (an absurd idea at best), I'm trying to focus on *who I still am* and kindly mutter, *You're doing okay. You'll get through this.*

It's like casting a vote of confidence in myself.

Sometimes, one vote is all it takes to see me through the day.

SAFE PEOPLE

Some people have not
learned how to be safe, yet.
They're still waiting to be
softened by suffering

or made trustworthy by
integrity and compassion.

Others are still searching
for the courage to accept,
forgive, and embrace
their own humanity,
so they can love and
accept yours.

Even if some of our stories are painful, they still represent a kind of *personal treasure* because what we think and feel are very important to us.

Most of the time, we are careful who we trust, and we share our personal information with discretion. But if strong emotions are surging through us, we may let down our guard. Then, in response to an almost overwhelming urge to *just tell someone*, we may blurt out our feelings and secrets to anyone who will listen, including strangers and gossipy neighbors.

At first, this gives us a great sense of relief, but later, we may be filled with regret and feel we have betrayed ourselves or someone we love. In any journey of grief, we discover people who value our confidences, who know how to hold the treasures of our heart in safekeeping. We also encounter people who are life-travelers still in training. People who can only be trusted with small pearls of truth here and there, and not all the treasures of our heart . . .

Yet.

REST

For now, recovery
may be found
more in rest
than in reason.

More in lullabies
than in logic.

So simply pillow
your weary head
upon my heart,
and let your
soul relax.

This invitation is an echo of the most comforting phrase I know.

A divine invitation spoken over two thousand years ago by a man who chose to be homeless himself so he could spend his life nurturing others. Giving everyone else a soul home.

Come to Me,
all you who are weary and burdened, and I will give you rest . . .
learn from me, for I am gentle and humble in heart,
and you will find rest for your souls.[2]
—Jesus

When we are grieving, we crave many things: answers, healing, action, justice . . . each one of these has its place. But often, we need to rest first, to simply *be* before we try to *do* anything.

We need to take time to honor our loss, gently nurture our health, and surround ourselves with safe people. We need to gather physical and emotional energy for the journey ahead and bask in the divine promise that if we come to God when we are soul-weary, he will give us rest.

COMFORT

Comfort may
change nothing
yet change
everything.

When grief lays your soul bare, there is nothing sentimental about your need for comfort. You crave it with a primal hunger beyond words, and sometimes you find it.

You discover the bliss of being in safe hands and being protected by strong arms. This experience can be so powerful and healing that you cherish the memory of it for a lifetime.

God knows, even today, you may long for a refuge like that, for a Safe Someone to shield you from shame's taunts and help you to carry your sorrows.

And if you do, you're not alone. For I crave such security too. Sometimes I've found it in the love of friends and family, and sometimes in the deep inner knowing that God's Spirit is called *The Comforter*. *A Being* full of warmth and truth who understands us and sits or walks beside us.[3]

When life's shadows cross your path, with all my heart, I pray you find the comfort and assurance your soul craves. And also that one day soon, you can step out into the sunshine again.

A first-century writer named Paul sent a letter to his friends in the Greek town of Corinth. He spoke with great tenderness about the *Father of Compassion* and the *God of All Comfort*. Yet, when Paul was young, the Bible tells us that he did not see God this way. He saw God as judgmental and stern, an echo of his own angry heart. Later, when he met Jesus, his whole perspective was transformed.[4]

Many of us are on a similar faith journey. We explore, with faltering steps, the nature of God, taking many detours along the way. But as we experience more of life, we become more compassionate and come to understand in a more profound way the value of divine grace.

Then we begin to love more deeply and naturally become more godly in the truest sense of the word. For, as John explains,

God is love.[5]

A FATHER'S ARMS

When I was a young child,
if I fell asleep in the car,
my father carried me upstairs
and tenderly tucked me into bed.

I wonder if he knew
how many times
I *fell asleep* on purpose!

I have a handful of friends who are very good at hugging. (The *well-padded* ones are the most cuddly!) And what a treasure they are. While others scramble for the right words to say, these friends just open their arms and their hearts. Instead of offering me glib answers, they offer me themselves, and I love them for it.

I picture God like that, warmhearted and friendly, standing with arms open wide, ready to hold me close whenever I run to him. But what happens on the tough days when I'm too weary to run to him? Or on dark nights when I am too confused to seek him? When I feel abandoned, bereft, and alone?

Then I picture God bending down and scooping me up, just as a loving father picks up a weeping toddler and lifts her onto his knee. Settling me on his lap, he tenderly wipes away my tears with his handkerchief. Snuggled in his strong arms, my whimpers fade, and my sobs gurgle to a stop. Then I lift my head, and taking a brave breath, I whisper all my sorrows into his ear. I know he understands how I feel, because he's had lots of practice carrying heartache.[6]

This may seem like a rather childish picture of God, and perhaps it is. But does that really matter? At what age do we outgrow hugs? And even as adults, can't we allow ourselves to be tender as well as tough?

Strong as well as vulnerable?

I think we can.

TOUCH

When you have no words
to ease my sorrow or lift my pain,
please reach out your hand and
touch me with your kindness
then I will hear your heart.

If you are brokenhearted, you may crave a strong shoulder to cry on. But the last thing you need is an eager stranger elbowing their way into your personal space, uninvited. When everything else is spinning out of control, you want control over who gets close and who touches you.

Because body language is very powerful.

When touch is used with care and discretion, it can be very soothing, even healing, because touch speaks volumes when words fail us.

When our grief is fresh, others may comfort us with their body language. But as we heal, our capacity and desire to comfort others in return will gradually increase.

Then our eyes can say, "I love you," even when our lips are too tongue-tied to speak. And our tears can whisper, "I'm so very sorry" at a friend's graveside when no one on earth can "find" and return the person who's been "lost."

Even our feet can "speak" words of compassion, guiding us through a field or forest as we walk beside a grieving friend, keeping in step with their sorrow. And our fingers can whisper endearments as we massage the knots from a loved one's shoulders or stroke a weary child's hair until she falls asleep.

Through touch, we can speak
before a word's been spoken.

We can refresh a friend's soul
with the touch of our hand
when the tea's been poured
but words have run dry.

We can speak in the sacred
timelessness of waiting,
when there's nothing more
to say or do except to be.

Be, and be with,
and that is enough.

ONE MOTHER

Each memory is imperfect,
a priceless shard of history
buried in the sands of time.

I scurried here and there across the beach, bringing treasures to my mother: strands of olive-green seaweed, lumpy with rubbery bubbles; luminous white shells, pearl-lined with pink; and gnarled brown fragments of wave-washed bark, frosted with salt.

We were making a sand village together, my mother and I, complete with tiny houses, winding streets, and open squares. She was the master architect, and I was her very important barefoot assistant.

As we built, the sea sent shimmering waves surging up the sand. Above our heads, the seagulls swooped and soared in the warm breeze and called out to the high blue sky, "Come and witness our aerial dance."

All was right with my childhood world then.

When our sand village was almost finished and it was time for lunch, I found a tiny red paper flag further up the beach half-buried in dry sand. With eager fingers, I dug it out and ran laughing to my mother. With great ceremony, she placed it on top of a miniature castle, and the village was complete.

My mother and I stood back and viewed our creation with great satisfaction. Then we brushed off our clothes, picked up the bucket and spade, and walked back to our caravan for lunch.

Turning our backs on the sea, we let the tide come in as it wished. We gave curious waves the freedom to explore the village streets which we had sculpted with such care. We let them knock with frothy urgency upon each sandy door and surge unbidden as bubbly guests in each tiny house.

The sand on that Somerset beach in England has shifted many times since my mother and I built our village there. And many tides have ebbed and flowed over the land. But in my mind, the houses still stand, and the flag still waves proudly in the summer breeze.

Memory itself is a curious thing. Part truth, part imagination.

We color it with the crayons of childhood understanding, then color it again with the vivid pens of teenage interpretation. We overlay it year by year with laughter and tears, with adult traditions, prejudices, and dreams. By the time we are adults, each story lies half-buried, waiting, like priceless treasure to be found. Brushed off. Explored. Renamed.

My memories of my mother are very mixed. Like kaleidoscope images, they have fragments of joy and sorrow.

Joy, because my mother saw the beauty in snowy fields, where blue-gray tree shadows sheltered the tracks of wandering sheep. Joy, because she taught me how to fill bird feeders with nuts and stand very still until our blue-feathered neighbors flew in to dine.

Joy, because she helped me trace with soft young fingers the hard lace of the ice patterns that *Old Jack Frost* drew on my bedroom window in the night. Joy, because she taught me how to knit my doll a scarf and patiently pick up the stitches I dropped.

And joy, most of all, because she taught me about kindness, curiosity, and love. How to enjoy creating beautiful things and playing with color. How to lisp my first prayers and find love in the warm security of her lap.

But my mother also taught me about sorrow.

Sorrow, because she sometimes role-modeled anxiety and showed me how to leave the door ajar for fear to enter. How to sift through the past for things to regret or look forward too far into the future and worry about the trouble stumbling our way.

Sorrow, because she taught me about serving others to the point of self-neglect.

Sorrow, because, through the years of her illness, she also taught me about the insecurity of love.

Through no fault of her own, she showed me that someone we cherish can be snatched away without warning. Strapped to a stretcher and carried away in the night by strangers. Swallowed up by the thunderous dark, while sirens wail.

That night, I realized that security can leave without saying goodbye. That all that's safe and normal can vanish into the darkness of a rumbling storm. Abandon us, whatever our age, as we stand barefoot in our nightgown peering down from an upstairs window, unseen, our eyes streaming.

I'm sorry you did not get to meet my mother or feel her friendly eyes turn towards you. I know she would have warmed your heart with her smile. Touched your soul with her luminous prayers and soothed your spirit with her tender compassion. She would have encouraged you with her creativity and faithful kindness.

She would have blessed you,
as she blessed me.

Two Mothers

We do not remember
our own history as facts;
we remember it as stories.

As we mature and grow,
we understand life better,
and our stories change.

Yet, each time we tell
our story, for us, it is true.

Although she died a long time ago, I have never *gotten over* the loss of my mother.

Such a fundamental loss is not a hurdle to leap over. No such loss is.

If you lose a career, a limb, or a dream, you do not bounce back the next day. And if you lose a partner, a son, or a daughter, whether you like it or not, you are shaped by that loss forever. (Even if you have some say in *how you are shaped*.)

When I faced the loss of my mother, one of the things which helped me the most was a gift I received. It came in the person of my father's sister Alice. Alice had never married; instead, she had made a successful career for herself in office management. When I was growing up, she was in charge of all the student accounts at a university.

One summer day when I was ten years old, Alice travelled three hours by bus to my boarding school to visit me. She had arranged to take me home for the weekend to celebrate my eleventh birthday. Because it was Friday afternoon, most of the students had already left. There were only a few boys on the front lawn playing a casual game of cricket in the sun.

After a quick "hello," my aunt led me outside, and we sat together on the sloping edge of the lawn. I could smell the newly mown grass and feel its prickly softness on my bare legs. All around me, it was summer, and every cell of my body was alive and brimming with birthday anticipation.

Then quietly, Alice told me, "I'm so sorry, but your mother died on Tuesday." And though I sobbed in her arms, crumpling my blue school dress, the story hardly seemed real. A few paces away, I could still hear the thud of the cricket bat and the boys laughing in the shining air. Still smell the new-mown grass of summer.

From that day on, Alice cared for me like a daughter. Every few months, she took Friday off work to pick me up from boarding school. As she had no car, she traveled by bus. In winter, this meant standing in the rain or snow between each bus change, then sitting in the drafty bus for several hours.

After she picked me up, we made the same slow trip to her home while the winter sun faded.

When the bus finally wheezed to a stop, we unbent our cold limbs and hurried along the lamplit lane in the icy dark. By the time we arrived in her kitchen, we were chilled through. But she had prepared for this because a large pot of vegetable soup was already warm on the back of the stove. I devoured that soup as one who was starving; often, three bowls full of it, until my tummy was warm again. Then we chatted and laughed in the cozy kitchen and nibbled salty popcorn, rolling the unpopped kernels around on our tongues.

Throughout my teenage years, wherever she lived, Alice welcomed me into her home. She gave me a chair by the fire and the benefit of her warmhearted advice, like, "Remember to have a place for everything and keep everything in its place!" She also welcomed my friends. Several times she folded out her ancient couch so another girl could stay the night. (Once the couch folded back up on us, and we had to be rescued from its creaking springs!)

Alice and I developed a special bond, and I came to love and respect her dearly. One day, when I passed a rack of Mother's Day cards, I picked one out for her. After this, I sent her a card each year until she died, aged ninety-two.

Alice did not replace Amy, my mother. No one, however kind they are, replaces someone else. Just as no family, culture, or lost dream replaces another.

Amy was a compassionate nurse, foster mother, and artist. As a young midwife, she had worked in the London docklands delivering babies, and I think of her whenever I see the series *Call the Midwife*. When I was young, she often welcomed sick children into our home so she could give them extra care.

She was also a confident public speaker, and when I was a child, I sometimes sat at the back of large halls on hard chairs, swinging my legs while she gave lectures on health. At home, I watched fascinated when she picked up her knitting. Hoping she would design a dress for my doll or a cardigan for me. I'm still amazed that she could knit shawls for old ladies in the local tenements and read a book at the same time without dropping any stitches!

By contrast, Alice was a scholarly accountant, pianist, and gardener. She walked tall and had an air of authority about her which concealed a kind and generous heart. Often, she quietly sponsored students who could not pay their fees.

She also loved to learn. One day when she was about fifty years old, she applied to take some courses at the university where she worked. The staff welcomed her idea, and she began to attend lectures in New Testament Greek. After each class, she cheerfully studied complex grammar with students half her age.

Amy and Alice were different in many ways, with their own quirks and flaws. But both were my mothers in terms of nurture and encouragement. Therefore, as long as I live, I will always be grateful for their warmhearted wisdom, faith, and love.

In word and memory, I still honor them, for they helped to shape the story I tell myself and the story I tell the world. As the years passed and I gained perspective, I gradually changed my dominant story from,

Poor me, I lost my mother when I was young
to
I'm so blessed. I had the care of two good mothers!

(Several years later, my mother-in-law Margaret also made a unique contribution to my life. She baked great bread and knitted me a fluffy cream sweater. When we visited, she invited me to explore her colorful garden where leafy trees and bright camellias edged a sparkling pond.)

*Like me, you did not choose the script of your child*hood stories nor control who scribbled their agendas on the first few pages of your life. If you let it, this can make you feel perennially powerless. But, whatever our past, you and I can choose *how we tell our stories now*.

Which messages we *believe are true*.

And what we write by our own words, and our choices, on the blank pages of today and tomorrow.

Latent Power

We cannot control every aspect of our lives. Or know in advance who we will lose to accident, illness, or death. Or who will walk away.

But we can choose, day by day, who we walk toward. How much kindness and love we bring to each relationship in our heads, our hands, and our hearts.

That much is in our power.

Prayer

In times of grief,
you may be lost for words
and not know how to pray.

But when words slip from your mind
and scatter like beads from a

broken necklace, don't be afraid.

God knows the words your heart
can only whisper. His Spirit longs
to string them together for you
and form your prayer.

The idea that God himself helps us pray is taken from an ancient letter written by Paul to the suffering people of Rome. In essence, what he wrote was this: *Even when you are too weary and sore to find the right words, God hears the deep longing of your heart and understands.*[7]

For me, prayer is a form of spiritual reflection that goes beyond meditation.

Whether I come to wrestle with big questions or simply whisper, *Here I am*, my inner being resonates with the deepest mysteries of the universe. And more than this, I feel in tune with The One who created the universe himself. At that moment, compared to God, I am smaller than I have ever been, and yet I sense that, through him, I am destined to be someone greater than I have ever been before.

Head held high. Healed and whole.

After writing this piece, I came across a short story about God and our prayers.[8]

The story is set in the throne room of the universe, where everything is glorious beyond compare, where the very air shimmers with rainbow light.

As we watch, twenty-four elders bow low before the throne. In outstretched hands, each elder carries a gift for God: a beautiful golden bowl. A bowl?

As I read a little further, my heart skips a beat, for the gift the elders bring to God in their bowls, while thousands of angels sing, is our prayers. My brokenhearted cries of grief. Your whispered pleas. Our joyful gratitude for life.

My heart was touched when I realized that each stumbling word we utter in the raw honesty of our humanity is carried all the way to the glorious, compassionate Throne of Grace where the God of love reigns.

Oh yes!

WHY?

The question "Why?" may take
only a moment to ask, but
God knows it may take
an eternity to answer.

If you are asking "Why?" today, I feel for you.

You are asking one of the biggest questions in the universe.

One that touches the heart of meaning and life itself.

In the beginning, when grief is still fresh, when we cry out "Why?" we may not want answers as much as comfort, to have someone listen to our pain, someone with arms strong enough and long enough, to embrace us in our tear-soaked rage. Someone whose heart is big enough to give our pain shelter for the night.

Someone—God, woman, man, or child—who has steady, unfazed, generous love to spare.

Love to share.

ALL THERE IS TO KNOW

Father and child were strolling along the beach,
wriggling their toes in the sand and
filling their pockets with shells.

"Father" said the child, flinging eager arms wide,
"I want to understand everything there is to know."
The Father chuckled.

"Can you hold all the sea in your hand?"
The child giggled, and jumped a splashing wave.
"No, but I can swim in it, just like you!"

"Good. Then can you dig up all the land?"
The child leapt over a skein of seaweed,
"No, but I can build castles in the sand."

"Perhaps then," He teased, "you can breathe
in all the air." The child skipped ahead,
"No, but I can turn cartwheels through it. Look!"

The Father cheered and scooped the child up
in his arms. They spun together laughing,
eyes shining, filling their hearts with love and

Sending white gulls swirling high into the blue.
Then, hand in hand, they strolled on along the sand
Mortal child, with Immortal Father. Content.[9]

IN MEMORIAM

When we mark life's milestones
and honor their significance,
we confirm our own value.

I had a dilemma. My wedding anniversary was approaching, and I was no longer married.

My husband and I had been through so much together. We had worked in several countries and raised two sons. He had endured a couple of bouts of cancer and still had the courage and tenacity to work long hours to support our family. But we had recently separated, and I was sad and sore. I had no idea what to do. How could I *celebrate* an anniversary alone?

At the time, I had no idea how common this *anniversary issue* is.

If a parent loses a child to cancer, how do they remember their child's birthday? Do they bake their favorite cake, then comfort themselves by eating slice after slice? Or make a donation to a children's charity?

Do they drive to the beach where they built sandcastles together? Then stand on the shore where the high gulls cry and stare, sightless with memories, over the empty sea?

If a beloved partner or friend dies, do you buy a bunch of red roses and place them to wilt, petal by petal, on the grass-choked grave? Do you call family around to your place to share memories over coffee and croissants and laugh until you cry? Or do you hike high into the wilderness with friends, muscles burning, until you can see forever? Then, when the light fades, tell stories while the damper bakes and wood smoke drifts upwards to the circling stars?

Because our culture tends to tiptoe around death and be speechless in the face of grief, we are often left to navigate anniversaries alone. And *alone* is hard.

If you have lost someone recently, several questions may be drifting through your mind, seeking solace.

How can I remember their love but not the pain of their loss?

Will it help if I ignore the coming anniversary and consciously focus on something else? Or should I take the day off work and wade into the pain? Bury myself in photo albums and weep?

Will I feel better if I do something practical, like repaint their bedroom or plant a tree in their honor?

Perhaps the most confronting questions are the ones we hardly dare voice, like, *How do I handle the surging rage inside me? Rage that my loved one abandoned me and dared to die?* (We can ask this question, even if logic tells us that our beloved had no choice in the matter!)

Questions may tumble around us for weeks, quietly ganging up on us as the anniversary approaches. Ambushing us.

How do I contain my resentment over the aching void they have left in my life?

How do I remember them in ways which honor the complex truth of our relation-ship? Acknowledge the strands of adoration and irritation woven throughout our days together?

When is it time for me to "move on?" To let the memories naturally fade?

Most of the time, we don't voice these questions. They ebb and flow just below the surface of our consciousness. This means that even if we are surrounded by other people, we can feel as if we are wading through a dark swamp alone.

And, as I said, alone is hard.

Because I have traveled for a while with questions like this, I have decided to share my story in case it brightens the path for you.

This is how I chose to celebrate my wedding anniversary.

Because I had no script to follow and no previous experience to fall back on, I was flying blind. But after several days of pondering, I made a plan:

First of all, I chose to mark the significance of the anniversary, not ignore it. I had devoted almost thirty years to my marriage and raising our sons—more than half my life. And I reasoned that if my life mattered, then this milestone mattered too.

Secondly, I wanted to take charge of the event. I wanted to turn something painful and puzzling into something healing and good, to transform it. So silently, I began to pray, *Please God, show me how I can make love, not pain, win the day.*

In response, this is what I felt inspired to do.

I decided to contact thirty people who had played a significant role in my life, one for each year I had been married, and write them a thank-you card.

After work, I started making the cards. On the front, I placed a picture of a butterfly because this symbol spoke to my heart. It reminded me that one day I, too, could emerge from my *cocoon of grief* to fly again.

I also included a brief printed message explaining the purpose of the card and thanking the person for their love. I prepared cards for a wide range of people. Beginning with my sons and close family members, I added former schoolteachers and university lecturers who had encouraged and inspired me.

Then I included significant friends, neighbors, and co-workers. Once I began the list, I was surprised at how quickly it grew. Soon there were twenty names on it, then thirty.

I found this process very healing.

Each evening after work, I sat down to scribble personal messages in the cards. And as I did, *my mind was constantly drawn out of my grief to focus on gratitude.* With each card and each happy memory, I began to see how blessed my life had really been. As the pile of cards grew, I realized something that meant a lot to me. I saw how many people had willingly invested their time, energy, and resources into bringing me up, teaching me, and befriending me.

I felt humbled by their generosity and comforted by their legacy of kindness.

Instead of looking in the mirror and seeing *a failure* staring back at me, I began to see myself through their eyes, as someone worthy of love, care, and attention. If each one of these friends, teachers, and family members had believed I was worthy of nurture, then maybe I really was!

By the time my wedding anniversary arrived, I was ready for it, armed with thirty thank-you cards to drop, with a satisfying thud, into the mailbox.

As my act of defiant gratitude in the face of loss.

My vote for hope in the face of despair.

My act of love.

CREATING MEANING?

Some experiences come
carrying meaning;
others bear a begging bowl
for us to fill.

Life has many defining moments, points in time that help us measure and discuss "before" and "after."

Sometimes these moments mark a great win, at other times, a great loss. It's the losses which seem to affect us the most. They touch us so deeply that we long to make sense of them. But sometimes, even after many months or years, all meaning eludes us. Then our loss can seem not only sad but senseless, a soul-searing waste.

When this is the case, and we cannot *find* meaning in the event itself, we may still be able to *create* meaning from it, to actively give it purpose ourselves by how we respond.

Many times I've struggled with seemingly senseless pain and spent a restless night resenting the loss and the waste. Then I've met someone a few days later who is going through a similar experience, and we naturally click. Because I have a gut understanding of their pain, I don't judge them or offer shallow advice. I don't rush to solve their problems. Instead, I simply accept what is, and in doing so, accept who they are, who we both are.

As we unite as equals in our common humanity, in our unfathomable losses, personal ego slips away, and a miracle happens. For we create a mutual empathy that dissolves each other's loneliness.

But what if you cannot find such a friend? What if you walk alone and never tell awestruck crowds your inspiring story?

Please don't give up.

Because you may already be encouraging more people than you realize. Every time you get out of bed and have the raw courage to simply put one foot in front of the other, you are sending us a powerful message. You are telling everyone who sees you that *whatever their own struggles, tough stuff can be endured*.

Sometimes just by living,
you give us the priceless
gift of hope.

Thank you.

VALUES

If you sail through stormy seas
and toss your values overboard,

What chart and compass will
guide you safely home?

Several years ago, I suddenly found myself tossed about in a great ocean of grief and change. Like a sailor washed overboard into the foaming deep, I felt abandoned. Left to drown. Nothing seemed sure or stable, and no life raft floated within reach of my desperate fingers.

In the stormy days and nights that followed, I sent many heartsore questions spinning silently out into the dark. For instance, *Does all that's happened mean my values are useless? Is faith in God a waste of time? Is love worth the pain, or should I just forget it?*

Suddenly, in the midst of all my anguished doubt, a voice deep within me responded in a way I did not expect.

Don't give up on your values, my heart said firmly in an echo of God's earnest plea. *Your beliefs and values are not void. This is the very time your values matter. This is their finest hour.* Really? Wow! I didn't think my finest hour would feel like this! I'm so vulnerable and scared, I almost missed it!

So I kept my values. All of them.

Even when life was tough, I held on. At times, my courage faltered, and my faith wavered. I mumbled and bumbled and wept. But one way or another, with prayer and the support of friends, each time I dropped my values, I scooped them up again and reinstalled them in my mind. I determined to act from love, kindness, and integrity, *however others acted*.

Looking back now, I can see this was a pivotal decision. Because when I chose to hold on to my beliefs and values, I asserted my right to choose for myself the kind of person I wanted to be. And this was a vital step in my recovery.

There are many times when life's setbacks and personal earthquakes have shaken me more than I care to admit. I have faltered and fallen because that's what human beings do. But my experiences have not undermined my conviction that faith, hope, and love are important. Instead, each experience has confirmed how vital these qualities are. Vital for my life today and for all my tomorrows.

As I write this, I am wondering what moral choices you are facing. Are you at the crossroads between telling the truth and living a lie? Is integrity wrestling with compromise in your heart? Do you feel like cheating, giving up, or giving in? Is all that's good in your mind and heart going head-to-head with all that's apparently easy or convenient? With despair? Can you feel yourself slipping into corrosive bitterness, when you know in your heart that forgiveness is the path to reconciliation and healing?

Whatever is happening in your world right now, please, as much as you can, turn towards integrity and choose to live by your highest values. Seek ways to strengthen your spirit and nurture body and soul. Give yourself permission to freely ask for help when you need it and gather friendly support. Vow to stick to your own deepest promises.

Because every time you decide
to do what's right in the dark,
all alone, when no one else can see,

It changes who you become.

With every brave decision you make,
you unconsciously leave a trail of light
in the world for us to follow.

So, thank you in advance,
and God bless you.

BROKEN HEART

Oh no, I've broken it again!

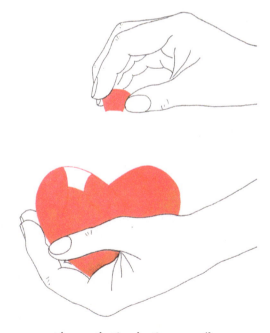

I know, that's why I've come![10]

Just when we feel we are "getting it all together," we may be hit by a new tragedy that shatters our hearts once more.

If this happens, we may lie awake and wonder, "This time, do I have the strength to make it through?" Sometimes the answer is "Yes," and when dawn comes, we rally and begin anew. Sometimes the answer is "No," and dawn does not bring relief, only the knowledge that we need help.

Help from someone, somewhere, today.

If you are facing repeated losses or setbacks, a sequence of tragedies or episodes of bad news, I feel for you. I pray you have the energy and courage to seek the local help you need.

And seeking, find it.

Healing Words

What are the most healing words
you've ever heard?

These are mine.

I found them in the writings of a first-century doctor called Luke, who took notes on a public speech he enjoyed. The main theme of the speech was this:

In response to God's loving Spirit
I've come to encourage you and
gently bandage up your broken heart.

I've come to heal your bruised soul
and set your spirit free.[11]
—Jesus

Adoption

We adopt fears
like children, then pour
our energy into raising them
as if they are our own.

There was a time when I was surrounded by fear.

Everyone I met seemed to be anxious about something, in pain of one kind or another: fragile health, money issues, fractured relationships. I also had a few fears of my own, and little by little, I became saturated with fear.

Busy with all my gloomy musings, I hardly noticed hope was on the brink of drowning.

One day, in the gray quiet of dawn, I realized I had been waking up each morning expecting things to go wrong, dreading more bad news. On edge. Walking on eggshells. Afraid that if I stepped boldly onto life, it would collapse under me, and I would fall beyond the reach of help.

And I was tired of living like this.

So, as the first birds began to sing, I sat quietly by myself while the others slept and really looked at my fears. To my surprise, I realized *most of them were not my fears*. They were fears of other people, which I had adopted as my own, then raised without realizing it.

They were absorbed and inherited fears that had moved in, uninvited, and stayed for years, lingering in my mind like mental squatters. Like toxic terrors determined to live rent-free, fed by my imagination. So, with great bravado, I firmly pushed them out of the door, turned the key, and refused to let them back in!

(Though, I will admit, they sometimes pop in through an open window, and I need the broom of prayer to sweep them out again!)

FEAR LESS

My concerns are really my fears
dressed up to go out in public.

Fear always seeks to defend itself,

But security is free to be curious.

To listen, explore and understand.

Since birth, each one of us has created a fear pattern. These patterns are like a network of red warning lights linked by strands of memory and emotion.

Our patterns naturally change as we grow up. With each stage of life, new fears come into focus, and others fade. For example, a child often fears the dark but loves growing older. In contrast, an adult may walk along a dark road with great bravado and appear fearless but then return home and open a packet of hair dye because he or she fears growing old!

When we mature or acquire new skills, some fears may disappear completely. For instance, most adults don't check under their bed for monsters or need the comfort of a teddy bear before snuggling under the blankets.

In addition to our common human fears, which help us avoid danger, we have added our own unique fears. We fear public speaking or launching ourselves into the swimming pool from the high diving board. We fear getting lost in strange cities or having a crowd of friends over for a meal.

One of the paradoxes of life is that *we can fear both failing and succeeding*. Perhaps because both separate us from the herd and make us visible.

Many of our subconscious fears have been handed down to us by previous generations. Others are new minted in our own minds. But whatever their cause, each fear stunts our life. It influences what we say, what we anticipate or dread, and the kind of relationships we form.

When we are afraid, we think small, act small, and shrink back from adventure. (And if we were turtles and carried shells on our backs, we would crawl into them and hide.)

Our fears keep us from sleeping. Then our loss of sleep makes us grumpy, reactive, and even more afraid. (Unless we consciously notice the negative loop we are forming and create circuit breakers of sanity.)

Because I long to live beyond my own, very human, fears I love Scilla Elworthy's tender and inspired idea. She suggests that if we are lying awake at night, paralyzed by fear,

"The only thing to do is to get up, make a cup of tea,
and sit down with the fear like a child beside you.
You're the adult. The fear is the child.
And you talk to the fear and you ask it
what it wants, what it needs.
How can this be made better?
How can the child feel stronger?
And you make a plan . . ."[12]

When I catch myself feeling anxious, I try to remember Scilla's words and stop long enough to ask *what's really bothering me?* Often, it's something I haven't even admitted to myself, a fear that's been lurking in the background, trying to hide. Once I discover and named it, I can make my plan, explore options, and decide where to focus my energy. Even if I only do something small, it makes me feel more in control, and that's a great help when my life feels messy and overwhelming!

You and I may face similar circumstances but make quite different plans because we have unique trigger points and different things which scare us.

Life is complex and challenging, and we will never escape fear completely (partly because some fear has a legitimate role in protecting us). But little by little, we can help each other to be brave, find ways to grow stronger and actively share ways to release the bottled fear we call anxiety. We can call a friend if we need to, or cry on their shoulder either figuratively or literally.

One day, when I felt anxiety building, I thought . . .

You know what?
Nobody needs my fear today.
Not my neighbor.
Not my husband.
Not my friend.
Oh my, I don't
even need it!

So I told my over-active imagination to hush and got busy making my plan instead!

On a personal note . . .

Many times, as I have been writing this book, I have been afraid, and my fears have stalled the work for days, even weeks, at a time. I have been afraid of making a fool of myself, of publishing deadlines, and of being misunderstood. I have been afraid of being successful and known and of being a failure and mocked. I have been afraid of being vulnerable and baring my heart.

Each time, once I recognized my fear, I found myself at a crossroads.

I could choose to abandon the book. Close the computer, shove my paintings into a drawer, and forget them. (On the one hand, this would have been a great relief, and on the other hand it would have caused me deep personal grief.)

Or I could choose to go on.

Instead of giving up, I paused for a while. I prayed. I dropped my head onto my arms and wept. Then I picked up my pen and my paintbrush and started again. You hold this book in your hands because I believed that somehow, someday, my story would bless you. And because, when I became lost in a maze of words, I had people who prayed for me and who cheered me on.

And also because, at the deepest soul level, I trust in God, the Being who whispers in all the world's languages, *Because of who I AM, you can live from love, not fear.*[13]

And I believed Him.

TABOO

The greater our fear,
pain, or confusion,
the more we wrap it
in silence.

Every culture has words that are taboo. In addition, each family selects their own taboo words and adds them to the local list.

Taboo words change with time. Each generation thinks they are braver than the one before, not realizing they have just chosen different words, or ideas, to send into exile.

Because taboo words trigger a sense of fear, shame, or embarrassment, people tend to tiptoe around them, sometimes unconsciously, and sometimes deliberately. A parent may even say to their son or daughter, "Oh, we don't talk about that in our family."

I wonder which words are taboo in your home.

Growing up, were you free to talk about divorce, body odor, or mental illness? Could you freely discuss politics, sex, God, or money around the kitchen table? Did your mother or father discuss depression, self-worth, or failure, and how to live beyond it? Were they open about both the tough and tender stuff?

Mmmm . . .

When we send words into exile, we rarely see we are reducing our own power to cope, to cooperate with others and to find solutions. For instance, if you could not talk about money in your home, how can you rally around to support an uncle who is going bankrupt? How do you speak to your partner about credit card debt? Raise his or her spending habits? The urge to gamble? Who will role model healthy money management to your children?

If two taboos are combined, the effect is doubly crippling on a family. For instance, if you cannot talk about *money* or *death* in your home, how will you discuss a succession plan for your business with your partner or children? How will you create a Will that honors and protects the people you love?

In challenging times, how can you say the *right thing* if all the painful words have been hidden? Tucked away in dark corners? Lost? How can you and your loved ones bond together in joy or in grief? Comfort each other and say, "You mean the world to me"?

If no one in the family is allowed to mention death, what do you say when your father is dying? Do you pretend nothing's happening? Do you and your father wear false smiles all day, then weep separately in silence at night? Do you wait until the funeral to sob, "I love you"?

And if all the tricky words have been banished, when your life becomes messy and embarrassing, *can you be sent into exile too?*

When you struggle with something taboo, are your friends and family *lost for words*? Do they talk endlessly about the weather and next door's new kittens instead of asking, "Are you okay?" Do they rush to turn on the television or try to look busy when you visit?

Some families are so well trained in being silent that a herd of elephants could waltz through the room, and no one would say a word!

If this sounds like your family, you may feel lonely, puzzled, or deeply hurt.

When times are tough, you may long for your mother's support but not receive it. You may crave your father's encouragement but notice he buries his face in the newspaper as you approach. If this goes on for a while, you may desperately wonder, *Can anyone see what I am going through? Does anyone really love me?* At times like this, it's easy to feel abandoned, cast off. *But their silence may have nothing to do with you.* Your family may simply be so tangled up in their taboos that at this critical time, they are literally *tongue-tied.*

So, what can you do?

For a start, you can acknowledge that your family may have developed a culture of silence for a reason. Some of the older folks in your family may even feel that it's not "normal" or "right" to discuss certain topics. For instance, some of my family members would routinely say, "We don't wash dirty linen in public" if something socially or morally awkward was even hinted at. By this, they meant that anything shameful or embarrassing had to be kept private.

One of my aunts used to say, "least said, soonest mended" if she saw a family or neighborhood row brewing. As a teenager, I learned to rapidly changed the subject if she said this, even when her shutdown sometimes frustrated me. Now I understand life better, and I can see that her verbal nudges were often useful. They stopped me gossiping or grumbling and helped me move on mentally and emotionally.

When we understand others more, *it helps us take their silence less personally*. We begin to see their silence *as part of who they are, rather than as an act of rejection of who we are, or are not*.

I've also noticed that many people who say very little *do a great deal*. Even if they are *lost for words*, they are often wonderful at helping out in more tangible ways. Without being asked, *they show up rather than speak up*. They bring homemade cake. They pop in to fix things. They mind the baby or offer to take the kids to the park. Without saying a word, they say by their actions, *I love you, and I've seen what you're going through. I can't find the right words to express how much I care, but I'm here for you, and I'm bringing you what I have.*

And what they have is often very precious!

Having said all this, you may still crave verbal reassurance or a meaningful discussion. If this is the case, you may choose to break the silence yourself. Be the one to retrieve abandoned words, then gently and courageously string them together to send echoes of hope into the social void.

Or you may keep looking around your extended family until you find someone wise, someone who can still speak, an uncle who has weathered adversity and been made brave by experience, a cousin who has gained compassion through personal suffering.

If you can't find anyone in your family to talk to, you may find a counselor, doctor, or pastor in the next street, someone with the courage and training to reach past social taboos and listen to your story.

One day, if you are especially blessed, you may even meet a friendly stranger in the local park and begin to chat naturally. Sitting together on a sun-warmed bench under blossoming trees, you may begin to share ideas without any barriers or expectations.

Later, when you part company, you realize that you have sent your life story spinning into the spring air, and someone has caught it with open hands and welcomed it with a kind heart. You feel understood, perhaps for the first time, as if you have bumped into a kindred spirit and been blessed.

A person who has developed the grace to listen like this is *an unsung hero*.

They know that life is complex, and they choose to understand you without judgment or prejudice. They are grounded enough to talk naturally and freely about emotionally volatile subjects without catching fire themselves.

They can do this, not because they are careless with words, but rather *because they have accepted their own gloriously flawed humanity, so they can be at ease with yours*. As you walk and talk with a person like this, you can feel yourself relaxing, feel your heart being warmed, embraced.

Instead of feeling isolated, you feel a deep sense of connection. You feel that, even now, even in the midst of all this, you are okay. You sense the healing bliss of being heard and understood. You bask in the warmth of their love until your shame starts to evaporate, and your fears begin to melt.

And hope stirs.

By and by, you grow stronger. You live through each impossible event. You become more comfortable with who you are and with the realities of life. Your wounds start to heal.

Several months later, you pause in the local park again. You admire the beds of summer flowers, slip onto a sun-warmed seat, and close your eyes. When you open them, you see a stranger sitting on the other end of the bench. They look lonely, so you smile. You begin to chat. And gradually, without thinking, you naturally reach beyond traditional taboos to listen to their story with all your heart.

You make the time to care.

Then, as you take your leave with a smile and a hug, you suddenly realize something profound. *You have grown into a healer yourself!* You are now the kind of person you needed earlier, a person full of compassion and courage, someone who can look beyond taboos to the beating heart of the matter.

You have become a safe haven, where wandering souls can come to lay their threadbare taboos to rest.

I experienced something like this when I was a new student at university.

I noticed that some of the staff wrapped themselves in a professional aura. They came to class with all their learning but did not bring themselves. They carried briefcases of knowledge but left their hearts at home. However, a few teachers spoke to us openly, as equals, and we felt they understood us. One young couple told us that married life was sometimes hard, that after the honeymoon, it took patience and kindness to get along with another person.

Because this couple trusted us with their truth and openly voiced their very human joys and sorrows, they gave us the courage to name and voice our own. In the classrooms and hallways, they took the time to *see us*. They helped us accept and explore our own humanity.

Their ability to reach beyond taboos and their authentic courage, warm and inspire me still.

Oh, the comfort, the inexpressible comfort
of feeling safe with a person;
having neither to weigh thoughts nor measure words,
but to pour them all out, just as they are,
chaff and grain together, knowing that a faithful hand
will take and sift them, keep what is worth keeping,
and then, with a breath of kindness, blow the rest away.[14]
—Dinah Maria Mulock Craik

RESTORE ME

When my pride
takes a tumble,

Or my heart
is wounded,

Please heal and
restore my soul.

King David was a warrior, poet, and composer. He was also athletic and charming, and the women adored him. They even made up songs about him and thronged the streets to sing and cheer when he rode by. As a young man David basked in their praise and adored them right back! [15]

But, there is something puzzling about David's story, because, although he became a prolific composer, we have no record of a love song for a woman. Instead, David chose a quite different muse. Full of passionate awe, he reserved his most lyrical poems for The Maker of the earth, sea, and sky.

By his admission, his ardent adoration stemmed from his own life experience.

Because, before David became famous, *he started life as a nobody child. The youngest son of a farming family where he was out ranked by a parcel of handsome and successful big brothers.* Brothers who probably thought David was just a naive kid with his head in the clouds. A pest. So they banished him with his songs and questions out to the fields to herd sheep. Out of sight, out of mind! [16]

But God kept David on his mind.

He noticed David out there alone under the big open sky. He saw how faithfully he nurtured the ewes and protected the lambs. The noticed his courage when he faced down lions and bears. He heard David's prayers and saw his alert and enquiring mind. So, one day, God sent a holy prophet to call David in from the fields and say, in effect, "*I want you to be a Somebody. Others may have missed it, but I see great potential in you. I've noticed your loyal spirit. Your* warrior heart, and I want you to care for my people and lead them."

Wow!

As he grew older, David pressed on through many setbacks and struggles. But, strengthened by God's belief in his potential and fueled by a passionate desire to serve, David repeatedly bounced back from discouragement.

Eventually, David was crowned king. But, even in the palace, surrounded by courtiers, he did not forget his humble beginnings or the fields of his boyhood. One evening, he stepped down from his royal throne, laid aside his crown and bent over his harp. Strumming it softly, and testing out lyrics here and there, he began to compose a song. A royal gift to the heavenly Good Shepherd, who remained his closest friend.

The LORD is my shepherd,
I shall not be in want.
He makes me lie down in green pastures,
he leads me beside quiet waters,
he restores my soul.
He guides me in paths of righteousness
for his name's sake.
Even though I walk
through the valley of the shadow of death,
I will fear no evil,
for you are with me;
your rod and your staff,
they comfort me.
You prepare a table before me
in the presence of my enemies.
You anoint my head with oil;
my cup overflows.
Surely goodness and love will follow me
all the days of my life,
and I will dwell in the house of the LORD
forever.[17]
—David

Whenever I hear David's song, I feel less alone and more able to face tough times with courage because I know God also walks beside me. *Calls me to be a somebody. You to be a somebody.*

Today you may feel fit as a fiddle, bouncing with energy and vitality. Or you may not. The rocky path of life may have left you physically drained and soul-weary, in need of a stroll through a green valley with a friend. Longing to spend time with someone who has the skill to soothe your soul and restore your life.

A holy Companion who still works miracles
in hearts and lives. The Healer whom
David sang about in his poetic song.

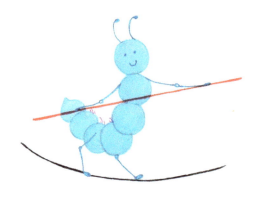

God restores my soul. David

Footnote 25

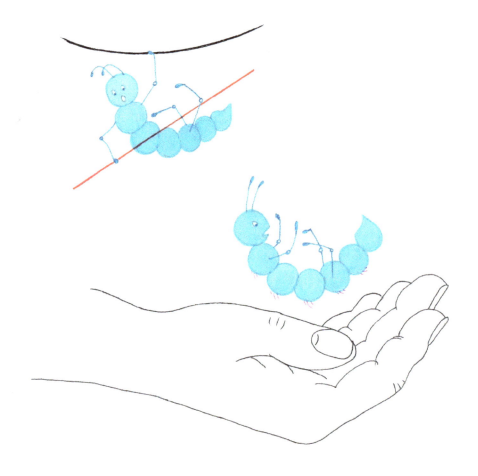

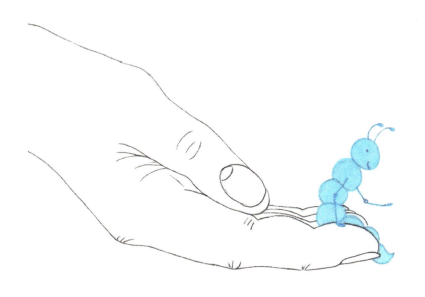

Recovery

In life, we face many head-on collisions.
Some even involve cars.

If a friend is in an accident, you have a rough idea of what to expect: lots of pain, tests, and waiting around—then, hopefully, a gradual return to good health.

But if the same friend experiences an emotional injury or a deep loss that affects their heart or mind, you are less sure what to expect. How long will they take to heal? You don't know. What can you do to help? You can only guess. The time it takes for a car accident victim to heal may give you some idea.

Most stories in an Australian setting would go something like this . . .

Sirens wailing, the ambulance carves a desperate track through the rain-slick streets. The ambulance scatters rush hour traffic and runs red lights because inside the van, the medics are hanging on for dear life, trying to keep their seats and trying to keep the patient breathing. The woman on the stretcher has been in an accident and taken a severe battering, and she is barely alive.

Finally, the ambulance screeches to a stop outside the emergency room. As the sirens fade, the medics unload the stretcher and send her skidding through the sliding doors. Instantly, she becomes the unconscious center of attention, the focus of everyone's hopes and fears. A few hours later, she gradually comes around. She begins to mumble questions and ask for water, but she's still too spaced-out to stay awake, or make any real decisions.

By the end of the week, she is much brighter. She can think clearly and speak coherently, and she begins to relive the accident in vivid prose. Her family listens and listens some more, then sighs with relief when the doctors declare she is out of danger.

The next day, the orderly arrives. He lays her flat on her back, piles her belongings around her, and unhooks the machines. Then he trundles her bed along endless shining corridors toward the ward. She can feel herself being pushed through swinging doors and around corners, but all she can see are the ceiling lights flashing by above her head.

As the orderly clicks her bed into place, she glimpses a row of beds on her right, then on her left. So many beds. So many people. She squeezes her eyes shut and pretends to be asleep. It's all too much.

The next morning, she manages to say "Hello" to the person on her left. Then on the right. She asks their names, then promptly forgets them because her own story and her own pain still fill her mind.

But gradually, as the days pass, she starts to recover. She tries a crooked smile at the lady on the right, and they swap magazines. Soon she is chatting with the other ladies. They share stories and manage a laugh. They share detailed medical histories, enough to make a teenager blush, and they learn the names of each other's children.

She eats her first real meal. Oh yes!

Each afternoon, she watches the news on television, but the events depicted there seem worlds away because the ward is now her world. And *her own news is The News*. It spills out in every conversation. She tells anyone who will listen about her scars, the fluid in her drip, and the latest X-ray results. The ward staff have heard stories like this a million times, but they know the drill, so they smile kindly and humor her self-absorption.

At last, she is able to go to the toilet in a wheelchair, and this makes the headlines. Without hesitation, she announces her triumph to everyone. Grinning from ear to ear, she tells all the intimate details to her doctor, the tea lady, and even the janitor who swishes under her bed with the antiseptic mop.

All day she beams down on the world like Victory herself riding in a chariot of sheets—clad, at last, in unsoiled pajamas. As the weeks pass, she becomes more than a patient, she becomes a connoisseur of catered sandwiches, a critic of scrambled eggs, and an expert on the avoidance of bedsores.

She becomes hope herself.

The physiotherapist senses this and begins to spin tales regarding the wonders of rehab. He describes its gleaming parallel bars in glowing terms. And so she waves farewell to the ward staff and enters rehab. But rehab challenges her in ways she has not anticipated. It demands that she think. Remember. Like a young child, she has to learn once more which is her right foot and which is her left.

Cast in the role of a beginner again, she feels almost sub-human, close to defeat. Sometimes the gleaming bars seem to mock her as she stumbles between them. But deep inside, she is determined to succeed, and increasingly, she does. Some days she struts between the bars like a model in heels. On other days she tumbles down to become, once again, a tantrum toddler, flailing on the floor with flabby fists.

When she graduates from bar work and can walk with a frame, there comes a splendid, terrifying day, the day she is sent home. On that day, the doctors and nurses come to applaud, even as they dismiss her from the pedestal of "special" and demote her to the ranks of "normal." Wiping streaming eyes, she assembles her trembling limbs in the passenger seat of a friend's car. All the way home, she braces herself against his dangerous speeding. She watches in bemused awe the fascinating cacophony of the city rushing past her window.

Finally, on his arm, she stumbles into the silence of her home and is deposited on the couch. She sits there like a sack of potatoes and stares stupidly at the familiar dust-coated tables and chairs, and she shivers.

She is home, but not at home.

Home is the hospital, the visitors, the wilting flowers, and the cheerful tea lady with the lukewarm tea and coffee. Home is being the center of attention. Cared for.

But there can be no return. She has been set free to be responsible again. Liberated to feel both empowered and lonely. Released to create, with all the determination she can muster, a new reality and new connections.

She is free to rebuild her life one day at a time and use her newfound wisdom to rise above her limits.

After any head-on collision in life,
this is what we all have to do.

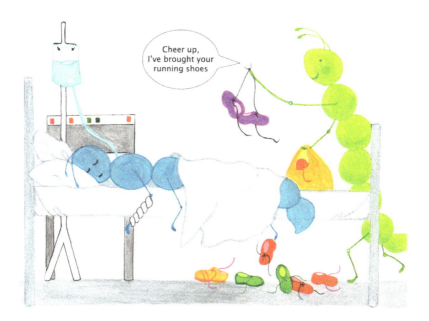

Guess Work

When we haven't a clue,
please give us one.

When we cannot read your mind,
please read your story aloud
so we can hear.

If your heart's been broken, you do not wear a sign around your neck that states, "Accident and Emergency, Quiet Please." So, even if you feel very fragile inside and tremble in the first acute stage of your grief, we may miss the cues. Blithely go on our way, oblivious. Sorry.

We don't mean to be careless or cruel. So, don't be too hard on us. And please don't measure our love or our friendship by how we respond. We are just caught up in our own lives, and sometimes this makes us deaf and blind to your life.

If you need a hand, please give us a clue.
Tell us what's happening
(though not in too much detail)
so we will know.

Because, as helpers,
we are beginners too.

TO FORGIVE?

Forgive,
so your soul
can live.

When some people hurt me deeply, I did not try to forgive them. I was too weary and soul sore. Instead, I just acknowledged my feelings and rested. For months I lived as simply as possible, guarding my meager emotional energy.

When the news on television became violent or sad, I turned it off. When I could neither think clearly nor pray coherently, I simply let myself wander around the garden without trying to make sense of life. After work, I ambled down grassy tracks or wandered under the fluttering canopy of leafy trees.

Gradually, I began to explore what had happened. I saw the part that I, and others, had played in the tragedy. I began to see that, even when things had gone wrong, and we had hurt each other, we were all trying to make sense of life, trying to do the best we could. Seeking pain relief of one kind or another for body and soul.

One day, several months later, it dawned on me that I had forgiven those who had hurt me. I had not tried to forgive at all; *I had only tried to understand, and* forgiveness had slipped into my heart anyway, gently and naturally. It had come as a result of being willing to view each person with compassion, including myself.

Throughout this process, I had also become increasingly aware of our common humanity. I think this helped in several ways.

Firstly, it toned down my self-righteousness. In some settings, there is an *innocent victim*, and we need to honor that. But most of the time, life is simply messy, and even with the best of intentions, we hurt each other. Therefore, if we rush to classify people as "good" and "bad" instead of seeing them as learners like us, we miss a lot of wisdom.

Secondly, recognizing our common humanity saved me from extreme forms of regret, judgment, and bitterness. It gave me permission to make mistakes without *seeing myself as a mistake.*

Thirdly, as I have mentioned, it also helped me to forgive.

Finally, it made space in my heart for hope and healing. For a new beginning.

I do not know who, or what, has wounded you. You may have led a sheltered life or been exposed to cruelty, deception, and betrayal.

But whatever your experience, I still recommend you forgive those who have hurt you, not because you should or must, but because it lessens your pain. Because it liberates your mind from spiraling in endless circles of regret and revenge.

It also offers you something else . . .

At a time when playing the role of a victim seems so tempting, it offers you the chance to reassert your leadership. Because, when you forgive, *you decide how to respond. You choose* your own attitude. *You choose* to be self-protective and not leave yourself open to further abuse. *You choose* to be kind and have healing conversations with your family and friends. And instead of waiting around for the other person to apologize, *you choose* to let the past go and move forward when it suits you.

And most of all, once the dust settles, *you choose who you want to be.*

When you do this, you demonstrate to the world, and especially to yourself, that even when life is tough, you have *the capacity to take the initiative.*

To be a leader.
Even now.

Even in this.

So, what is forgiveness?

Perhaps you already have a clear idea. For me, forgiveness has an intangible spiritual quality that I find hard to define. I know it is not about forgetting—our minds are not capable of that. Nor about pretending nothing's happened. That's absurd. To say, "It's nothing," is also a lie. A lie which disrespects both the truth and our own value. And forgiveness is not about allowing others to hurt us again and again. That makes no sense at all. We each need to be accountable for who we are and how we treat others.

Rather, forgiveness seems to be about honoring my own humanity and the humanity of the person who has hurt me, about choosing to be gracious, not just this once but as a way of life, *as an expression of who I am*.

And another thing . . .

If we get into the habit of forgiving others, we are more likely to forgive our-selves when we mess up. In the little daily ways where we forget, stumble, and fail. *And this is a big deal.*

My hope is that, gradually, as we reflect God's forgiving grace, we will learn to be more gracious at our very core. We will make kindness to ourselves, and to others, a way of life, as illustrated by these two luminous quotes from the works of Henry Wadsworth Longfellow.

In the lives of the saddest of us, there are bright days like this, when we feel as if we could take the great world in our arms and kiss it. Then come the gloomy hours, when the fire will neither burn on our hearths nor in our hearts; and all without and within is dismal, cold, and dark.
Believe me, every heart has its secret sorrows, which the world knows not, and oftentimes we call a man cold when he is only sad.

If we could read the secret history of our enemies,
we should find in each man's life sorrow and
suffering enough to disarm all hostility.[18]
—Henry Wadsworth Longfellow

The Grace Cascade

God is tender hearted
and forgives you,

So you can
pass on his
grace and
forgive
others too.
(Footnote 19)

FRIENDS

Friends keep loneliness at bay,
even when they don't know what to say.

When your life changes for better or worse, your group of friends tends to change too. Some friends make themselves scarce, and others linger or rush to your side.

One lady told me, "The worst thing that happened to me after my husband left me was that some of my friends left me too. Just when I needed their support, they disappeared. I was really puzzled and deeply hurt by their actions. I felt abandoned once again."

So why do some friends leave us when we need them most?

Who knows?

The reasons are as varied as the people themselves.

Some friends may be "lost for words," so put off speaking to us, then feel so bad they had nothing to say that they avoid us. Others may be scared our pain will overwhelm them or our illness may be catching. Some may be barely holding onto life or sanity themselves.

Whatever the reason, spoken or unspoken, you know it hurts to be abandoned. And you know, when night falls, how doubts and questions crowd into your mind: *Is something wrong with me? Did they ever really like me?*

When friends leave us, it adds an extra layer of loss to our grief. It can feel more painful than if someone dies because it seems as if a friend has actively chosen to walk away.

If you have lost a few friends lately, by all means, ask questions. Explore options to restore the relationship. But as you grieve, also remember to be kind to yourself. Find little toeholds of comfort where you can, small finger-holds of hope. And hang on. The instability and the questions will not last forever. You will heal and discover new friends in unexpected places.

Just as you are patient with yourself, be patient with your ex-friends; do not judge them too harshly. Just like you they are trying to make sense of life.

After a major crisis or interstate move, you may lose some of the friends who shared your past, but the world is still filled with people who can help you create your future, ones who will, even yet, be witnesses to the wonderful milestones and achievements ahead.

Some may even bring you chocolate!

When we think of those we love, sometimes friends feature before family. Friends know about the griefs and questions we hide from the world. They know what we ache for and dream about. But sometimes, when we are bursting to share what's on our hearts, they vanish.

This is especially common when a couple separates. Some friends feel a greater empathy for him and his story. Some are loyal to her. And so they take sides. Others, not wanting to take sides, talk to neither side until the silence and the distance have grown.

But it doesn't have to be this way.
Even if we don't know all the answers, even if we stumble over words, we can do something to show we care.

As I discovered.

My first husband and I separated a few weeks before Valentine's Day when all the shops were brimming with cards declaring undying love. As the day approached, I braced myself for waves of sadness. I vowed to be strong. And I was, all through the long day at work as colleagues beamed and boasted over floral deliveries.

After work I returned home, my emotions still under control, relieved the painful day was almost over.

Then the doorbell rang. A man was standing there, half hidden by a huge bouquet of beautiful flowers. I thanked him but barely had time to close the door before I started sobbing. On the card, a friend had simply written, "You are not alone."

And in that moment, I wasn't.

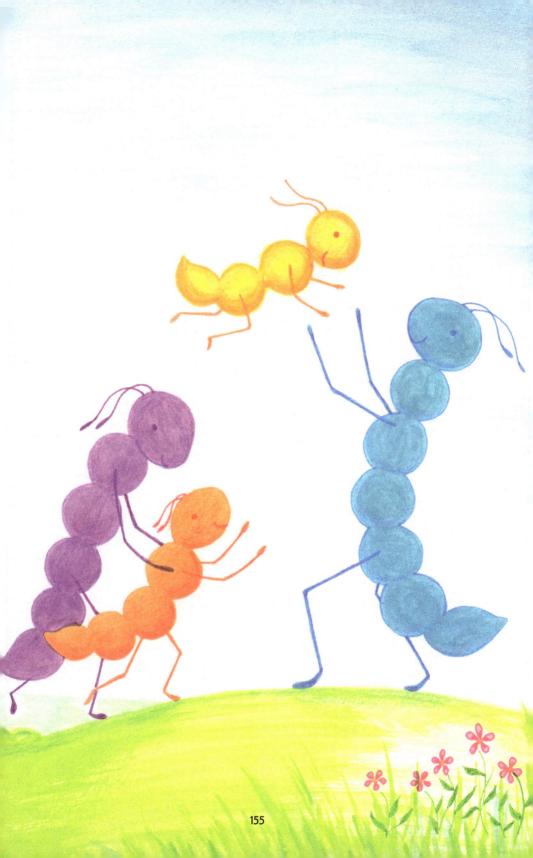

BEST FRIEND?

When you learn how to be loyal to yourself,
you will naturally know how to be loyal to another.

Imagine you are strolling with a friend in your local park or forest. Suddenly, mid-sentence, your friend stumbles over a tree root and sprawls face-down in the dirt.

How do you react?

Do you turn on her? Hit her on the head with your water bottle and scream into her muddy face, "You stupid idiot, why don't you look where you're going?" Do you begin to kick her in the stomach with your hiking boot and shout, "When will you get your act together? You're always falling down!"?

No?

The very idea horrifies you. You're a nice person and wouldn't even dream of it.

Great.

Then why do you sometimes say such cruel things to yourself when you fall down? When you forget the car keys or a colleague's name? When you run late, again? Why do you berate yourself so easily and moan, *I'm so stupid, I could kick myself*?

When did hitting a person when they were down ever encourage them to get up? When did a swift kick in the guts ever make someone's heart glow with fresh hope?

Never.

And yet you campaign so ardently for social equality . . . *for others*. How kind!

One of the most insidious things about slipping into self-condemnation is that you unwittingly take on two roles. It's pretty obvious that you become a victim of your own mean thoughts. But you also adopt the personality of a bully. When you are simultaneously a bully and a victim, your thoughts tend to go around and around in painful circles wearing down your hope and resolve. If this happens, where can you go for mental relief?

Because both of these roles bring a heavy burden of negative soul-destroying emotions, if they become habitual, you're likely to become weary and discouraged. Too disheartened to pursue your own goals or try again. Wallowing in self-pity and shame, you're more likely to lash out at family, friends and colleagues, spreading the social angst.

So, next time you mess up (and there will be a next time), instead of calling yourself cruel names, try being kind to yourself instead. Try being *friendly*. Say gently to your poor beleaguered self, *Are you okay?* Then follow it up with a bit of moral support, *Come on, I'll help you up. You'll soon be fine. You'll learn from this, and next time, you'll be wiser and stronger. I've seen you bounce back before and you can do it again.*

Decide to be your own champion!

Beneath good manners, lies respect.
And beneath respect, lies love.

Love for *all* humanity,
including yourself!

You will walk with many people in your life, some of them for a long time. But there's only one person you will walk with all your life, yourself.

So why do you and I sometimes treat our most constant traveling companion, our own selves, so badly? Is it because, lurking beneath all our self-criticism, we harbor a sneaking suspicion that we are unworthy of love? Or do we believe that our constant falls provide *evidence* that we are flawed beyond repair? I hope not because, if we believe these lies, we add to our brokenness penance. And to our grief, shame.

But penance and self-punishment, whether brief or extended, have never wiped out regret, healed a crushed spirit, or mended a broken heart. Only love can come close enough to do that.

And love does.

Because long before we knew it, Love knew it. Knew that we would fall, we would fail, and shatter in a thousand pieces. Broken.

And so Love came.

Love that is the bedrock of faith, of hope, and all healing. A love that has the power to change, not just our words but the intent behind them. Even how we see ourselves.

And this Love is open to everyone. It tumbles down in a great cascade of love from the heart of God Himself.[20]

If we are open to receiving this love,
we become kinder to others when
they fall, and kinder to ourselves.

Music

Music can heal the wounds
our lips can barely voice.

Turn sleeping dreams into
symphonies of possibility.

When I was a teenager, my aunt offered to pay for piano lessons. So I went. The teacher was very patient, but her pupil not so much. A few months later, the music teacher and I parted company by mutual agreement.

Unlike me, you may be a skilled musician and find great joy in playing the piano or guitar. Or you may love to sing. But whatever instrument you play, you may sometimes lose the song in your heart.

Many years ago, a group of singers were held as prisoners of war. Their captors wanted some entertainment and commanded, "Come on, sing for us!" But the people hung their musical instruments on the nearby trees and sadly responded, "How can we sing when we've lost our homes and our homeland?"[21]

Like them, sometimes you may feel too sad to sing or play. Weary from repeated setbacks and losses, you may forget the power of your voice. It's as if sadness, despair, and shame are holding you prisoner and silencing your song.

If this describes how you feel today, I'm so very sorry.

Sorry for your sadness but also sorry because our world needs the music of your voice, needs to hear you sing or play your Love Song to Life.

When you have rested and
healed, please, will you sing
your song for us again,
the song of your purpose?

When we are sad, we may long to turn down life's volume for a while. Seek refuge from noise in an open meadow or in a deep forest. Anywhere our frayed nerves can bask in wraparound silence. But soon music calls us to return. It urges us to come and listen, to be soothed and restored.

Even when we lack the heart or the energy to sing or play ourselves, we can tune in to the earth music all around us, the whisper of the wind in the trees and the sigh of the sea, the birds' dawn chorus and the hum of bees on a drowsy summer afternoon. Gradually, when we relax into nature's melodies, our hearts begin to heal, and one bright morning, we discover our own song has returned.

While it's still our song,
it's more rich, full, and
glorious than ever before
because it's infused with
wisdom and holy awe.

Our grateful love gift
to the listening world.

King David was mostly a wise and successful man, as we have already discovered, but he had some significant flaws and some very low times in his life.

He lost his first wife to another suitor, grieved for friends killed in war, and was betrayed by leaders whom he trusted. Sometimes David felt so battered and alone that he descended into dark despair. At times like these, he often withdrew from the royal court to shape the lyrics to a new song. It helped him voice his feelings and make sense of his emotions.

I have blended two *restoration songs* for you because they have a similar theme. At least one of the songs is attributed to David, and the second may also be his.

I was so miserable I could barely drag my feet through the day.
I felt like I was stumbling through deep mud,

that I was doomed to be sucked under.
But just when I thought, *I can't go another step,*

God heard my cries.

He reached down and rescued me from the pit of despair.
He restored me to the path of life and gave me hope.
Now laughter bubbles up inside me, and I can't stop smiling![22]

LONG WEEKEND

Not all long weekends
turn into a holiday.

Some far exceed
the promise of this.

My favorite example of a person making meaning from apparent defeat is found in the familiar, and moving, story of Easter.

Like real life, nothing about the Easter story[23] is easy, and I like life to be easy. Perhaps that's why I'm sometimes reluctant to read the story. But when I do, I discover it's full of ordinary people, men and women, much like me, who sometimes struggle to make sense of life. People who want purpose and adventure but scramble for safety when everything around them begins to unravel.

And that weekend, life not only unraveled; it descended into betrayal, tragedy, and death. Therefore, you could be forgiven for thinking that, as long weekends go, it was not a winner. In fact, all that weekend had to redeem it was one strong man. And by Friday afternoon, He appeared to be beyond help himself. If the story ended there, we could argue that all suffering, and even life itself, has a hollow ring to it. Or that, when things get tough, we have every excuse to succumb to despair. But thank God, the weekend did not end on Friday. Nor when the dead hero was laid out to rest in the dark hand-carved cave on Saturday.

Instead, on Sunday morning, that one man made good. He made good, even in the face of apparently wasted, tragic suffering. He made good so splendidly and with so much vitality that we still remember who he is 2,000 years later. We carve his name in stone, wood, and gold: *Jesus*.

And we still pass on his story.

I wonder why.

Is it because Easter captures, in the space of one dramatic long weekend, all humanity's grief, pain, and hope? All our longing for healing and transformation? The promise of acceptance and personal salvation which we all crave? If this is the case, then Easter belongs to *us*, and we can claim it as *our story*.

A story which so eloquently declares,

Whatever happens in my life,
I believe that love will win.
That God's eternal joy lives
on in me, and no one,
and nothing, can quench it.

PASSIONATE MOTIVES

Love is not passive.
When love has the
power to act,
love acts.

Some time ago, I was eating a casual lunch with friends. We were chatting about this and that when our conversation wandered to areas of spiritual experience and faith. Suddenly, a man turned to me and asked out of the blue, "Why did Jesus have to die?" I paused mid-bite.

Mmmm . . . What could I say?

I felt it was a question I couldn't ignore. It's not only central to the story of Easter; it's central to the lives of millions of people worldwide. But I also knew it deserved more than a flippant answer. So I decided to give it some thought and get back to him later.

The question wandered around in my mind for a few weeks seeking a place to rest.

Firstly, I realized that Jesus did not have to die. He could have ignored our plight and turned his back on our suffering. Walked away. Because he had the option to wash his hands of us, *Jesus did not have to die. He chose to die.*

Next, I turned my attention to what motivated him to give such an extreme gift. I came up with several ideas but quickly dismissed them. None of them seemed to show strong enough motivation. After all, *if you're willing to die for someone, you're really motivated!* It's not something you do for fun or drift into casually one sunny afternoon because you're bored.

You know the stakes are high. The consequences are permanent. Once you've died for someone, you can't say, "Oops, my mistake. I won't do that again." When you die for someone, you say, in effect, *Your life is more important to me than my life.*

That's commitment!

The kind of commitment a loving parent has for a precious child . . .

While I was still thinking about the question, I had the opportunity to visit my sons and their families in Canberra. Because of all the lockdowns and shut-downs prescribed in response to the pandemic, I'd not seen them for a long while, so when borders re-opened, I sped to see them.

Every moment I spent with them was precious. I tried to cram as much love as I could into every day, and so did they. In between their work commitments, we played board games, shared meals, and spent one golden day at a leafy park where animals played. We even heard a lion roar.

On the day I was leaving, I woke up while it was still dark. My flight was early in the morning, and I was afraid to go back to sleep in case I overslept. So I got up and showered and dressed. By the time my son came down to wake me, I had everything packed, and we chatted briefly in the sleepy predawn silence.

As he carried my suitcase into the kitchen, ready for the long trip home, he asked, "Have you got everything you need?" I assured him that I did, but he wasn't convinced. Going to the pantry, he began to pull out drawers searching for snacks, anything he could find to give me. I was very touched. At last, he found some snacks and pressed them into my hand, urging me, "Please take them." Smiling, I unzipped my carry-on bag and slipped in a handful of wrapped treats, including an apricot bar, a date brownie, and a bag of nuts.

As we neared the airport, we were sitting in the car together but not together because I was already bracing myself for the parting. At the airport, we hugged goodbye. Then hugged again. I watched and waved until his car merged with the other early morning traffic. Then I let my arm drop. He was gone.

About an hour later, I prepared to board the plane. The staff had just checked my boarding pass, and I began to walk down the sloping corridor to enter the plane. Suddenly, I heard a voice from behind calling urgently, "Mom!" then a little louder, "Lorna!"

I turned around to see my older son waving. I hurried back up the corridor to meet him, but the security staff would not let him pass. He was only a few paces away, but I could not touch him. A few arms lengths from me, but I could not hug him.

I saw a small bag in his hand, and he tossed it to me past the guards. It was a bag of chocolate orange balls, which I scrambled to catch. Hurriedly, he called out, "I thought you'd like something from England to take on the plane." I was very touched and longed to hug my thanks. But all I could do was wave and make hugs in the air with my arms. For a brief moment, we lowered our masks, and when he went to the window, I blew kisses.

I was the last to board the plane and had to hurry, but I turned to see him one more time, treasuring up his face in my mind. Then I was ushered onto the plane. Sitting there, strapped in, I looked out of the window through a blur of tears. As the morning sun rose above the brooding grey hills, it shone on several billowing white clouds. Beautiful.

Both my sons had woken up well before dawn to care for me, the first to drive me to the airport, and the second to drive all the way across the sleeping city just to see me for a few minutes and say goodbye.

As the plane lifted off, I thought of both of them, of the love they, and their families, had shown me for several weeks. As the plane surged higher, we entered the clouds, and for a few moments, we were blinded by fog. Then we burst out above the clouds, and sunshine flooded my face.

Suddenly, with a full heart, I knew, without hesitation, why Jesus had to die.

Love.

When you love someone, you want to do all you can for them. Protect them and provide for them. Hug them. Lavish them with gifts. Do whatever is in your power . . . If they are hurting, you hurt too and want to heal them. If they are dying, your own soul dies with them, and you think, *If only I could fix this. Give them life! What on earth can I do?*

Did God ask that question too?

Did he look at humanity from his golden throne? Look at you and me with great tenderness and say, *"I can't just leave them to suffer and die. I have to do something!"*

Is that why we celebrate Easter? Why the weekend begins with Good Friday, when, for Jesus, that Friday was anything but good?

Did God see generations of humanity falling and dying, and *it broke his heart?*

Did he reach a point where he said to himself and to all of heaven, "I can't stand this anymore! I have to go? *Go and die in their place?* I'm willing to die for everyone . . . for the tidy people and the messy people, for the wrinkly old ones and the busy young ones. For the rebels and the tough folks trying to hide their wounded hearts behind a shield of bravado. I'm willing to die for the reason-weary cynics and the misty-eyed dreamers weaving castles in the air. For the sinners and the sorrowful. I'm even willing to give my life for the people who hate me. The very people who are out to destroy me!"[24]

Does Easter begin with Good Friday
because Jesus' sacrifice redeems us?

And end with joyful celebration

because his resurrection liberates us?

No Contest

It was almost bedtime, and there was a lull after the storm of a busy day.

As the fire glowed in the hearth and the silent stars came out, the children climbed around their mother on the couch and competed with one another to snuggle on her lap. Once they had settled down, one brave voice suddenly piped up.

"Mommy, who do you love the best?"

The new-bathed children were very still, washed faces shining, eyes wide with hope, and hearts a-tremble with fear. There was an eternity of silence, then, finally, the mother shook her head.

"No" she said, "It's no use. I can't decide between you. I'll just have to take a deep breath, expand my heart, and embrace you all."

Quivering down through the ages of earth's long day, there came a whisper and a wail, then the rising crescendo of a million voices.

"God, who do you love the best? What color skin? What gender? What age?"

The mountains trembled. The roaring waves lay still. The air held its breath.

Then, finally, in the awe-filled silence God spoke.

"No," He said, "It's no use. I can't decide between you. I'll just have to come down to earth, open my arms wide, and embrace you all."

Home

Wherever you have been roaming,
in fear or shame, in doubt or sorrow,
please, come home to love.

Wherever you are on life's dusty road, no travel-stained clothes can dim your value. No detours permanently delay your arrival. And your story, even now, can have a happy ending.

So says an ancient tale.[25]

The story begins in the heart of a young man who is all grown up but still at home. Well, his feet are still at home, but his head and heart have already left. For, in his imagination, he roams the land, seeking adventure and travel, longing to be anywhere but home.

One day, bubbling over with thwarted wanderlust, he looks at his father and thinks, *My dad could live forever!* The thought does not fill him with joy; it makes him sick with frustration. Silently, he broods, *I'll never get my hands on his money!* A devious plan worms its way into his mind.

Emboldened by imagined freedoms, he approaches his father with a cunning plot wrapped in fake affection. Shrouded in smiles, he mumbles something like this, "I know I've been restless lately. So, if you give me all my inheritance now, I'll get out from under your feet. Leave you in peace."

His father is no fool. He knows the story. He understands a rebel's heart and what it needs to heal. So, with eyes full of grief and love, he agrees. Elated, the son gives his good old dad a brief hug and almost dances from the room.

For days, he checks his bank balance. He looks first thing in the morning. He sneaks breaks during the day to slip in and check it again, waiting for his inheritance to pop up. Then one morning, while his eyes are still bleary with sleep, he sees it. Wow, he's never seen so much money in all his life! So many zeros! Letting out a muffled *hooray!* he rushes to dress, then hurries to pack his bag, stuffing it with all it can hold.

So long, Dad.

Finally, he's free. Free of all the imagined constraints of home, and he hits the road, ready to party! And he does. With pockets full, he gathers *friends* wherever he goes. The locals can see him coming a mile off, and they're always willing to laugh at his brilliant jokes and eat at his expense.

He never checks his bank balance. Money like that will last a lifetime.

If only.

One morning his credit card purchase is denied. Red-faced, he mutters an excuse about a bank error and makes a quick exit. Finally, he checks his account.

Zero.

He can't even pay for his room. He grabs what he can from the small fridge and stuffs it into his bag. But soon, even this is gone, and his pockets are empty. He checks each pocket twice, only fingernail fluff.

With a pounding head and growling stomach, he wanders down the city streets, kicking aside wastepaper and dead leaves. He passes bakers pulling crusty bread from their ovens and checks his pockets again. He smells hot coffee brewing . . . Desperate now, he hikes across town to knock on the doors of a few friends. As he approaches, he's sure he hears voices within, but no one answers the door. Once more, have they seen him coming a mile off?

That evening, he slides into his usual restaurant, grinning broadly. Bluffing and banter has worked for him in the past, and he hopes it will again. The waiter glances at his unkept hair and muddy shoes, then smiles stiffly and shows him to a table. But when the young man quietly asks if they offer deferred payment options, it's too much, and the waiter grabs his sleeve and firmly escorts him to the door.

Stumbling out into the cold night, the son peers in through the steaming window and sees all his friends feasting in a quiet corner. They seem to be looking his way and laughing, but maybe he's only imagining it.

That night he is forced to sleep rough. He wanders around for a while, checking out doorways, back alleys, and broken park benches. Finally, he hunkers down behind the hotel, where a vent blows out just a little warm air and all the savory aromas of the kitchen. Sinking onto the cold concrete, he wraps his arms around himself—the only hug he's had for a while—and shivers through the endless night. His only company, the alley rats. As the sun rises, he shakes out his chilled limbs, swiftly looks right and left, then rummages in the hotel bins for breakfast.

He lives like this for a while, wandering unshaven and unwashed through the blur of days and nights, unloved by man or beast. After a brief dead-end job on a farm, he curls up on a sack in a fetal position. He's reached rock bottom, and he knows it.

And yet, what's this? The edge of a memory, half-buried? A snatch of song? The whiff of his mother's bread baking?

Home?

Fueled by desperate resolve, he stumbles to his feet and peers down the road. Which way? Unsure, he heads in the general direction under the feeble light of a half-moon. He tramps through tunnels of specter-black trees, shivering. Across wastelands, where the sand drags at his feet like treacle.

He passes through villages where homes nestle in cozy groups. *The homes of other people.* Seeing them, he feels a whispered yearning growing louder, heart and soul crying out to be heard. Determined now, he picks up the pace.

He may be dirty, penniless, and starving, but he's on a mission. His clothes, like his life, may be in tatters, but his mind is blessed with brilliant clarity. As he plods on, snatching drinks from streams where he can, and berries from bushes, no one pats him on the back. No one smiles. Instead, other travelers gag at his body odor, which reeks of self-sufficiency gone sour, and holding their noses, they cross to the other side.

But what does he care? He's following a thread of hope, and he's unstoppable.

He carries no visible baggage, but he's weighed down with internal baggage: Regret. Guilt. Fear.

He also carries one more thing. It's tucked away safely in his imagination where no one can steal it. It's a picture of his father. He looks at this picture often and holds his father's smiling eyes in his mind. He tries to remember those eyes, their warm understanding and their love and laughter.

Every step of the weary way, he practices what he'll say, *Dad, I'm so very sorry. I've messed up big-time. I've dragged your good name in the gutter. I'll do anything if you'll just let me come home— scrub floors, muck out the calves, clean toilets—anything.*

Waiting at home is his father. He's worn a hole in the carpet by the window, walking back and forth, hoping. One morning he finishes his breakfast and checks at the window, as usual. He peers down the road through the morning mist, once, twice. Can it be?

He shades his eyes and looks again. It is. It's his son. He's about a mile off, but the father can see him coming. He would know that walk anywhere. He flings open the door, tightens his belt and runs flat out toward his son. He doesn't care about success or failure, about catching germs or getting grime on his tailor-made clothes. All he cares about is his son, hugging him tight and never, ever, letting him out of his sight again.

Precious One,
How fast do you think God can run,
arms outstretched, to welcome you home?[26]

Section 3: The Cocoon

Part 2 Resilience, Renewal, Healing

In the misty dawn, before the sun gilds their feathers with gold, the birds begin to stir. They hop from branch to branch and lift their beaks to carol a love song to the Creator of Morning.

Roused by their symphony of praise, the garden creatures stir. The dragonfly shakes out her gauzy wings and skims across the liquid light of the waterlily pond. A stripy yellow bee soars into the air, takes his bearings, then heads for the center of a climbing rose. Far below, a colony of ebony ants hold a whispered conference of wiggling antennae, then scurry off in single file to harvest a crumbling log.

Only the caterpillar stays in bed, snug in his silk pajamas. What is he thinking?

Is he dreaming of days gone by when he starred in the dawn parade? When he wriggled and looped with the best? Or with every fiber of his being, is he planning a new beginning?

The Seed

Buried by life's setbacks and sorrows,
unable to see the sunshine under
layers of rejection and regret,
you may be tempted to give up.
But, hold on a minute, what if
you were *created to be a seed*?

From compost
comes growth.

In the garden, many a blooming rose owes its beauty to compost, its fragrance to waste, and its velvet petals to the rich loam of leftovers. In the forest, many a sturdy sapling is protected and nourished by yester- day's cast-off leaves which fluttered down to cover its roots last fall.

A seed seems so small. Of no consequence or value. But, not everything is as it seems. Within a few months, tiny seeds can grow into plants that bear beautiful flowers. And within a few years, small seeds can grow into tall trees. Where nature is concerned, I think God actually has fun surprising us! Taking something apparently insignificant, wrapping it in his love and saying, "Look what I can do with that!"

I wonder, does he takes as much delight in surprising us?

Taking the experiences we resent, the ones we sullenly label "a waste," and using them to make something magnificent out of our lives?

Even now, is he inviting you to open your heart? Blossom into someone more wise, compassionate, and kind?

What if your most productive

and beautiful days still
lie ahead?

Days when you
burst out of your shell
to heal and bless the world?

Courage

Hope arms us with the courage
to outwit fear.
And, love and purpose
steady our stance.

Whenever I hear the word *courage*, I immediately think of a storybook hero, a brave knight in shining armor riding to the rescue of a swooning maiden or a besieged village. A strong man of legendary valor, who is generous and brave. I picture him ready to help at a moment's notice. Something like this . . .

One day, a villager bursts into the knight's hut, gasping for breath,

"Quick . . . the dragon's back!"

Instantly, the knight flings down his rustic bread and cheese to grab his scarlet-plumed helmet. He whistles for his trusty steed, leaps into the saddle, and digs in the spurs. As he thunders through the village, all is still. Sackcloth peasants cower near their battered huts, and children peer out from behind their mother's skirts. But the knight has no time to comfort those who weep. Yet.

He has a job to do.

Bending over low over the stallion's back the knight gallops down the scorched track *toward* the fiery dragon, sending clods of earth flying. Rounding a bend in the trail, the horse suddenly rears high in the air, legs thrashing, for the great beast has been waiting for them.

Poised, ready to pounce, the dragon fills the whole path. With each swipe of his thrashing tail, he sends great trees crashing to the ground. And, after every gulping breath lethal spurts of fire snort from each nostril searing the dust.

The knight trembles but refuses to flee, even when the smoke makes his eyes sting, and he catches a whiff of his own hair singeing. Lowering his visor, he advances upon the dragon. This makes the hackles on the dragon's back quiver. Full of vengeful fury, he growls until the rocky gully resounds with his roars and the air of Earth crackles with his defiance.

Determined to succeed, the knight dodges left and right to outwit each clawed attack. For hours, he battles for life, and for right, under the blistering sun. But, the battle is more intense than any mortal man can stand, and the knight begins to slump in the saddle. Sway with exhaustion. Heart pounding and weary to the point of death, he holds his cracked lips in a determined line. *He cannot fail, or all will be lost.* Finally, with the last of his strength, the knight raises his mighty right arm and lands a fatal blow.

For a moment, all is still.

The birds stop singing. The earth trembles and the knight forgets to breathe. The scaly monster shudders briefly, then with a great bellow, he crashes to earth, sending a plume of sulfurous smoke spiraling high into the quivering air.

It is finished.

With a regal cry of triumph, the knight wheels his horse about and gallops back up the path to the village.

Hearing him come, the people burst into wild applause and begin their traditional victory chant. Every voice joins in until their chorus swells into a great crescendo, "Gospel! Gospel! GOSPEL!" In response, the knight thrusts his unbent lance high into the sky. And on his gleaming, blood-splattered shield, the heraldic lion throws back his head and roars.

With great joy, the villagers pour into the road to claim their hero. The children run beside his horse, their hair flying. As he skids to a halt on the village green, the old folks, overcome with trembling relief, trip over their water buckets to shake his hand.

Everyone begs him to stay. So he does.

With trembling fingers, he unbuckles his armor, dropping each piece with a sigh of relief on the grass by the well. Then, as a gaggle of giggling children pump the handle, he cups water in his bruised hands to wash his face. Refreshed, bear-like, he shakes his great head, and sparkling droplets from his beard shower over the children, and for a moment they scatter, laughing.

An old man offers him an earthenware cup of fresh-crushed grape juice, and the knight gulps it down eagerly. As he passes back the cup, he smiles his thanks, "Ah, that was good." A motherly lady bustles up and hands him a bread roll, still warm from her clay oven, and he takes a big bite. A young man unrolls a lamb's fleece and flicks it across their best stool, and all the people settle down around him. Some sit on handmade benches or old logs, but most sit on the wiry grass, their feet tucked comfortably under them.

They want to hear all about it. Retell and relive his thrilling story.

But somehow, the knight always manages to steer the conversation back to them. He acts as if it's their stories, and their feelings that really matter to him.

And so, all afternoon he listens to their tales.

Hearts warmed as never before, the village folk pour out their lives before him in word and song like a great libation of gratitude. Some tell tales of loss, and his eyes glow with compassion. Others are blessed with the gift of good humor, and he leans forward, his eyes crinkling with joy. At the punchline, his merry laughter joins theirs, filling the valley.

Feeling safe in his presence, little children play at his feet.

Toddlers run tiny toy carts over his toes, bump, bump, bump. Other children clamber onto his lap, hoping for a hug. A young boy offers him a wilting wild-flower, and the knight lifts the flower to his nose and smiles. A young girl pats his cheek and traces the line of a lingering scar with her tender finger. Sensing his pain, she stretches higher and brushes his face with her lips, hoping she can kiss his hurt better.

Out of the corner of his eye, the knight notices a handful of village boys struggling to lift his armor from the grass. As they loop it clumsily over their shoulders and strut before their friends, his heart fills with a warm glow as he realizes *they want to be just like me.*

The knight looks over the crowd once more, and his face seems to welcome them all. Crippled and whole, sandaled and barefoot, his eyes embrace them. No one is turned away. Even the brokenhearted village outcast feels accepted and dares to edge closer. Drawn by a yearning long buried under years of rejection, he gathers his tattered courage about him and comes to sit at the knight's feet. When he is settled, the knight lays a warm hand on his shoulder and beams, "Welcome."

Reluctant to part, the villagers linger, telling tales and sharing bread until the crimson sky fades to gold and the first star begins to shine.

At last, the villagers push back their stools with a reluctant sigh. The young men pick up their buckets and wander off to milk the cows. Mothers gather up their children for dinner. One or two old men stroll over to a bonfire and, bending down, kindle a flame with a few dry twigs. Soon the whole heap of wood is burning, and the villagers eagerly return. They circle the blaze with glowing faces, hands outstretched for warmth.

Then the fiddlers fiddle, and the children skip as living sparks of fire fly high into the sky. And the village maidens, emboldened by the knight's courage, slide closer to his elbows, each one hoping in her tender heart that he will catch her up in the dance . . .

So say the legends! The stories of long ago.

But you and I cannot live in legends, nor bask in another's glory forever. So, reluctantly, we must close our mental picture book and lay it on the shelf. Wave goodbye to the fluttering pennants of yesteryear, and let the brave knights march back into the mists of time. We must farewell the dragons, as, one by one, they hang their heads and slink back into history.

For, of course, no dragons live near us. They have all bowed to time's command and fled.

And yet . . . I'm not so sure.

Because I've noticed the Dragon of Loneliness lives near me. If I lag too far behind the hurrying crowd and quickly turn my head, I catch him haunting my heels, eager to drag me into his lair.

And the Dragon of Lies still labors to claw great craters in the self-healing Road of Truth.

Failure lurks 'round here somewhere too. Like a highwayman, he hides on blind bends and lingers in shadowy gullies just beyond ambition's arrows.

And The Dragon of Doubt has loitered for ages by the Pathway of Faith. Pacing the borders there he taunts passing pilgrims, and with diabolical leer, he mocks their sacred quest.

Debt, too, has resisted all humanity's attempts to banish him. He brazenly trips along behind Greed's lumbering feet or stalks the erratic steps of Injustice. On his scaly shoulder, Debt carries a coil of rope to lasso unwary travelers and tie them up in knots.

Wherever I turn, even today, I catch a glimpse of a scaly tail or a puff of smoke. In remote villages and soaring city towers, in crumbling castles and dark alleys, I notice Poverty still languishes, wearily grinding his yellowing teeth.

And on every far-flung shore, where the people of earth stray, you can still trace the footprints of Grief in the sand.

For so it has always been.

But where dragons abound, warriors also gather.
Warriors who shake so hard with fear, their armor rattles.
Warriors who doubt themselves but dare anyway.
Warriors who know the risks, but live large, *because large is needed*.

Warriors like you and me.

Adult, child, or teen, we are no paper cutouts, no fabled heroes of yesterday. We are the living knights of today, and in our hearts we sense this. So, whatever the weather, or foe, we refuse to be defeated, or deflected from our purpose. With hearts that yearn to be brave and true, even as they quiver with fear, we choose to face each dragon head-on, whoever we are, wherever we live.

And we choose to do it together.

Even when we are wounded and weary and look like easy prey. When we are tired of wondering and tremble before a vast galaxy of quivering questions, we refuse to run scared.

For our hearts still throb to the beat of the original Knight's heart, and his glorious eternal bravery runs in our veins.

This holds true, even when the Dragon of Mortality breaches the ramparts of the local hospital, and his acrid breath, tainted with despair, wafts down the sterile hallways. Still, we refuse to surrender. Even when our only armor is a pair of wrinkled pajamas and our only weapons are a rolled-up magazine and a paper bag of crimson grapes,

We still trust that our keenest
weapons are spiritual.
That Love and Faith
already stand beside us,
shoulder to shoulder.

Undaunted and unbowed,
by the power of God's grace,
we choose to cherish life, and right,
while we have breath.
Even when eternity beckons.

And, in honor of all humanity,
we strike a match to the
fireworks of hope, till our lives
light up the sky, so our
children's children can dance.

Long ago, when sages spun stories by spark-spitting campfires, the legends of dragons were born.

Or were they?

Some say dragons predate humanity. Well, one dragon at least, the Chief Diabolical Dragon, from whom all threats and fears spring, the author of all lies, misery and war, and the infamous ancestor of all lesser dragons.

Others say that, long before any dragons clawed their way into history, there was an eternal Source of Life, a Knight called Faithful.[1]

Who knows?

Who knows?

OUR ARENA OF COURAGE

Whether you measure it in
giant leaps or shuffling steps,
courage is still courage.

In legends of old, knights fought in the public arena while everyone cheered
or jeered. But today, most of our battles are fought in the private arena of
our minds.

It is in our minds that we challenge Anxiety until it surrenders, in the labyrinthine corridors of our heads that we joust with Despair. In the silent cacophony
of our thoughts that we ride out against Guilt with the lance of forgiveness,
and in the musings of the night that we decide to stride into life carrying the
Banner of Integrity, whatever the social cost.

We don't always win these private battles. Sometimes we fall hard.

We're flung to the ground and trampled by Temptation and routed by Habit.
But all is not lost. For strong values, heartfelt prayers, and small wins still
make a difference.

They give us the courage to face the challenges we would rather flee. They help
us tackle stacks of paperwork undaunted, sort through mountains of smelly
socks, and attack tangled piles of weeds, and do all this without a swirling
crimson cape or shiny armor!

Each battle we win matters because it gives us hope and the motivation to
plod on, step-by-step. It gives us the tenacity to feed our kids day after day.
To sit at the kitchen table chopping onions, alone, without a visored helmet,
even when our eyes stream with tears. It gives us the commitment to pay our
rent faithfully year by year, even in tough times.

Hope helps us act like *a legend* on the messy front line of life when we would rather linger at home, invisible and safe.

It gives us the courage to stand up for the downtrodden and be a voice for the voiceless when we would rather slink away in silence. Hope also helps us graciously applaud another's success when we secretly dream of taking a victory lap ourselves.

Whatever we face, we are buoyed up most by a quality often lauded on flowery cards: love.

For, when all else crumbles under the weight of our sorrow or fear, when even faith and hope falter, love, in its deepest sense, comes to our aid. It gives us the strength to keep going *anyway*.

Love leads us through life's darkest nights.

It helps us to climb out of bed, ragged and weary, when duty calls. It guides our steps as we stumble half-asleep through the house *toward* the wail of our teething baby. It helps us lift the tearful face closer to our ringing ears.

Day and night, we keep going. We stir the vegetables and spoon out the rice. We serve, and bless, and heal. As parents and friends, sons and daughters, we do all this.

Who says service has to make the headlines to be *real*? Or courage has to result in a public parade to be called a *victory*?

Who says you need to slay a dragon
to be worthy of the name *hero*?

THE MAKING OF A BRAVE

To start small,
may be empowering
after all!

Several years ago, life was hard for me. In the face of repeated setbacks and losses, I had almost run out of *brave*. Although I wanted to break free of inertia and despair, I was so, so, tired. Everything I wanted to do or achieve seemed to demand an energy I did not possess. To require a mountain of effort. I was almost ready to give up, but not quite. Deep inside, a tiny spark of hope still lingered, and in my braver moments, I wanted to coax it back to life.

One gray day, as I wandered around town on my lunch break, I passed a bank. Suddenly, an idea popped into my head, *Why don't I pay myself to be brave?* The idea sounded so silly that I began to smile. Maybe it would work. So, I retraced my steps and bought a small bag of coins.

That evening, I hunted through my kitchen cupboards for a glass jam jar. After washing off the dust, I cut a slit in the lid. I stuck on a white label with the word COURAGE printed in bold black letters. Then I placed the jar, and the little bag of coins, in the center of my kitchen bench.

Now what?

As I stared at the jar, I felt a tiny whisper of excitement. I began to wonder, *What can I do to earn my first coin?* Because I was so weary, I knew it had to be something easy, something small. Looking around, I saw a tumble of dirty dishes in the sink. Ah yes, the dinner dishes. Rolling up my sleeves, I filled the sink with hot water.

As soon as I had placed the last dish in the cupboard, I reached for the coins and dropped one into the jar. I had made a start. But the single coin looked very lonely, as if it needed a friend. So, I thought to myself, *What else can I do? Fold the washing?*

Over the next few weeks, every time I acted out of bravery rather than cow-ardice or discouragement, I dropped a coin into the jar.

Climbing out of bed instead of cowering under the covers? One coin.
Going to work when I felt like calling in sick? Another coin.
Paying my electricity bill on time . . . weeding a small flower bed . . . writing one letter . . . more coins.

As the sparkling pile of coins grew, so did my optimism. I no longer had to drag myself out of bed or use fake self-talk to convince myself I was brave. Right there in front of me, glinting in the sunshine, was the tangible evidence.

Evidence that I had the courage to rebuild my life. One washed cup and one small coin at a time.

Several years ago, I came across these words of Amelia Earhart, and they have resonated with me ever since. Amelia had the amazing temerity to fly solo when planes were in their technical infancy. She must have summoned courage to be her co-pilot every time she took off!

Courage is the price that
Life exacts for granting peace.
The soul that knows it not,
Knows no release
From little things:

Knows not the livid
Loneliness of fear,
Nor mountain heights
Where bitter joy can hear
The sound of wings.[2]

—Amelia Earhart, Pioneer Aviator

THE MASTER ARTIST

I'm no artist, you say, as you turn away,
but think again, Dear Friend,

My days were blank, life colorless gray
till you saw my despair

And cared.

With bold flourish of gold you swirled
joy on my soul.

Sketched paths for my wandering
feet. Then lifting hope's mirror

You urged me to see, framed in love's
hands, your living masterpiece,

Me.

ENCOURAGEMENT

When one person encourages another, they
don't hide the truth nor fake a happy ending.

They just draw different conclusions
from the same evidence.

It's a curious paradox, but the more I search for opportunities to encourage
someone else, the more quickly I forget my own woes. The more I search for
the right words to lift a friend's mood, the more I rekindle my own passion
for life. *It's as if my soul hears the voice of its own hope, amplified.*

Therefore, for my mental health, do I need people to encourage even more
than I need people to encourage me? Is being a helper, in itself, healing? If so,
this makes the holy proverb true which states,

It's more blessed to give
than to receive.[3]
—Jesus

TWO GIFTS

Two people longed to bring a gift
to lay before the throne of God.

One person stepped up and boldly said,
You've made me strong and smart.
I place my skills and talents at your feet;

with them, I'll heal and train humanity.
And they did a splendid job!

The second person shyly came
and laid their wounded heart
in tender hope before God's feet.

Moved with deep compassion,
God stepped down from
his golden throne and wrapped
the seeker in a warm embrace.

Then, unseen behind the seeker's back,
a vast procession formed
as the lonely, scorned and broken
risked coming forward to be healed.

I had always assumed that strong, smart people had the most to offer God, that they could make the greatest contribution to the world. Now I'm not so sure. It's obvious that we rely on skilled people to run our schools, workplaces, and hospitals. That we need loving, wise, and strong parents who are willing to commit to raising thoughtful, healthy and happy children.

But the mentors I remember with the most admiration and affection are not the ones who seemed to *have it all together*. Instead, I remember the mentors who had the courage to be real, the ones who showed me how to be vulnerable by being vulnerable themselves. Showed me how to hope when I feared I had messed up too badly to be of any worth, or use.

For instance, when I was at university, a lecturer was absent from class for a few days. When he returned, he told us that he had been sick. He could have stopped right there, and we would have accepted his excuse without question. Instead, he took a deep breath and told us why he had been ill. From memory, his comments went something like this, "I read that going without food for a time and fasting was a good idea. I heard it was a traditional spiritual discipline and it helped to create enlightenment and inspire devotion to God, so I decided to try it myself. At first, I was fine and proud of my ability to resist food, but soon I became too shaky and nauseous to work or even stand without support. As I lay trembling on my bed, weak and discouraged,

I realized that a spiritual practice may suit one person, but not another, and this is okay." Then he added with a smile, "I don't think I'll try fasting again!"

As he spoke, we all sat very still with our eyes focused on his face. Not a pen moved as we listened to his brief story. We sensed that something special was happening. Instead of giving us a lecture or talking down to us, he was sharing his own spiritual journey with us, as if we were his equals. Fellow travelers on life's road. We felt the weight of his vulnerability and knew, without him spelling it out, that he was trusting us to understand him, to be gracious and kind.

I have no idea what his lecture was about that day or what he planned to teach us. But I remember what he taught me with his testimony and how he reassured me. How he told me that:

I am free to be an authentic human being before God, myself, and others because God understands my unique personality and already loves me.

I can therefore risk being an explorer who sometimes fails, without becoming a failure. I can make mistakes without losing my status as his beloved.

One event does not mark the end of my story because whatever my life journey has been up to this point, my future is untarnished. It is totally clear and blameless.

Even in the mess and muddle of today, God can still use my story, and who I am, for good.

That day, my professor had the raw courage to live his lesson.
No lecture required!

SHAME AND HOPE

There are only two subjects
taught in every school.

Two lessons
all the students learn.

For a start, he sat too close. Even though we had just met, he pulled his chair up to touch mine. Then he leaned over into my personal space and let his shoulder brush my arm. I tried to remain professional, but inside, I cringed. I fought down the urge to push him away or to run. As the hours passed, I became increasingly anxious. I took urgent bathroom breaks just to get away.

I felt intimidated, threatened by this know-it-all stranger who was literally breathing down my neck. The man who had come not to teach me, but to parade his knowledge.

My supervisor, *with a dubious stab at wisdom,* had hired him to explain the new computing system at work. She expected me to understand it all in a few hours (no pressure!), then teach it to our team. But as the trainer bombarded my brain with increasingly complex levels of information with no time for questions or to take notes, he was really teaching me something quite different. He was teaching me to feel fear, fear in the form of shame.

While his words were carefully polite, and he spoke with exaggerated patience, his tone screamed, "How dumb can you be?" And his raised eyebrows and deep sighs shouted, "What kind of idiot are you?" So, on that memorable day, as his words and sighs poured over me like a poisonous flood, I did not become wiser. I became paralyzed.

I was too busy bracing myself against his veiled sneers to pay attention to something as insignificant as a computer program. *I was in survival mode, busy building ramparts against an intellectual bully and defending myself absorbed all my attention.*

When the roles were reversed, and I was the one teaching, we were constantly reminded, "No one cares how much you know, until they know how much you care".

I wonder if the trainer had been told this too, but just forgotten. Perhaps, in his haste to share his knowledge, he had misplaced the idea. Maybe, as he drove to work that morning, he had earnestly wanted to do a good job. Rehearsed in detail all the things he would say, then started to panic, goaded by the belief that, "I have to rush through this or I'll never cover everything". Is it possible that, in his quest to "get it right" and his desire to save his reputation as a good trainer, kindness had simply slipped off his radar and fear had taken its place?

May a teacher fear failing as much as a student?

May a trainer's stress be contagious?

But, what if the trainer was not afraid? What if he was simply passionate about his subject and his head was so crammed with facts, that he forgot *I was a person?*

It's easily done.

Whatever the cause, when a teacher, leader, or manager, creates a fear-dynamic or focuses only on facts, it has far reaching effects. Because, whoever we are, *we relate to life as a person first, and students, family members, or workers second.*

We long to be respected, far more than we long to hear information or advice! We want to feel seen and heard, far more than we want to remember the role of a verb in a sentence. We crave emotional and physical safety far more than we care that 2 + 2 = 4.

Thankfully, I have been taught by many people who deliberately, or instinctively, understood that I was a person.

My parents started the ball rolling by cradling me in their laps when they taught me to read. They awakened my curiosity with simple picture books and stories. *They hugged and loved me into learning.*

My mother hummed little songs and taught me "finger plays". How to tell tiny tales with my hands. She helped me build villages out of sand at the beach. Learn how to knit and paint and make use of scraps of wool to create pictures in latch hook rugs.

My father took me into the garden and placed a single blossom on my tender palm. Then he invited me to lift it close to my face and peer into its heart. Explore, and describe, the exquisite detail painted there by the original master artist.

My father loved nature and he taught me to glory in the wonder of creation. Appreciate each changing season. He showed me how to find as much delight in a lacy snowflake swirling down to melt on my mitten, as in discovering, hiding shyly among the leaves, the first ripe strawberry of summer. He also strolled with me down winding country lanes, where thatched cottages snoozed in the sun. Sometimes we paused to watch fat ducks waddle past. Or trace the liquid path of moorhens as they paddled on the village pond, or prodded rushes into nests with their scarlet beaks.

When I was older, I was also blessed to have a few exceptional teachers who knew how to pour creativity into their classes and make learning fun. And a scattering of mentors and leaders who noticed my fumbling attempts to learn new things and cheered me on to success.

All these people had the rare skill of being able to combine a love for their subject, or job, with a love for their students. This made their enthusiasm catching. Instead of creating a fear-meets-fear dance in their home, classroom or workplace, they were secure enough to relax. To enjoy passing on the flame of their knowledge, then cheering as it kindled afresh in my heart.

Most teachers are hired by a school because they are skilled in a certain area. They may therefore believe they are training the students to sew, or solve mathematical problems. To cook, or understand chemical reactions. While this is partly true, I know now that the main role of a *teacher is not to teach a subject or skill.*

It is to teach a person. A teenager, adult or child.

Teach them about love in the form of self-respect and about the wonder of life. Provide a safe place so each student is relaxed enough to learn, and free to be curious. Free to use all their mental capacity to focus on, and naturally grasp, the idea that

$2 + 2 = 4.$

IMPOSSIBLE

Impossible
may simply be
a premature
shroud for possible.

Your current situation may seem impossible, and perhaps some aspects of it are beyond your capacity or control. But before you consign your whole life to the "Too Hard Basket," consider this: You have already done many things which seemed impossible at the time.

For a start, you figured out how to breathe after living under water for nine months.

Then, you learned how to pull on your shoes and tie your laces after running barefoot.

In school, you unscrambled coded squiggles on a page and coaxed them into yielding their stories.

And when you returned home, you learned how to balance on a bicycle in spite of a few tumbles.

You could say, "All my friends learned to do similar things," and that's fair enough. *But you still faced each of these challenges personally*. You still kept at each task until you had mastered the skills yourself.

Did you have some help along the way? Sure. We all did. A teacher who showed us the meaning of ABC. A parent who held the back of our bicycle seat as we wobbled down the path. So perhaps, with a little help, you can decide which of today's *impossible* tasks to leave well alone, and which one to tackle.

Which ONE!

Unless, of course, before you begin, a treacherous idea worms its way into your mind. And you secretly realize that you *want the task to be impossible*. Because *impossible* has many advantages. If something's impossible, there's no pressure to perform, no shame in failure. Phew, what a relief!

Whatever our age, before we begin any new task, we silently gather evidence and ask ourselves, *Am I likely to fail or succeed?* The answer helps us decide how much energy we want to invest. If we believe we'll fail, we try to slip away unnoticed. Make excuses for not even trying.

Or *we create* an internal tug-of-war.

We place Curiosity at one end of the rope. (We hope she will help us imagine what success looks like and motivate us to try.) Then we hand Fear the other end of the rope. Even though we know he will say something nasty like, "Imagine mud on your face and a crowd of your peers laughing."

As Curiosity and Fear begin to tussle, they use up lots of our energy. They drain our mental and emotional batteries so much that motivation wanes and momentum wanders off with a shrug. Eventually, if someone pushes us enough, we may try the task a little. Give the rope a little tug, just to see what happens. But we're not likely to throw all our effort into trying. No way. Especially if we listen to Fear's whispers, "You'll stumble for sure, slip up, and end up flat on your face, with the taste of goop in your mouth."

To our fragile ego, being publicly shamed seems like a fate worse than death, and the idea of being labeled "a failure" is like a life sentence.

So we don't really try. *Until not trying becomes a habit.*

When this is happening, we rarely see that our subconscious ego-defense behavior is drawing us deeper into caves of despair. Or see that we are whiling away the lonely hours, scratching paintings of ourselves as cowards on the rock walls of our self-made prisons.

When I was teaching, I saw this happen more than once.

I saw smart, capable students playing mind games like this, spiraling down into defeat. Many of them were teenage boys. After failing in front of their mates a few times, coming last in a test, or missing a line when reading out loud, they quickly disengaged from schoolwork and refused to try. Burned once, twice, three times through the years, they had learned to be as cunning as wild animals sniffing a trap.

As teachers, we knew that whatever we tried, there was no way these students were going to risk getting caught out, being exposed to further ridicule. Being hurt or humiliated in front of their peers. For their part, they pretended they had lost their homework. They shrugged off knowledge as if they didn't care. They sat at the back of the class, rocked on their creaking chairs, and mocked the students who tried. They yelled out, "Loser!"

To save face.

These students desperately needed someone to see them. Really *see* them and befriend them safely. A mentor. A parent. A fellow student or a teacher. Sometimes they found such a person. Sometimes they did not.

When I managed the library, I watched teachers herding groups of students through the doors, hoping they would study. I helped the teachers find books for their students and I observed how each teacher treated the teenagers in their care. Some teachers turned their backs on the rebels, then sat in a corner reading the newspaper. Others tried briefly to engage them, then dismissed the students as hopeless and sent them to the principal.

Other teachers seemed to have a knack for helping reluctant students get past their fear of failure. Without yielding to inappropriate behavior, they quietly worked with prickly students. They helped them to take tiny, private risks. They patiently encouraged them and gave them small sips of success until they developed a taste for it.

Gradually, these students achieved a string of wins, *and they began to believe in their own competence.*

The most dedicated teachers also helped struggling students shine in the subjects where they excelled. They displayed their woodwork or encouraged them to join one of the school's sporting teams. They put their art up on the noticeboard or gave them a lead role in the school play. They deliberately put these students into situations where others could see them win and applaud their success.

As the months passed, the curiosity and hope of these students became stronger than their fear, and they stood a little taller. They also saw less of the principal and more of the inside of a book!

The most steady and courageous teachers went a step further. They did not just teach theories or give lectures; they *role modeled* resilience. They showed their students *what healthy adult behavior looked like.*

By their own example, they helped their students to see that all of life is a series of experiments, mini skirmishes with fear. The students quietly watched these teachers "have a go." They saw the teachers win and lose. They watched them laugh at themselves and bounce back from defeat with good humor. They saw them crippled and vulnerable in the face of tragedy, limping back to life, faith, and wholeness—scarred but undefeated.

In doing this, the teachers showed their students two key things: how to succeed and also how to recover from failure. And even more, that a person's identity is not measured by either failure or success. In a million ways they showed their students that failure is neither fatal nor permanent. Rather, it is a natural by-product of having the courage to live a life of authenticity and purpose. Day by day, the students saw, in practical ways, how life was done, how to be human, how to say sorry, how to be brave and how to be loyal to those you love.

When I was about seventeen, our biology teacher developed a brain tumor. As you can imagine, he was away from class for several months. One day, he came back to talk to us, even though he was still sore and his head was still shaved and scarred.

He did not give us a biology lecture, instead, he talked to us about life. About resilience and faith. As his gaze scanned the room, he looked at each one of us in turn, his eyes burning into ours, willing us to understand. What he said went something like this,

"The last few months have really challenged me. Been painful and tough. Sometimes I've felt like crying. Sometimes I've felt angry or afraid. Some nights I couldn't sleep as my mind swirled with "Why?" questions. But through it all, I've known one thing for sure. *God loves me.*" He paused and looked at us again. "Please, please, remember that whatever happens in your life, God loves you too."

A few months later, we filed into church for his funeral. Row on row of students in matching uniforms, sitting, for once, in silence, clutching soggy tissues in our laps.

Apparently, his teaching career was over.

But things are not always as they seem, for his faith and hope did not die that day. They lived on in his children and in my classmates and me. For, in his life, we caught a glimpse of raw courage and steadfast faith. Qualities to carry into our own futures. We also saw, beyond any doubt, that he valued us. That there was some intangible quality in us, and in him, that made him climb out of bed when he was dying, to come and speak with us. To care.

Teachers, like our biology teacher, just by living, give their students a thousand lessons.

In response, some students risk
having a go at life too, while
their teachers cheer them on.

So, hooray for all who teach!

For parents, mentors, and friends
with the love, commitment, and vision,
to wrap life-skills in words of hope.

THE MERRY-GO-ROUND

Some merry-go-rounds
are child's play.

Others make us sick!

As I glanced across the park, I could see the children's playground between the trees. There, in the center, was the merry-go-round beside the shiny yellow slide and the blue swings.

As I ran closer, I noticed that the circular base of the merry-go-round was scuffed and worn. Most of the red paint had been rubbed off the sturdy central pillar and off the slender metal bars, which radiated from it like spokes on a wheel. All around the base, there was a deep groove in the dirt, as if the mud had been trampled down by generations of childish feet running in circles.

I was the only child in the park, and I reached out a hand to give the merry-go-round a half-hearted push, expecting it to turn easily. But it was heavier than I thought, and it just sat there, unmoved by my gentle touch. So I pushed harder, then harder still, bracing my legs firmly on the ground, pushing with all my might.

Finally, it began to move, slowly, at first, then a little faster.

Encouraged by my success, I pushed it round and round a few times until it was spinning nicely. Then I leaped aboard for a ride. It was fun. As the wheel turned, I felt the wind in my hair and the warm sun on my face, then on my back. I watched the slide and swings glide by and birds soar high in the sky.

I was master of my destiny, free.

But suddenly, a large group of children swarmed into the playground. Before I could step off the merry-go-round, they grabbed the handles and began to run round and round, spinning it faster and faster. Big boys leapt wildly on and off, laughing. They dared each other to hold on by one hand and lean further out. As their bodies swayed over thin air, they taunted the younger children edging closer to the middle, the ones hanging on for dear life, wide-eyed.

Like me.

Too scared to speak, I grasped the bar with all my strength, feeling giddy and sick. I squeezed my eyes shut, trying to blot out the spinning playground, willing the boys to stop.

Finally, when I was sure I couldn't bear another second without losing my breakfast, I heard the scuffing of feet and the big children's voices tumbling away toward the swings. The wheel began to slow down, and relief washed over me. I opened my eyes and saw the trees gradually sliding back into focus.

At last, the spinning stopped, and I stepped off the wheel. But to my surprise, the ground itself was now spinning. Giddy and sick, I staggered to a park bench and crumpled there, motionless, waiting for the awful whirling in my head to fade.

As you may have guessed, I haven't ridden a merry-go-round for a while now. And yet I have, repeatedly, for there are many kinds. I'm guessing you sometimes ride one too.

Maybe, like me, you've found yourself at a new school or in a new job. You begin full of anticipation and joy, but it's harder than you expect. But you keep at it, pushing yourself to succeed until you start to make progress. There's a smile on your face, and the winds of freedom are blowing in your hair.

But suddenly, or little by little, the pace picks up. Others start to expect too much of you. They demand more work, give you more assignments, or they schedule more exams. Suddenly you realize your world is spinning out of control, that you are lurching through each day giddy from lack of sleep. Anxious and sick at heart, all you want to do is close your eyes and yell, "Stop! Please stop! I want to get off!"

One evening, several years ago, I knew this was happening to me. The pressures at work were building to a fever pitch. I was rapidly losing control, losing out on precious family time and forgetting how to laugh.

I desperately needed to press pause and regain control of my life, give myself time and space to make sense of the events that were swirling around me. Listen to all the emotions that were circling deep inside my soul.

So, one evening, while the rest of the family slept, I sat down at my desk and switched on a small lamp. As I sat there in the soft circle of light, many of my emotions and fears rose to the surface, and I found myself whispering a little seven-word prayer that went something like this,

Dear God, please tell me about uncertainty.

Though my head was wearily bowed, I did not close my eyes. Instead, I reached for a sheet of paper and a pen.

At the top of the page, I wrote "Uncertainty" and boldly underlined it. Now what?

I decided to write down any similar words that came into my head like, "chaos, change, fear, opportunity and mystery." Next, I drew a line down the center of the page. On the left, I began to list all my miserable emotions. Because I was alone, I felt free to pour them out unedited. The list began something like this.

I feel:

Sad
Flat
Tired
Lonely
Unmotivated
Afraid
Lost
Confused
Tearful

Just listing these feelings helped me.

As I poured out my heart, I felt I was honoring myself, that I was giving myself permission to feel what I was feeling without judgment or shame. I was taking the time I needed to hear my own heart's call.

After I had listed all my sad feelings, I looked at them for a while. Then, with a sigh, I added a few more.

Next, I looked at the blank column on the right of the page and wondered, *What shall I write there?* Not knowing what else to do, I began to work down the list of words on the left and deliberately write the opposite emotion or attitude next to it on the right. For instance, next to sad, I wrote *glad* and on down the page.

Glad
Buoyant
Full of energy
Understood

Inspired
Courageous
I've got a clear purpose
Focused
Joyful

Naturally, it took a fair bit of effort to think of cheery words when I felt low! At first, it also seemed superficial and fake. But I had the framework on the left to help me, so I simply worked down the page.

At first, I did this without any real enthusiasm. But as I selected opposite words line by line, I began to feel something shifting inside me. Surprised, I realized that *the process itself was beginning to change how I felt*.

When I reached the end of the page, I saw something quite striking, for there, laid out before me, were two clear *attitude paths*.

Seeing these columns, I felt a whisper of hope. Hope that I could reclaim my own feelings and then, step-by-step, find the wisdom and power to reclaim my own life.

Instead of being a passive victim of others' "spin", I could re-center myself. Be still long enough to choose who I wanted to be and where I wanted to go.

I've whispered that little prayer many times since that solitary evening, and each time I've changed the last word to fit my circumstances. For instance, when people were too demanding or rude, I wrote, "Dear God, please tell me about bullying," or if I started comparing myself to a beautiful, talented, popular friend, I wrote, "Dear God, please tell me about jealousy." When I was enjoying a budding romance and wondered if it was for real, I wrote, "Dear God, please tell me about love."

Whenever I have made the time and space to do this, I have sat up straighter than before and often felt inspired. Been blessed by many "Ah-ha!" moments of clarity and gained insights into others' views and values *and more aware-ness of my own*.

ONE IN A HOLE

Good questions act
like rungs on a rope ladder
leading us up toward the light.

It's great to find the *right* answer to a question, very satisfying.

But if we become obsessed with seeking glittering answers in life, faith, or work, *we may grossly underestimate the power of good questions*. For instance, if you repeatedly find yourself falling into the same hole and making the same mistakes, you may be tempted to ask:

How could I have been so stupid?
What's the matter with me?
Why did I mess up, yet again?

These sound like valid questions. When we ask them, we can fool ourselves into thinking we are being accountable, ready to be honest. But these questions have nothing to do with accountability and everything to do with blame. Therefore, they don't help us find real solutions. All they do is rob us of joy, motivation, and hope—just when we need these qualities the most.

If we routinely ask *blame questions* like those above, all we do is burrow ourselves deeper into the mud of defeat. Once there, we tend to wallow in self-recrimination until we become bogged down in despair. Why on earth would we actively train ourselves, or anyone else, to be so helpless and hopeless? So miserable! The whole idea is absurd, and yet we do it anyway!

Almost on autopilot, we slide into repeating words and phrases passed on to us by our parents and grandparents, words that lead us down, not up. But, in our saner moments, we long to ask intelligent, productive questions, like:

How did I get out last time?
Who can give me a hand up?
What new options are available today?

We want to learn from our mistakes and teach our children to do the same. We want to forgive ourselves, and others, and find healing solutions. And little by little, I believe we can.

In life's toughest times,
let's choose to ask creative questions.
Questions inspired by love, purpose and hope.

TWO EMOTIONAL PATHS

Life is unfair.
I know that!
Now what?

During my final year of school, my friends and I were under a lot of pressure. In our eyes, we were being bombarded by assignments and essays which were coming at us from all directions. One day, when a teacher gave us yet another assignment, we stormed out of class and dumped our school bags on the ground. Then we gathered in a ragged circle to fume and fuss. We took turns stressing about how hard our lives were. We muttered, "It's not fair" in a million ways and complained how out of control we felt. At first, letting off steam like this was cathartic. We felt understood and less alone. But our discussion soon descended into an unproductive whinge session, which made us feel even more powerless.

As our energy wound down, I noticed one of my friends had not joined us, so I wandered up the hallway to see where she was. As I pushed open the door to the library, I saw her quietly studying at a table by the window, the sunshine spilling over her head and books. When I approached, she looked up with a smile. Coming closer, I saw, to my chagrin, that unlike me, she was already halfway through her *unfair* and *impossible* assignment. Bother.

I can see now that her approach was light-years ahead of mine in terms of maturity and productivity. While I procrastinated, then tried to justify my attitude by blaming my teachers, my friend quickly adapted to the new circumstances. She did not squander precious time or energy on blame or on creating emotional static. Instead, she made the best of the time she had.

Today, that schoolgirl is a successful doctor, teacher, and spiritual leader who invests many precious hours in healing and encouraging others.

Therefore, with a nod in her direction, I choose to challenge a lifetime habit of resisting and resenting change! Of pouting when others call the shots, as if I'm powerless! Instead, I'm going to drag myself, kicking and screaming, out of procrastinating and whining and pour my creative energy into making good use of my time, energy and influence. Well that's my plan!

Whatever others say or do,
I'm going to use what I've got,
however small, while I've still got it!

SINK OR SWIM?

A drowning soul
is rarely polite.

After anticipating the break for months, you arrive at the beach and spread out your towel. The day stretches ahead of you forever and the blue sea sparkles all the way to the horizon. Ah bliss!

You snooze for a while in the sun, then decide to go for a quick swim before lunch to cool down. As you bob gently on the swell, all your cares wash away and you feel buoyed up in body and soul. When your tummy rumbles, you reluctantly head for shore, but after a while you sense something is wrong. You are swimming *toward* the shore but being *dragged away* from it, pulled out to sea in a strong rip. Panic begins to bubble up inside, and you paddle furiously. You turn, as best you can to face the shore, and scan the land and sea for potential help.

On the beach, you notice several families relaxing in the sunshine. Young children are running to and fro building sand castles, and behind them an older couple are throwing a ball for their dog. The person nearest to the waves is sitting in a beach chair and idly flicking through a magazine.

Sensing you are being sucked out to sea, would you casually call . . .

"Hello there. Sorry to trouble you, but I'm in a bit of bother. Would mind giving me a hand, please? There's no rush. If you're in the middle of a story, feel free to finish it first. I can wait."

Or would you shout? Scream? Wave your arms in the air to attract their attention? Yell at the top of your lungs, between gurgling gulps? Try to span the widening distance between you and the shore by increasing the volume of your voice?

Why?

As I said at the beginning, a drowning person is rarely polite. People who feel overwhelmed by life's turbulent sea are often close to panic. Especially if they they feel their resources are not equal to the demands of the situation.

It's true that some yelling is habitual, or just plain nasty. Some anger is destructive and the snarling words have real bite, but often we cry out because we're scared.

Because we feel broken and abandoned. Low on energy and hope. This can happen at any age, and in any culture.

One dark night, we look at our lives, and we sigh. We see no way out of the pressure and responsibility that is slowly sucking us under. Weary of swimming, and keeping everyone, and everything, afloat, we are desperately tired. Physically and emotionally exhausted and longing for relief.

Sometimes we dream of having a simpler life. At other times, we only have the energy to doggedly tread water hoping that someone will see us struggling and care. Offer us a hand, or at least show us the way to solid ground. To a rock of rest, relief and hope.

So how do we end up in deep water in the first place? Sometimes we leap into it ourselves!

Convinced we can handle the current, we take on wave after wave of responsibility. We strive for a promotion. Or we accumulate more debt trying to spend our way to "a better lifestyle." But there are days when our earnest quest mocks us, and we find ourselves floundering rather than floating.

At other times, we are swept out to sea by a flood-tide of adverse or demanding events.

We are buffeted by repeated waves of illness, accident or misfortune. We lose someone we love, then have a huge mess to clear up in the wake of their passing. We cry over mounting utility bills, or we inherit the sole care of an ailing parent. Even positive life events can leave us reeling. We may adore our twins, but not the fact that they teethe together and bawl for attention in stereo.

When someone in a team or family has a "short fuse" it's easy to cast blame. Tell them to "get a grip" or change. Believe they are the problem, then gossip behind their back. In most situations, it's easier to fix blame, than look for creative ways to reduce the workload. Easier to expect more of ourselves or others than downsize our demands or let go of a few cherished expectations.

If several members of a family are taking on water at once, things can get decidedly desperate. There may be a fair bit of yelling! This may have nothing to do with how dearly the people love each other; more to do with each person's weary hopelessness crying out to be heard. Their lonely striving begging to be seen.

If this happens, we may be tempted to call everything quits. Flee into entertainment, an apartment alone, or into working overtime. But sometimes all the situation needs is one brave person. Someone willing to voice the collective angst and say, "Things have been tough for us all lately. I'm sorry if I've sometimes made things worse by my attitude. What can we do to ease things up around here?"

Then look around the table and ask, "What do you think would help? What do you need most right now?" Asking such questions takes a lot of good timing, wisdom and courage, for some things can be fixed and some can't, and no one needs life to get harder. But, given a bit of goodwill, there's a chance that talking about it will help.

Some family members may only ask for a few more hugs, or hot meals. Others may mutter, "I just need more sleep!" A perceptive teenager may offer a more challenging answer, "I think Dad's stressed out and needs to change jobs" or,

"We've often talked about moving to the country, so why don't we just do it? I'd love a horse!"

Whatever suggestions flow in, at least you'll know what people think and have a fighting chance of exploring options. Working together to make life easier for everyone.

As human beings, we call, "Help!" in many languages.

We thrash about making a lot of noise and fervently hope that someone nearby spots us in the water. We hope they look beyond the silt and mud we are stirring up with all our thrashing, and care enough to get involved. Pull us to dry ground, (or at least point out the way). When we are drowning in work, or despair, we hope that someone has the energy and skill to send a life-ring, or a kind word, skimming across the waves in our direction. Or, better yet, they launch a lifeboat, speed to where we are, and reach out their hand. Then says with genuine warmth,

"Climb aboard friend. You're safe now, I've got you."

It's amazing the change that happens in a person when they're no longer all at sea. When they feel safe. When they have the resources to cope, and have hope. They tend to relax and say "please" and "thank you" much more readily.

They may even smile!

THE TALLY

May I present,
an ordinary mortal,
one with skills and flaws.

The only kind
Dear Old Planet Earth
can offer you to love.

Relationships have a lot in common with mathematics. For, wherever you live, there's plenty of scope to add and subtract!

If you like, you can choose to make a detailed tally of all your loved one's flaws. Create a hefty ledger of all their faults. Each time you add an item to your list, you can then subtract a little respect. A little affection. But when you do this, love tends to wane, nagging multiplies and scorn compounds!

If it suits your mood, you can also demand longer hours and increased accounting fees, then publish your list as frequently and loudly as you like. You may also add lots of *fine print* to reduce the interest you have to give on their account. Then you can add multiple requirements thinly disguised as "To Do" lists. (So your beloved—whether adult, teenager or child, can clearly see how to earn a better rate. How to pass your frequent audits!)

On the other hand,

You may choose to create a detailed tally of all your loved one's endearing qualities and add to it daily. Then frequently scan the list, eager to mention with warmth and good humor an item or two. Make a game of showing how much you *already* love and appreciate them.

If you feel especially passionate, you may even take delight in adding bonus interest to your joint account in the form of hugs and kisses!

In the end, the way you calculate in any circumstance, relationship, or setting, is totally up to you!

Just in case you're wondering . . . you may keep a similar running tally on yourself.

Then find yourself in credit or debit!

101 WAYS

Showing we are vulnerable scares us witless.
Literally. Afraid of being vulnerable
we slip into the lunacy of choosing
isolation over connection.

We barricade ourselves within

a citadel of loneliness
rather than say to a friend,
"You hurt me," and let them see
and heal our wounded heart.

But even if our lips are still, we have developed a thousand ways to say,
"You've hurt me."

We slam doors,
We scowl and shun.
We bristle with anger and
Go silent and withdraw.

We hunch our shoulders and slouch off.
We nurse grudges like teething babies.
We shoulder physical or verbal guns
Loaded with "comeback."

When we finally open our lips, it's often to gossip behind our friend's back. Tell others the story over and over again, building the drama. Circle through endless loops of, "he said, she said," hoping to successfully abdicate all personal responsibility and bury our former friend under all the blame.

Unaware that, by default, in making them powerful, we have abdicated our own power.

Sometimes, we cast our friend in the role of an ogre, then we fear and despise the being we have created. Finally, after wallowing in our own propaganda for weeks or for years, we convince ourselves that our former friend is dangerous. That they are plotting against us and we have to defend ourselves against them.

We tell ourselves that all hope of reconciliation is lost and that, after all they have done, they are not worth befriending anyway! So we pull up the drawbridge of our hearts and mount cannons in the castle of our souls just in case they approach us. We may even *launch a pre-emptive attack!*

Why?

Wouldn't it be so much easier, in the long run, to simply say, "I was hurt by what you did yesterday"? Then give them a chance to explain? And, if we can muster the courage, add, "I really value your friendship, so please don't do it again."

Oh, what a lot of life we miss when we dismiss friendships too easily. When we expect ourselves, and others to be flawless before we can be friends! When we lean towards being tight, tense and brittle, instead of relaxed and easy-going.

Why do we let misunderstandings divide us when we could continue to have such fun working and playing together? When we could relish the thrill of combining our skills, talents, and resources to enjoy life and make a real difference in the world?

THE LAMP

Her story

It's almost my birthday.

The idea had been tingling in her spine for days, popping up in unexpected moments, and making a warm glow spread through her whole body.

At last, the morning finally came, and she woke with a sense of joyful certainty. *Today's my birthday!*

She sprang out of bed and dressed, alive with anticipation. Laughter and giggles chased each other through her mind, making her grin into the mirror as she combed her hair. *Sixteen, wow, I'm almost a lady!*

Tossing the covers over her bed in a hasty attempt to make it, she raced for the stairs and leapt down them two at a time. Seconds later, she burst into the kitchen, calling out a cheery "Good Morning!"

Her father was there, stirring porridge in a battered tin saucepan. He turned and smiled, "Happy Birthday!" Then he resumed his stirring. She laughed, and said, "Thank you" to his back, and glanced at the table. She saw a large lumpy gift by her plate, the frail brown paper gaping here and there to reveal something made of wood. A little frisson of warning shivered through her, but she brushed it aside, nurturing her buoyant excitement, clinging to joy.

When her father turned off the stove, she collected two spoons from the drawer, the milk, and a small bag of dark brown sugar. Then she pulled out her chair and sat down. Her father began to ladle out the porridge and divide it between their bowls. He scraped out the pan carefully, making sure that not one oat was wasted. With deliberate steps, he carried the empty pan to the sink and splashed it with water.

Why on earth is he so slow!

Finally, he sat down, bowed his head for grace, then said, "You can open it now." Her hands flew to the paper, and she tore it off with eager fingers. As she did, the joy in her heart curled up and died, for there was the lamp, the old lamp she had seen for years in the untamed junk corner of her father's bedroom. The one lying on its side, abandoned, among the broken furniture.

As she pulled the last scraps of paper away, she regarded it with dull eyes, her gaze sweeping over the chunky base, which was little more than a rough-hewn block of wood, where traces of time's dust still lingered. Not knowing what else to do, she turned the lamp around and saw one side of the shade was creased, as if a dent had been smoothed out. Close to tears, she silently stroked the cord with one finger and pulled away a tiny cobweb still clinging to its coils.

It was so hard to say it, but she knew she must, so, without looking up, she said as bravely as she could, "Thank you." Even to her own ears, it sounded hollow.

"I thought it would be useful by your bed."

She nodded and picked up her spoon.

They both busied themselves with their porridge then and ate silently, as if it took great concentration to lift the spoon to their mouths, to chew. Finally, when she had scraped up the last mouthful, she scooped up the lamp and fled to her room. She didn't need the mirror to tell her she had tears in her eyes or a doctor to explain why her stomach felt sick.

It wasn't just the ugliness of the gift that hurt her, though she dearly loved pretty things. It was the lack of creativity, the lack of thought, as if *he hadn't even bothered to know her* or what she might like.

As she sniffed and wiped her eyes, logic tried to argue that he loved her.

While she tumbled her schoolbooks into her bag, logic urged her to remember his devotion, his practical care: the hot porridge, even now warming her, the rainy days when he drove her to school so she didn't have to cycle alone or face the thundering trucks blinding her with muddy spray. The times he picked fresh lettuce from the garden for their lunch or chose pink and cream roses with the dew still clinging to their buds so she could decorate her white hat. The length of fabric he helped her find so she could sew herself a summer dress . . .

Logic was right, of course. As it always is. Yet it was also wrong, for she craved something more than logic. *She wanted desperately to be seen and accepted, understood and cherished. To be the most important person in the world to somebody.*

His story

Weariness was his constant companion now.

He felt wedded to it even more surely than he'd been wedded to his wife of twelve years, the wife who had faded before his eyes and drifted too far into illness for him to reach her, too far for him to save her.

He hadn't expected his life to turn out like this.

Growing up, he'd been the strong one. He was the one who took over the family business when he was fourteen, and his father died. He was the one who kept it going and provided for his mother and siblings. In those busy years, when he found brief moments to dream, he'd imagined he'd have a family himself one day, gather his children around the table, smile across their heads at his beautiful wife. Build a home filled with love.

Nothing had prepared him for the crushing loneliness of his nights now, the aching void through which he trod day by day, the routine that rarely varied. He was bored with it himself, but he didn't have the energy to be creative, so he got up, ironed himself a shirt, packed his bag of books, and checked the day's appointments. Then he scrounged in the pantry for some bread . . . again.

He'd been in survival mode for years, but somehow, he'd always kept on top of things, found just enough energy to make it through the day, scraped together enough money to pay the bills. Sometimes, for a fleeting moment, he envied people with happy families, but steadied by his faith in God, he pressed on. Managed to summon a resolute smile. On frosty mornings, when he longed to stay in his warm bed, he swung his legs out anyway. He stood up, even as his toes cringed and curled with the cold as they hit the threadbare mat.

He had a daughter to support. The light of his life, his one and only child. A precious but puzzling teenager. In quiet moments, he sometimes asked himself, *Who is this young woman under my roof? What does a teenage girl think anyway?*

He hadn't a clue.

Shaking his head, he checked the mirror and laid down his shaver. It was her birthday in a few days, and he still had no idea what to give her.

Sixteen. Only yesterday, she was a child, sitting on her mother's lap. Then came the awful years. He sighed. *The years when I had no idea what to do. I was so torn between my dying wife, my little daughter, and the need to go out to work to keep the whole thing going. Such bleak years pretending I was fine and having to be strong for everyone, making wise decisions, even when I was drowning myself. Out of my depth, floundering.*

Then, in the end, having to say goodbye to everything anyway, watching, helpless, as our family disintegrated beyond repair. Visiting my dear Amy in the hospital, kissing her pale lips for the last time and walking away.

Driving Lorna to boarding school. Plodding up all those creaking stairs in the dark and lugging her battered suitcase. Every step a betrayal. Climbing higher for her sake, even as I sank into despair myself. Kissing her curls and driving away. Away. My heart urging me to turn around and wrap her in my arms. My mind pressing my foot to the pedal and speeding me home to loneliness.

Did I really do all I could back then? Who knows?

I chose her school with care. Wrote to her each week and gave her my best advice. Took packets of chocolate biscuits when I went to visit. Prayed for her with all my heart and soul. I brought her home for holidays . . . even when all I could manage was an attic room. Leaving her alone there while I was at work.

Where did all the years go? Who is this girl? My daughter?

He shook his head again and hung up his towel. *Maybe I can buy her a new dress, but where would I shop? How much do dresses cost these days, anyway? If only my sales were better . . .*

He plodded upstairs, praying for ideas, and began to make his bed. As he pulled up the blankets, he happened to glance across the room where the spare furniture lay. At first, he only saw what he always saw, reproach: a heap of chairs and appliances that would come in useful one day when he had the energy to finish extending the kitchen. Then he spied the lamp. Maybe that would do. *She loves to read in bed*, he told himself. He walked over to the corner and began to rescue the lamp from the legs of an upturned kitchen chair.

He pictured his daughter curled up in bed, her face bathed in lamplight, reading. *Brilliant! She won't have to scramble out of bed to turn off the light, then fumble her way back in the chilly dark. She can read in cozy bliss, then turn off the light whenever she pleases.*

It was as if a weight had rolled off his shoulders. At last, he had a plan, a solution to the birthday dilemma.

OUR STORY

That night, he tapped on the door of his daughter's bedroom and went in to say goodnight. She was already in bed, propped up on her elbows, a book spread out on her pillow. The rest of the room was in shadow, but the lamp glowed above her head, shining on her hair like a halo.

She looked up from her book and smiled at him.

For a moment, he stopped breathing. *How precious she is. How beautiful!*

As he bent to kiss her cheek and murmur a prayer of blessing over her head, he wondered if she had any idea how much he loved her. How, even when words failed him, he tried to tell her in a million ways *that everything he did was for her*.

MIRAGE OR MIRACLE?

Seeking perfection in place, person, or profession,
our hands forever outstretched toward a mirage,
we may trip over the glory and wonder of real life.

I have to confess that a restless quest for perfection has shaped many aspects of my life. Starting with bricks, mortar, and apple trees!

I could blame my father for leading our family on a semi-nomadic journey, but I have a feeling my mother had itchy feet too.

I began life in a sturdy two-story house built by my grandfather. It was on the main street of a small town, and he had fitted out the large front room as a shoe shop. As mentioned above, my father inherited this business as a teenager of fourteen, when his father died.

Years later, when my parents married and I myself was born, I listened for the little bell above the door to ring. When I could walk, I toddled in to gaze up at customers as they selected slippers or handed my father boots to repair. Even now, whenever I breathe in the warm smell of good leather, I remember my father. I hear him bending over the iron shoe "last" hammering on new soles, his lips full of tiny tacks, ready. Or I see him placing my sandals on his workbench, to cut them open here and there so my growing toes had room to wriggle.

Our house had a long garden at the back with space to grow vegetables. Late one summer afternoon, my parents pruned some bushes, and we had a big bonfire. As a treat, my mother wrapped dough around sticks and helped me hold my bread out to the flames. When it was cooked, she pulled it off the stick and filled the hollow center with butter and strawberry jam. It tasted yummy, even if most of the filling melted and ran down my hands and I ended up licking my arms as well as my lips!

By the time I was three years old, my parents had sold the house and the business, and we made our first move.

Hoping for a more rural life, my parents selected a place in a small village several hours away. The large rambling red-brick home was called Nut Tree House, and it's still there. It had two huge walnut trees in the front yard and a tiny slide my father made underneath. My mother was a former nurse, and there was ample space for her to bring home sick babies or foster children, or loan a room to a single mother until she found her feet.

I loved sitting on the lawn and making daisy chains or running to the shed to watch tiny yellow chicks hatch. Once, I found some frog's spawn in a nearby pond and carried it home in a glass jam jar with a handle made from a loop of string. I often paused in my play to peer at the tadpoles swimming in the old sink. One day I went out to the shed as usual and found they had grown legs and escaped. So I chased them giggling, as they hopped all over the floor!

To me, the house and garden were perfect, but not to my parents, so they sold up and moved.

With the funds from its sale, they bought a stone cottage on the edge of the same village. It was tucked down a lane behind the old church. The huge veg-etable garden was edged with beautiful lilac bushes in ivory, mauve, and deep purple. In spring and summer, I ran free in the orchard. It was full of ancient plum trees and the air was fragrant with the drifting petals of thirty-seven apple trees. (Yes, I counted them!) Our land was surrounded by fields, and sheep brought their lambs to drink at the pond opposite our kitchen window. I learned to ride my first bicycle at this house, wobbling up our rutted flowery drive while my father clung to my seat and puffed along behind.

But something about this house didn't suit them either. So, we moved again.

Our fourth house was just up the road in the next village. It was much smaller, and the garden was only a narrow strip. But I was thrilled to make friends with another seven-year-old who lived three doors down. We cycled to school together, and in the summer holidays, we went, just the two of us, to the local river estuary. After filling our pockets with shells, we pedaled home. Once there, we carefully swooshed off the sand in warm water and spread the shells out on the back steps to dry. When her mother gave us tiny bottles of nail polish, we dotted the white shells with soft shades of pink, making delicate spotted butterflies.

While I was busy making friends and shell-painting, my father laboriously laid stones for a crazy paving path to the washing line. When his path was finished, you guessed it . . . we sold the house, and moved!

This time we landed in the bustling port city of Bristol where we settled in a tall town house at the end of a shabby, but formerly elegant, row. I walked to school alone there, careful of my step, as cars whizzed past. By the time the house was painted to my parents' liking, my mother was too sick to care for me. So, she packed my bag and hugged me goodbye. Then I picked up my teddy bear, climbed into the car, and waved her, and my fifth home, goodbye.

A family in the nearby town of Cheddar kindly gave me refuge. At their home, I had white toast for breakfast and feasted on the local cheddar cheese. Sometimes their daughter Sarah and I were allowed to make a cubby house under the kitchen table, and we created our own little world. Hidden there, wearing paper tiaras, we were secret princesses, and fairies fluttered out of story books to play with us.

But I was not so keen on school, on being a stranger again and a novelty to be stared at. But after the school bell rang, life picked up, especially when we had a few coins. Rushing for the door, we leapt on our bicycles and pedaled furiously until we reached the village sweet shop. Propping the bicycles haphazardly against the wall, we scrambled inside.

Now time slowed to a crawl, for how could we possibly choose what to buy from all the bright bottles and gleaming jars? Finally, we settled on a few lollies sparkling with sugar and promise, and clutching our tiny paper bags in triumph, we flew home.

Unfortunately, neither the lollies nor my home in Cheddar lasted. Within a few months, I was moved again, this time to boarding school. I was about nine years old by now, and this was my fifth school, and seventh home.

Phew!

Looking back now, I'm filled with nostalgia, but also a keen desire to embrace each one of those homes.

Why?

Because every single one had something unique and beautiful to offer: lanes to explore, flowers to pick, or friends to play with. As a child, I had time for reading, for dolls and drawing, but none for perfection. I didn't even know it existed.

All I wanted was love, joy, and stability. A puppy or kitten to stroke, and a place to run and play.

I did not understand my parents' restless search or why they moved so often. But I know they never found perfection, never discovered the ideal house or neighbours, and never earned an easy, reliable income.

And, what is more, they never caught a glimpse of an ideal person in the mirror either.

Oh, how I would love to go back in time, fling my arms around their necks and soothe their seeking souls. Tell them through laughter and tears,

For goodness sake, don't push yourselves so hard! Leave time for play! It's not your job to save the world!

This side of eternity, perfection doesn't exist.[4]
Please, put down roots.
Lay down your anxious quest and rest.

Here is fine. Right here is enough.
You are enough.
Just love me, and love each other.

That is all. That is ALL!

Half a Mind?

Imagination springs from
the same mind as action.

When I arrived at boarding school, I was two years younger than any of the
other students, who started at eleven years old. Some of the teenage girls
were kind and supportive. But some of them took delight in telling us younger
girls scary stories after lights-out. They knew, and we knew, that there was
nowhere else we could go. We were their captive audience.

When a story began, some of us children would squish our pillows up to our
cheeks to block our ears. But the girls were good storytellers, and their muffled words soon drew us in. Little by little, we eased the feathers out of our
ears to listen. After all, if we didn't hear their words, how could we know
which ones to block?

If the girls had a flashlight, they also made grotesque faces to illustrate their
stories. We alternated between squeezing our eyes tightly shut and peeping
out between our lashes to see what they were doing. Soon, in spite of our best
efforts, we were carried along by their tales. Lying rigid under our shroud of
blankets, we hung on every whispered word. We were mesmerized by their
mimes, and we fell prey to their storytelling power. For better or worse, we
had to know how the story ended.

After the taletellers finished, they turned off their flashlights and wandered off
to bed. But as younger children, we trembled in the living darkness. United
in our fear but alone in our thoughts.

Of course, right then, when my imagination was animated with fantasy monsters, I needed to visit the bathroom. My mind told my body, "Forget it!" But
my body replied, "Hurry up and go!" Eventually, after much internal debate,
I slid silently from under the covers and tiptoed to the bedroom door.

After a quick glance over my shoulder to check nothing nasty was following
me, I peered into the long, shadowy hallway. It was lit by a single dull lightbulb. With all my senses on high alert, I looked both ways. The other doorways, which, in daylight, were storerooms and bedrooms, were now dark
caves where hobgoblins waited, ready to pounce. At last, heart thumping, I

stepped into the gloom and padded silently along in my bare feet, hugging the wall as I went.

Afraid of being alone, yet hoping I was alone.

The old school building with its creaking floors has been demolished now, and all the hobgoblin caves have been exposed to the light.

But elsewhere in the world, hobgoblin caves remain. Some of them, tragically, are all too real, and terrors lurk there. Some people are so traumatized by the horrors of war or abuse, that even after years of counseling, painful memories and scars linger. And, if we want to, we have plenty of opportunity in libraries and online to tap into the horror stories of overactive minds. Into the written or graphic inventions of folk who seem to find pleasure in exploring darkness. Who are fascinated by evil, and drawn into its mesmerizing thrall.

This is true in every town and country.

For instance, one Saturday night several years ago, when I was hoping to relax for a while, I flipped on the television. A lady with a broad grin and syrupy voice began to list the programs. What she said went something like this, "For your viewing pleasure this evening, we have a great line-up of programs. At 7 p.m., there's a wonderful murder mystery. At 8 p.m., we have a gritty police drama for you. Then at 9 p.m., you can finish off the night with a probing investigation into a terrorist attack. Enjoy your evening!"

Enjoy my evening? Was she mad?

But no, she smiled before she disappeared, as if she was doing me a favor, as if her list pleased her.

Have we forgotten how odd this really is? Are we appalled by the gory games of ancient gladiators, yet blind to the nature of our own "entertainment"? If all the events listed in her programs really happened, no one would be having an "enjoyable evening." We would be fleeing for our lives, trembling in terror under the bed, or distraught with grief.

Thankfully, this time when the scary stuff came on, I had more than a pillow. I had a remote control in my hand, and I could press the "off" button.

Maybe this smooth-talking lady thought evil was fun, but I doubt it. She seemed friendly enough, the kind of lady who would pat dogs and smile at children. Instead, I think she was simply doing her job and buying into the popular belief, which goes something like this, "My mind has two separate compartments, one for reality and one for fantasy."

Really?

There seems to be a flaw in this argument somewhere. Surely, if half my mind is busy feasting on mayhem and murder, the other half cannot focus on living a more compassionate life. And if I pour hate, anger, and fear into one *side* of my mind, there's no way I can make more kindness and peace flow out of the other *side*.

Not if I want to be whole.

To have integrity of being.

Harmony and *integration*
between who I am on the inside
and who I am on the outside.

MIND TRAVEL

Nomad or settler?
Explorer or builder?
You choose.

Long before the first plane sped down the runway and lifted into the sky, people traveled to the ends of the earth in their imagination. Without a ticket or a boarding pass, they soared through time and space, entirely free, and you and I can do the same.

While some mental journeys demand more concentration than others, ultimately, for better or worse, we all choose where our thoughts go. So where will you travel today?

IMAGINATION AIRWAYS	
Your carrier of choice	
Today's flights	
Train wreck Pass	Cancelled
Despair Gully	Cancelled
Sanctuary Cove	Boarding now
Hope Health Spa	Boarding now
Green Valley Farm	Go to gate

Will you board a barge to the
mosquito-ridden swamps of Resentment?

Pitch your tent on the mudslide of If Only
and slither into the Valley of Despair?

Will you climb into the wire cage of Revenge
and plummet down the mine shaft to Bitterness?

Or will you

Sail to the balmy tropical island called Hope
and pluck the fruit of Motivation?

Board a train to Kindness and link arms with a
fellow traveler at the Humanitarian Ball?

Hike to the peak called Love and fill your
lungs with the rarified air of Gratitude?

No one will ever know where your thoughts go, but you will. And, in time, your face, and then your life, will eventually tell the world where you have been. Because the mental flight you board today *will change who you become* and profoundly influence where you land tomorrow.

PERSPECTIVE

Windblown seeds
of weed or flower
all grow when watered.

One gray morning I woke up sad. Snug and warm in my nest of soft blankets, I felt too weary to move. As I delayed getting up, I let my mind wander to several painful events in my life, and I sighed. *I guess my life has always been sad,* I thought gloomily, *and it always will be.*

An hour later, after a shower and some breakfast, I went outside to water the flowers. The clouds had blown away to reveal a brilliant blue sky. As the water splashed onto the pink and purple petunias and sparkled on the dainty white alyssum, I drank in the beauty of the morning. I felt myself smiling as I turned off the hose and left for work. What a glorious new day!

Once again, I had literally changed my mind within an hour.

Logically, we know our moods can be fickle, but when we're in the middle of a mood, it's hard to remember this. Our gut feelings can seem so logical! Sometimes they do reflect reality, *but this is not always the case.* If we make a major decision based solely on our fleeting emotions, it's like gazing at a lone cloud drifting across the summer sky and using it to predict next week's weather.

For instance, if we believe everything our emotions tell us when we are sad, we can begin to believe we have always been sad. But this is not true. Even in the middle of sorrow or loss, we know we have experienced some happy times. Little pockets of joy. Moments of laughter. Days when we flew kites in the sunshine.

When we deliberately remember all these times, our emotions can shift within minutes. And this helps us realize *how much power we have over our own thoughts. How liberating it can be to actively choose our own moods.*

At first glance, flying a kite seems like a frivolous pastime, an outdoor activity to keep children busy on long summer afternoons.

But there is something more to flying a kite than getting a small piece of fabric or plastic to stay in the sky. Flying a kite takes more than enthusiasm; it takes skill. It demands total concentration and a resilient determination to succeed. Each time the kite is dumped by the wind and crashes to the ground in a crumpled heap, its limp form asks us a silent question, "Will you pick me up and try again?"

And each time we say, "Yes!" We grow a little smarter or we run a little faster until, finally, our persistence pays off, and the kite begins to rise, to soar. Higher and higher. Then, filled with relief, we stop running, skid to a stop, and gulp in great lungfuls of air.

But even when our feet are still, our gaze rises with the kite. We watch it dip and sway and soar. We sense every sky-high movement echoed in our earth-bound fingers. We feel the kite tug on the string like a live thing as it darts here and there in the blue, like a bright elusive sailboat among white galleons of clouds. And as we focus on the sky, we forget earth. We forget that life is serious, and we smile. And as we smile, we remember that we, too, want to live, to rise against life's wind.

To play and soar again.

THE WHOLE TRUTH?

Would you prefer to visit a thorn
garden or a rose garden?

Depending on the season,
they are one and the same.

Once upon a time, a lady gave each of her neighbors a bunch of roses from her garden. Each neighbor said, "Thank you," and carried the roses inside to her kitchen.

The first neighbor hummed a cheery tune as she snipped off the thorns and carefully wrapped the stems in damp tissue. Then she pulled on her coat and went to her car. Settling the roses on the passenger seat, she drove to work. As she placed the fragrant roses on her desk, she told everyone, "I have such a lovely neighbor. Her gift has made my day."

The second neighbor tossed the roses onto her kitchen bench and pulled out her scissors. One by one, she savagely clipped off the blooms and flung them into the bin. Then she snatched up the thorny stems, and clutching them tightly in her hand, she stomped off to work.

A colleague noticed the stems jammed into a mug on her desk asked, "Why have you got a mug full of thorns on your desk?"
"That's what my neighbor gave me this morning," she spat out. "I'm keeping them to remind me of how much she's hurt me." And as she spoke, she uncurled her fingers to reveal the evidence of her neighbor's cruelty on her wounded and bloodstained palm.

The evidence, which told the truth, and yet lied.
Told the truth about the thorns
but lied about the character
and motives of her neighbor.

I wonder, how many times have I unconsciously caused myself a lot of unnecessary pain by the memories I have chosen to keep and the memories I have chosen to throw away? How many times have I ended my day with a bunch of stored wrongs, slights, and criticisms jammed into my mind? How often have I used this "evidence" to form a negative opinion of myself or others?

Oh my. Too often! What an absurd way to live!

Have I experienced a few thorns? Sure. We all have. But looking back, I cannot remember one totally awful day. Every day of my life has contained some joy, something which redeemed it, like a friend's smile, a cup of hot chocolate, a green traffic light, or a bird's song.

I wonder, *what would happen if we tossed more of our thorn-thoughts into the bin?* Would we tell a more rosy story to ourselves and to the world?

The idea for this story came from a few lines I read many years ago about a lady named Ellen. One day, Ellen received a letter from a friend. Delighted, she tore it open, only to find the letter was full of grumbles and littered with gloomy complaints.

That night, Ellen dreamed she was walking in a beautiful garden with this lady by her side. The owner of the garden was happily showing them around. He invited them to select some flowers, and Ellen picked a few and lifted them to her nose to breathe in their fragrance.

But the gloomy lady refused to be pleased. Instead of seeing the flowers all around her, she searched out some weeds and thorns. Heading towards them, she waded through their prickly stems then loudly complained to the gardener that they were in her way.

In response, the gardener kindly advised her, "Let the thorns alone, for they will only wound you. Gather the roses, the lilies, and the pinks."[5]

Paul explores a similar theme in his letter to friends in the Greek town of Philippi. He understood they lived in uncertain times. He sensed they were starting to become paralyzed with dread and overwhelmed with worry. Paul's heart was touched and he quickly sent a letter to encourage them.

In case this messy world is tying you up in anxious knots and stressing you out too, I've paraphrased a little of his letter below.

Please don't be anxious.
Instead, remember
God is near, so you can
tell him all your cares.

He's eager to share his peace
with you and help you relax.
Trust in his capacity to
guard your heart and mind,
in Jesus' name.

Please, relish this freedom he gives
you and delight in life itself.

Seek out all that's good, true
and lovely. Everything wise,
beautiful and worth celebrating,

And enjoy the rich bounty of this
Spirit-led life to your heart's content![6]

THORNY MOMENTS

This difficult moment does not define you;
therefore, you don't need to crumple,
or shrink, to fit it.

A million minutes ago, or was it a lifetime, I was living through a thorny moment, a very prickly time.

As the days passed, I could feel myself becoming exhausted, growing smaller and smaller. Compromising here, ignoring my feelings and values there. Trimming off hope and believing, vainly, that if I was less, I could fit in. That if I was small enough, I would be invisible and others' expectations, opinions, and criticisms would pass me by. That they would miss their tiny target, *me*.

But somehow, I could never shrink small enough to escape pain.

One night, during this flat, dull time, I tossed and turned but could not sleep. The whole sane world may have been deep in slumber, but I was wide awake. Eventually, bored and restless, I got up and wandered into the kitchen. Clicking on a small light, I started to flick through a magazine, listlessly turning the pages, aimlessly wandering through time and space. Suddenly, my eye caught the name "Canary Wharf," and I stopped abruptly.

Memories flooded my mind, memories of my older sister Gill in England. We had spent most of our childhood apart, so when we became adults we treasured time together. Because I lived in Australia, and she lived in England, she only visited me "Down Under" once, and I only visited her in London a few times.

One year, the flights to England seemed to last forever, and I was so grateful to finally arrive, give her a hug, and drag my battered suitcase into my bedroom. In contrast to the grey London streets, Gill had painted the guest room a sunshiny yellow, and just being there, I began to revive.

The next morning, when I stood by the window, I saw the sleeping city spread out below me. As the sun came up, the central building of Canary Wharf gradually emerged from the mist, and the dome turned to gold, a fitting color for the financial hub of London!

After breakfast, I wandered into Gill's living room, slid open the glass door, and stepped out onto the balcony. The sounds of Canary Wharf and the busy streets of London came up to me like a dull hum. But when I leaned out a little and looked over the railing, I saw a narrow waterway below me. I realized it was a remnant of the network of Dockland canals which had been used for centuries to carry freight inland from the wharf. As I watched entranced, a long canal boat slid into view. It chugged slowly past on the grey, oily water, as if it was being pulled by the horses of yesteryear. Then it rounded a bend and slipped back into history. As I paused there between two eras, I heard church bells chime the hour in an invisible steeple.

But I couldn't linger long, for Gill was eager to show me around. So off we went.

Although she was shorter than me, I quickly learned to wear walking shoes whenever we explored the city together. I also learned to keep her in sight as she buzzed in and out of shops, rapidly leading the way past glitzy hotels, then down shortcuts through back-alleys, where the red-brick walls were stained black by centuries of coal smoke.

My sister was a woman on a mission, and her enthusiasm was infectious. She seemed to have eyes everywhere, pointing out this, calling me over to see that, always on the lookout for bargains. Once she spotted a bargain, whether it was yesterday's bread on sale or Christmas decorations at half price, she pounced on the treasure and carried it home in triumph.

Just remembering her zest for life made me smile.

I was no longer standing half asleep in my Australian kitchen, sad and bored. I was on top of the world again, striding down the streets of Canary Wharf, head held high, looking life in the eye!

Suddenly, I realized that wherever I lived, I didn't have to live small.

I didn't have to crumple in defeat in the face of setbacks, criticism, or sorrow. I wasn't just a victim of this "thorny moment." Like my sister, I was alive with purpose and full of stories.

I am full of stories.

My own stories of adventure and triumph.

I am the wide-eyed toddler inching closer to the soaring flames of my first bonfire to toast my bread, absently licking melted butter from my fingers, gazing at the fire, fascinated.

I am the child on holiday at the Cornish coast, racing my cousins to the sand dunes. Launching myself into space and tumbling down the golden sand, sending it flying high into the blue sky.

I am the little girl wearing a hand-me-down swimsuit, holding her uncle's hand. Braving each giant frothing wave, leaping with delight as they come all the way up to his knobbly knees!

I am the teenager hiking with friends through the muffled chill of a winter forest, seeking the path by moonlight while in the distance, owls call. Pitching my tent in the snow.

I am the young adult working in Norway for the summer, taking the ferry to the Faroe Islands across the choppy North Sea. Lifting my bicycle off the ferry to ride it, legs pumping and breath puffing, up and down the local hills of the capital Torshavn. I am the girl on the front row of the touring choir, singing with other young people in five languages. Then later, searching in local shops for hand-spun wool to knit, in memory of the rugged moorland sheep.

I am the new university graduate working in a land where civil war simmers. I enter a shop slowly, quietly, *wary* . . . I lift my arms high, so the little old man who sits on a stool just inside the door can search me for weapons.

I am the bride-to-be, sewing my own wedding dress from scratch, spreading cream satin on my bedroom carpet and crawling around on the floor, trying to cut the cloth to the right shape for a graceful train.

I am the young mother, rocking her babies to sleep in the dark, bringing their screaming lips close to her ears, patting their backs, soothing them, and humming softly. *Calming herself.*

I am the teacher, inspiring sixty teenagers to create an Easter program for the whole school. As the only adult on duty, I am wading through a rough sea of teenage noise and chaos. Clinging to the frayed remnants of my patience as they jostle and scuffle around me. Two hours later, I am the teacher in awe, listening to the students tell the sacred story of Easter to the hushed assembly. Watching in delight as they leap to their feet, right on cue at the end, to wave their sparklers in the air and eyes shining, declare in triumphant, light-dancing joy, "*He is risen!*"

From toddler to teacher, I am all of these people.

And I am Me.

Today's thorny moment does not define who I am. Not even close. *So, I choose to defy its limits.* Defy them—not with argument or war—but with the glorious courage and joy of life. My life.

For I am more than this thorny moment.
And so are you! So are you!

RUMINATING

Some memories yield more wisdom
each time you *chew them over*.
Others just leave a bitter taste
in your mouth!

The first winter rains have come now, and the dusty summer fields are covered with a fine haze of green. Outside our kitchen window, behind a narrow band of bush, I can see our sheep. They are nibbling scattered hay and grain, and searching, with delicate lips, for tiny new blades of grass.

By midmorning, they have eaten enough, and they wander off to rest, settling down in scattered groups like randomly placed lumps of grubby cotton wool. Then they placidly re-chew their breakfast. This *ruminating* makes their diet of grasses and grains more digestible.

As humans, thankfully, we do not re-chew our food! But maybe we do something even more distasteful. Instead of reworking grains and grass, we mentally rehash old mistakes and chew over yesterday's blunders. Day after day. Night after night.

Why?

A little chewing may help us learn a thing or two, but what if we chew the same events over and over for days, weeks, or even months?

What if we re-chew our sorrows and blunders for years? What happens? We get a pain in our guts, that's what!

We feel sick at heart, and we leave our soul to starve, *even when new grass is growing all around us and the sun is shining*. What a waste of our *mind time*, of our emotional energy.

Ruminating serves the sheep well, but even ruminants only re-chew their food once or twice. They do not chew the same soggy ball of grass for weeks on end. Once they have taken what they need from the hay or grass, they send it on its way.

Smart idea.

They also snooze and snuggle up with their lambs in the sun. And they play, especially near dusk, when the parting sun, in a gesture of goodwill, paints the fields with gold.

The evening ritual usually starts with the lambs. No one calls them, but as the sun begins to set, the young lambs leave their mothers and gather in a restless group by a fallen tree or on the bank of a dam. Within minutes, they begin to chase each other up and down the bank. They leap into the air or scramble up to perch on a log. Even newborn lambs, who linger by their mothers, often arch their downy backs and bounce up and down on all four tiny hooves.

Last night something rare happened.

When the lambs began to play in the new spring grass, the whole flock seemed to catch their spirit of joy. First, the stocky teenage lambs started to skip and run around, then the mothers and babies. Soon the whole flock was racing up and down the field. As we approached, the flock turned and raced toward us, then it skidded to a stop, paused, looked us over, and wheeled around to race off again. Under the glowing sky, woolly lambs, baaing babies, and heavily pregnant ewes ran together as synchronized and graceful as a flock of birds in flight.

Now that's an experience I want to remember and revisit again and again!

And while I am talking about sheep . . .

One day a flock of sheep was pouring into our sorting yards. Looking them over, I spotted a tiny lamb in a forest of legs being jostled by the restless mob. Afraid the lamb would be trampled, I pushed into the flock and scooped him up in my arms. While the mob flowed on, I stroked the lamb's soft fleece. He nestled closer in my arms, relaxing his whole body. I was really moved by his confidence in me and felt honored by his trust.

When someone trusts us, it's always a great honor.

Later when the sheep spread out, I returned him to his mother. But the warmth of his fleecy back still lingered on my arms and reminded me of a story my husband tells . . .

One day, a middle-aged man was dying in the hospital. His local minister went to visit him, concerned he would be resentful at having his life cut short. After sitting and chatting for a while, the minister kindly asked, ". . . and how are things between you and God?"

The man's eyes lit up, and a smile spread across his weathered face, "The Lord's my Shepherd, and I'm His sheep," he replied, "and that's good enough for me."[7]

ENTITLED

We may be *spoiled* by both
our wounds and our luxuries.

By being neglected, or
pampered and idolized.

For both make us insatiable,
hungry for more ease or attention.

This is the tale of a journey, a journey I am taking, step-by-step, along a continuum.

A very long continuum.

I love the word *continuum*; it rolls off my tongue with ease. But I like the concept even more because it gives me hope. It tells me that, even if I only take one tiny step in the right direction, it makes a difference.

Way back when I was thirteen or fourteen, I deeply resented the loss of my mother. I was very jealous of friends who had good mothers. Mothers who sewed special dresses for their Valentine's Day parties, and mothers who took them shopping for girl-becoming-woman things.

I used to look with wistful eyes at families sitting together at summer picnics and dream about linking hands to say grace around the table at Christmas. Whenever I gazed at all these happy families, I felt wronged by life, as if I was an outsider, looking in through a window to an untouchable world of bliss.

As I saw it, the universe had shortchanged me. It had mislaid my life-script and forgotten to give me the proper deal. The deal which all children deserve. At times I wondered, *Why me?* and at other times, I wanted more. *I wanted compensation.*

While I waited for a fair deal or a knight in shining armor (whichever appeared first), I mentally sat and pouted at the "owed" end of the continuum. And without realizing it, I began to take on the personality of a victim.

I drifted into being passive.

Sure, I did my schoolwork, but I lacked initiative in other areas of my life. This was partly because I subconsciously felt *it's not my job to fix things. After all, I haven't broken anything.* And partly because I didn't know what to do.

Perhaps in response to the love I had missed, I also developed an insatiable desire for attention and affirmation.

In recognition of my suffering, I also rather hoped I would be let off any further tough stuff. So, in many situations, I looked for the easy way out. When I was a teenager, I could not describe or name these feelings. But now I understand that a sense of entitlement was settling deep into my psyche.

But all was not lost, and resentment was not inevitable. Because, while I waited and moped, other factors were nudging me along the continuum toward gratitude.

One of these was seeing, firsthand, what other school students had to cope with. For instance, one of my roommates was so crippled with back pain that she dragged her mattress onto the cold floor to sleep there, hoping for some relief.

Another classmate was sponsored to study at our school through an overseas aid program. At first, I was jealous of her pocket money, but then I realized how isolated she was in a strange country. How much she missed her family back home in Africa.

One of the boys in another class struggled to walk and speak coherently. On the playground, his classmates pretended he was invisible or snickered and turned their backs when he stumbled by. In contrast, I was blessed with healthy legs and many friends.

As I grew up and met people from different countries, I realized how self-centered and narrow my view had been.

Although some people have a far easier life than others, *no one escapes some form of struggle, loss, or grief*. Pain of one sort or another touches us all. It affects the rich and beautiful who own sparkling swimming pools. It touches the families who wake after a storm to find floodwater pooling around their mats from a leak in the roof.

As I read more widely, and watched the daily news, I came to realize that many *normal things*, which I took for granted, would seem like luxuries to folks in neighboring communities. Unlike them, I did not have to shelter in a basement because bombs were falling, nor draw water from a muddy river with a battered bucket, desperate to quench my thirst.

Although I was reluctant to admit it, I also saw that *I was not the recipient of a broken deal because the universe had not promised me anything. No one on earth is born with their fingers curled around a guarantee that promises an easy life.*

As the years passed, it gradually dawned on me that if I was ever going to move forward at home or work, I had to leave my crippling sense of entitlement behind.

If I wanted to escape tragedy.

What tragedy?

The tragedy that, if my dominant story is, "poor me", I will forever see myself as poor. Treat myself as less-than, and voluntarily self-limit! I will give a tragedy in my past permission to dominate my present. Make me grovel as its slave. In effect, I will crawl at its feet asking for permission to live. Or spend night after night teetering on the brink of oblivion, my toes curled around the edge of the abyss of despair. Yet be blind to my own skills, even in broad daylight! Overlook opportunities that are staring me in the face which I could grasp at home, in my community or in the wider world.

Why will I miss these opportunities? I won't see them because I will not be looking for them! They are simply not on my radar.

Another thing that challenges me is that, if I abandon my poor me idea and start to see myself as rich in talent, blessings or opportunity, *I will have to change my ingrained, familiar story*. Maybe even change my role in my family, community or club! The very idea is unsettling, lonely and terrifying. For who wants to be a lone voice, singing of hope, when everyone else is singing from the *poor me* song sheet?

But oh, how we need the courage to do this! The vision to step beyond habitual inertia.

It also became obvious that if I wanted to be a *victor*, I could not simultaneously play the role of a *victim*. I had to choose which I wanted more. And this was harder than I expected. To find out if changing from being a victim to a victor was worth the struggle, I asked myself some tough questions like:

What benefits am I gaining from all my self-pity?
Do I really want to go through life being "needy"?
Do I have the courage to step up and take responsibility for my own life and decisions, or would I rather blame someone else?
If I constantly shift responsibility to others, who am I empowering?

Gradually, I realized that being pitied for what I lacked was not as fulfilling as I had hoped, that waiting around for rescue and compensation was a fool's ploy. A joyless game that isolated me from love and hope when I craved connection, and paralyzed me when I craved action.

I also saw that the longer I was passive, the more I resented others. In effect, I was muttering under my breath, *Don't they know the script? Don't they know they are destined to rescue me? Make my life easier?* Obviously not!

With some reluctance, I came to see two more things.

Firstly, I realized that my self-pity was an old protective coping mechanism I had unwittingly created when I was growing up. It had been useful at a time when events seemed to randomly swirl around me and I feared I could not cope. It shielded me from unrealistic demands because, when a dominant person pitied me, they naturally made fewer demands on me. They sometimes even became my protector. This gave me some wriggle room, some space to gain skills and confidence. It also saved me from creating boundaries or upsetting more powerful people by saying "No," two life skills I had yet to develop.

Becoming aware of this helped me see that *we do not have to deny our own past in order to move forward*. Instead, we can say to ourselves, "This is what happened to me, and it was real. It was tough. It shaped parts of who I am and I will always honor that. I will respect all aspects of myself and of my story. I will also choose to be honest and see what was good, in me, in others, and in the situation. If I need help, I will ask for it, and if I can use my story to encourage others, I will do that too."

"But here I am right now! What can I do with today? How can I live today so that my tomorrow is better and the tomorrow of those I love? Finally, *who do I want to become*, and what steps can I take to grow into that kind of person?"

Secondly, I saw that my sense of entitlement had a trace of unconscious arrogance in it. Why arrogance? Because, by my self-centered attitude, and my mood of entitlement, I was implying that *my own suffering was greater than the suffering of others*. (Why else would others owe me anything?) Embedded in this attitude was also the idea *that I was more important than them*.

Having said this, I'm not minimizing real trauma. There are times when our suffering is acute, and we need to focus on ourselves in order to survive and heal. But if, long-term, I decide that my suffering is worse than yours, I effectively put myself on a "suffering pedestal." And by my words and actions, moods, and sighs, I demand your attention and your service.

But living on a suffering pedestal is so lonely. So isolating. So limiting. For, who among us can dance freely on a pillar?

If I habitually indulge in self-pity, I can also slip into being chronically self-centered and acting like a spoiled brat! Then, without realizing it, *I begin to use everyone*. I expect them to adapt their day to my needs, my goals, and my whims. To jump when I say jump, to rescue me from the consequences of all the decisions I make. If they don't, I label them "selfish," hoping to divert attention from my own selfishness.

I may also slide into devaluing other human beings, routinely attempt to rob them of their humanity and begin to use them as "resources". Or I may dismiss their very real needs, emotions, and challenges *in case I have to help them*. Of course, others will soon get wise to my ploys and notice how manipulative I am. They may even become so offended, drained, or hurt by my behavior that they are tempted to walk away.

If I get into a habit of acting like this, I can be plagued by a succession of shallow, one-sided relationships. Ones that leave me insatiably empty and chronically immature. Lonely and lacking the self-respect and love I crave. I can become so greedy for attention, that I completely miss seeing and celebrating all the wonderful blessings I have already received.

Therefore, in recent years, I've made a conscious effort to step down from my suffering pedestal and forget myself once in a while. Walk with others and listen to their joys and sorrows. When I do this something miraculous happens; in the light of their stories, my own woes fade. I become fascinated by their narratives, and travel with them in my imagination. I feel the rawness of their grief and the joy of their triumphs.

Little by little, as our lives and stories entwine, we create something magical. Like a healing circle of compassion. We begin to celebrate precious moments of shared humanity. We notice each other's life milestones and honor them together.

This creates a new kind of "wonderful". One that's far better than rescue and more rewarding than compensation. It's more exhilarating than pouting and throwing adult-sized tantrums.

More healing than payback.

As I began to make more healthy mental choices, my desire for revenge slipped into the background. I slid further away from the "entitlement" end of the continuum and closer to the "gratitude" end.

In doing this, I saw something profound,
that self-pity cannot acknowledge
its blessings, or it will self-destruct!

It will die.

Faced with this confronting truth,
I chose to let self-pity starve
rather than feed it.

I deliberately cast it aside to die.

Though I found it hard to break the habit of self-pity, when I look at my life through the eyes of gratitude, several things begin to happen:

I naturally reframe some of the stories I tell.

I'm less likely to wait around for someone to rush to my rescue.

I'm beginning to *make things happen* instead of passively *waiting around* for others to take the initiative.

I'm more willing to do the tough, boring stuff instead of leaving it to others so I can do the fun stuff.

I'm more creative and willing to brush off my own talents. Invest in attitudes and actions that help me grow.

And, I don't expect others to compensate me for any perceived or real wrongs. Instead, I'm beginning to relish my life and celebrate all I have.

I saw that living with an "owed" mentality is like squatting in a dim room bitterly complaining that no one has come to change the wallpaper in a long while. Like moaning about the poor food and feeble lightbulb, when we have the capacity to fling open the door and walk out into the sunshine!

Why, oh why, do we choose to linger in the dark, cursing it, or the ones we think created it, when adventure awaits?

Why do revenge, or being passive, seem more compelling than being alive?

What are we afraid to give up?

What are we afraid we'll find?

As I wrestled with questions like this, I decided to take another step along the gratitude continuum and consciously look around for blessings. The wealth of what I saw stunned me.

For instance, I became enamored with glass: simple, clear, window glass. Have you ever looked at a window? Not through the window at the neighbors to see what they are up to, or at the clouds to see what the weather is like? Nor even at the smudges on the surface?

But looked at the window itself?

Have you ever imagined what your life would be like if, instead of glass, you just had a big empty hole in your wall? What would your room be like in winter? How safe would you feel to snuggle down to sleep on a dark moonless night? In summer how many bugs would buzz in unimpeded to crawl down your collar?

Folks, we have something kings and queens in ancient times would have paid for in jewels and gold. We have a way to let the sunlight in, but keep the winter wind out. Amazing!

Then there's electricity, and hot and cold running water.

There's school, and free libraries. The fantastic ability to read and write anything we choose.

But this is not the end of the story.

For, even when, logically, things are going well, the habit of "entitlement" still tries to sneak back in to dominate my thinking and stall my progress. Sometimes, secretly, I still crave attention or feel entitled to pity. And when I do, I want to draw on others again, drain their energy to boost my own.

So I've developed a silent strategy to address this. Whenever the old feelings of self-pity surface and I feel "needy," I consciously whisper a little prayer and mutter the word *full* under my breath.

Why *full*?

Because *full* is the opposite of empty, of needy.

When I remember I have a full pantry, a full tummy, and a full life, when I remember how fully God and others love me, I no longer need constant affirmation or attention.

Instead:
If I am full, I can freely love and affirm others.
If I am full, I can lavish attention on others—not to be a hero and get the glory, but because I see them and really care.
And if I am full, there's no longer any room for self-pity, envy, or entitlement to live like squatters in my heart. So these grumpy fellows reluctantly plod off and look for lodging elsewhere.

After all I have experienced, do I still believe the universe has been unfair to me? Yes, I do. But not in the way we usually mean. Because the God of the universe has lavished color and opportunity, grace, and love on me and *more blessings than I could ever be entitled to by my own efforts.*

And, for each one,
I'm eternally grateful.

If you would like a practical and entertaining example of how to live beyond entitlement, I recommend reading Albert Facey's autobiography, *A Fortunate Life*. His fascinating story is set in the frontier days of Australia when the land was being cleared for farms and the first towns were being built. I found the tales of his courage and resilience more than remarkable; they were inspiring. In comparison, my life looks like a summer picnic![8]

Colin Thiele is another author who writes with wit and passion about life in rural Australia. His stories in the book *Sun on the Stubble* are dramatic, colorful, and full of warmhearted humor. Enjoy![9]

Spring Clean?

What is the use-by date
for regret?
The expiry date
for shame, or for joy?

When the spring sap rises in the trees and the sky is high and blue, do you ever get the urge to throw open the windows and spring-clean? I do.

If you do, where do you begin? Do you start by rummaging in a bedroom drawer and hunting for lost socks? Or open the refrigerator door, sigh deeply, and fill your rubbish bin, garbage bin, or trash can with items which have passed their expiration date?

Whatever your cleaning style, I doubt you aim to make things worse, even if you create more chaos and mess at first!

Have you ever . . .

Swept your arm across a dresser shelf and sent your mother's antique tea set crashing to the floor, then arranged broken beer bottles in its place?

Carried your best white shirt to the garage to mop up spilled engine oil, then hung up your tatty gardening jacket on a padded satin hanger?

Dragged your most beautiful carpet out onto the muddy road to be run over by farm machinery, then carpeted your living room with moldy newspapers?

And, as evening falls, have you ever snuffed out the rose-scented candles in your bedroom and scattered rotting fish heads across your pillow to help you sleep?

No?

That would be absurd! When you spring-clean, you carry rubbish and garbage, trash and mess *out*, not *in*. Always.

Always? Are you sure? Can you honestly say that you never look for physical or mental rubbish to collect? That you never archive wounds, failures, or regret for further reference, for instance, to use in evidence against someone? And you never, ever, dismiss happy memories and choose to preserve your sad stories instead?

Do you?

No?

That would be absurd. And yet, we all do it. We carefully archive all aspects of a wrong so the *facts* are ready to pull out, as needed, years later. We stay up half the night to nurse sleepless wrongs as if they were teething babies. We grant our woes unlimited mind time but silence our joys with selective amnesia.

Why do we do this? I don't know.

We are complex beings with complex minds. We cannot simply spring-clean our minds with a mop and a feather duster. We cannot toss out regret like odd socks or our grief like old magazines. But even so, perhaps we can choose not to let our thinking stink, especially if we change the life-stories we habitually remember and retell. If we focus on the love we have given and received, on what went right, rather than what went wrong.

Maybe then, instead of sniffing something fishy while we dream, we'll be able to remember and savor the sweet things of life. The bright balloons and starry nights. The picnics and hugs. The holy glow of candles on Christmas Eve.

And all the other good memories, which,
like honey on the kitchen shelf,
never spoil.

THE HONEY POT

I'm no Pooh Bear,
but I like my honey.

I like it drizzled onto porridge, stirred into spicy hot chocolate, and baked in gingerbread, moist and crumbly. This quiet craving makes for a rounder tummy and also some empty, round pots coming to rest in my cupboard.

One day, in honor of the fact that *honey is the only food that never spoils*, I decided to put one of my pots to good use. I wanted to make it into a Happy Memory Jar. Cutting some pretty paper into small slips, I began to scribble down memories, memories from that morning and from my child-hood. Whatever floated to the surface . . .

Australia, March 2:
I was blown home from my walk this morning. The sun was warm on my back, but a scattering of raindrops fell on my hat and arms. When the shower passed, I looked up and saw a rainbow shimmering over our home and sheds. And there, softly glowing within the curve of the arch, was a translucent silver moon. Beautiful.

Australia, April 3:
I cuddled my new grandson for the first time today. He's got very cute toes!

England, aged five years old:
My mom is busy sewing, and I'm standing very close, watching her feed the fabric under the needle. Her Singer sewing machine is filling the kitchen with a whirring noise, and I'm trembling with excitement, trying very hard to be patient. Finally, she snips off the last thread and holds it up for me to see. I step within the circle of her arms, and she slips the blazer on. As she does up the shiny gold buttons, I can feel the soft royal blue wool embrace me like a hug, and I stand very tall, my heart full of smiles.

When I began to write these happy memories on slips of paper, I was really moved. I began to see my own life in a different light.

In the past, when I told others about my childhood, I tended to speak in terms of loneliness and loss. Because the sickness and death of my mother cast such a shadow over my early years, *it was as if that was all I could see,* as if the lingering grief shrouded every story in gray.

As time passed, these sad stories had become so familiar, so easily shared, that I had no idea how much I was letting them shape me, or that I was basing my whole identity on only half the story. The sad half. The very idea really shook me. What if *the truth was that I had experienced a happy childhood?* What if I lost the sympathy vote? The excuse for self-pity?

More memories flooded into my mind, and as they did, something healing and magical began to happen, something I did not expect. As I focused on writing down one happy memory after another, my view of my childhood began to shift. I remembered summer days, sitting in my crinkly blue swimsuit on our front lawn linking daisies into chains.

I remembered waking to the rare magic of falling snow and my dad surprising me with a sled he had made, one with real metal runners! I remembered tugging on the string and feeling it glide with a swoosh and an icy squeak across the snowy path.

I remembered winter evenings and my mother dressing me by the fire after my bath. Helping me into my favorite pink pajamas with the roses on, buttoning up the jacket, and wrapping my whole body in the warm smell of toasted cotton.

Soon, so many good memories crowded into my mind that I could hardly sleep for excitement.

I felt like an explorer hiking through rough terrain, who pauses for a break and casually picks up a handful of pebbles. She idly blows off years of dust to discover in astonished awe, that she is staring at a palm full of priceless gems sparkling in the sun.

We often associate memory-making with retirement, with idle old folks sitting in sagging armchairs, reminiscing about *the good old days.*

But even a young child can create a Happy Memory Jar.

And sprinkle a little glitter around!

Cultivating Joy

In the soil of happy memories
gratitude and contentment grow.

Speaking Up!

You are not
just matter;
you matter!

One afternoon, when I was a teacher, I overheard an adult ridiculing a teenage boy. Before discussing it with the adult, I paused to comfort the teenager.

"I'm so sorry for what he said to you," I soothed.

The wounded teenager shrugged, looked at his toes, and began to scuff at the dirt. Quietly, he muttered, "It doesn't matter." I was indignant and hotly replied, "Yes, it does matter." Surprised by my tone, he lifted his head. I looked deep into his eyes and said, *"It matters because you matter."*

Whoever you are, abuse always matters.

Whether it's physical, mental, social, spiritual, or financial, abuse is never okay. Although many scars of abuse are invisible, it's easy to recognize that an abused person loses out, but it can be harder to see that the abuser loses out as well. *Because whenever one person holds another person down, neither can stand tall.* Both become chained to limiting behaviors. Both people waste their power.

One in manipulating and bullying, the other in appeasing or pleasing.

One in oppressing, the other in trying to struggle free.

Both waste their talents. Their creativity. Their lives.

So why do we so easily slip into saying, "It doesn't matter" or "I don't mind"? What fear-based behavior is driving us? And is our fear justified, or only imagined?

Do we say, "It doesn't matter" to keep a fragile peace? To avoid social embarrassment and "making a scene"? Because we're afraid to "rock the boat" and be dumped at sea? Tossed overboard from an important relationship, battered and bruised? Or because we're too world-weary to take on any more challenges?

Whatever our motives, if we learn to be dishonest, by default, we soon create relationships tangled up in lies, even in relatively safe settings.

"Where do you want to go for Christmas?"
"I don't mind; you choose."

"Did I say something to upset you?"
"No, I'm fine. It must be hay fever."

"Is the noise of my hammering keeping you awake?"
"No, you go ahead. I can read a while longer."

If we hide our feelings too often, or habitually talk in code, real communication quietly dies, at least in the short term. We may even *lose the ability to feel our feelings, forget how to express ourselves, or even forget how to tell the truth.*

We may slip into talking in code and hiding our true feelings under veils of lies because, at first, it seems safer than telling the truth. It appears to protect us from being too vulnerable in risky settings. It saves us from making an effort to know, and then share, what we think. (In some settings, this is a vital survival strategy.)

But, sadly, in the end, our cowardice comes back to bite us because we eventually discover that we're part of a relationship where two people are talking but not communicating, speaking but not being heard. For instance, two masks may be politely discussing the weather over breakfast, but behind each mask, two lonely people may be raging, or silently sobbing.

I wonder, what would happen if, little by little, we rediscovered how to tell the truth? The truth of heart, and soul, and mind? What would change if we had the courage to share what we really cared about in a spirit of generous love?

Then we learned to listen, and the another person did the same?

Would we rediscover our personal dignity? Our volition and hope?

Would two people begin again the thrilling journey of seeing, hearing, and loving each other, *for real*?

Would our children learn how to speak their own truth with integrity and courage?

Would each voice on earth matter more then?

The Hearing Test

Some people have ears that cannot hear.
Others have hearing-impaired hearts.

Several years ago, I told a friend of an event that had shattered my world, about a major health threat in my family only the week before.

With hardly a glance of sympathy and no word of understanding, she blithely told me of another lady who had faced a similar challenge. Then she launched into a detailed account of her own health worries, listing all her symptoms in vivid detail.

I left her home as lonely as when I had entered it, perhaps more so. For, though she had made me welcome, she had not really seen or heard me. When she dismissed my concerns, I felt as if she had dismissed, even devalued, me. I did not enter her home expecting her to fix what was broken. But I did hope she would pause long enough to see the world through my eyes. Sense my fear. Understand and be touched by the pain in my heart.

Many of us have very good ears
but hearing-impaired hearts.

Busy with our own concerns, we block another's message and rush to change the subject. Conscious of our own limits, we offer pre-packaged solutions when all a friend requires is that we acknowledge their journey and pause to pay homage to their life-milestones.

Whatever your knowledge or skill,
when you hear me with your heart,
you give me one of the most respectful
and healing gifts one person can give another.
Thank you.

The Shield of Good Humor

Life aims many
arrows at us.
Some miss!

People send many glances and words in our direction. Some words are friendly and we welcome them into our hearts. But some words are sharp and if we're good with words ourselves, or fleet of foot, we dodge them.

When we move into a different community or family we're likely to do a lot of this type of dancing, for humor has its cultural quirks. As a result we can easily become baffled by others' insider jokes and deeply hurt by their teasing. But in return they may be equally baffled by our response and ask, "What's the matter with you? Why are you upset? We were just joking!"

When I was editing this story I paused to chat on the phone to an Australian friend. After one good-natured barb he said in a teasing voice, "Don't listen to me through your English ears. Listen to me through your Australian ears!" His amusing comment echoed what I was trying to write here, and I laughed.

Laughter itself is a mixed blessing.

If we are in an unfamiliar setting, and we hear laughter all around us, we may assume it's directed at us. That they are mocking our values, dreams, and goals. Belittling us. While this may be true, if we assume it every time, we will either silently cringe and curl up in despair or become reactive and touchy. Ready, at the drop of a word or sideways glance, to flash into fiery defense of our identity.

But are these our only options?

Maybe instead of taking every teasing comment to heart and reeling in pain, as if we've been struck, we can borrow at least one idea from the gallant knights of old. Men of stout heart, smelly feet, and often misguided zeal, who galloped off to glory. In a move more wise than many of theirs, we can choose *to carry a shield with us*. Not a clumsy shield carved of wood, nor a costly shield cast from molten metal, but one far lighter.

An invisible, magic shield called The Shield of Good Humor.

The beauty is, we can take this shield wherever we go and use it to deflect barbed words with laughing retorts (or at least good humored thoughts!). This shield reminds us that *we do not have to take every comment seriously!* Instead, we have several other options.

For instance, we can actively choose to develop a buoyancy of spirit that's strong enough to rise above another's put downs. Even when we are misrepresented and misunderstood, we can grieve in private, then step boldly into life once more. We can quietly exercise the muscles of our resilience until they are strong enough to shake off shame. *Until our spirit is secure enough to laugh, to scorn, scorn itself.*

While humor's shield is light enough for everyday use it's also strong enough to weather life's soul-battering storms. Why? Because it's toughened by a kind of sturdy joy. A love of life.

This shield also has our own unique "coat of arms" emblazoned on it. Our royal ancestry and God-given worth etched in letters of faith and fire. They are carved there to remind us in no uncertain terms that, whatever the circumstances, or whatever others say, we are sons and daughters of the King of Kings![10]

Humor's shield is
tough and strong
to deflect shame's
taunts and repel
life's slurs and slights.

Padded with joy
this regal gift
comforts our hearts
and arms our souls
with quivers of chuckles!

PLAY

Water
of Life.

At our local toddlers' group, the discussion drifted toward stress. After a while, the group leader asked the young mothers, "What relieves your stress the most?" Instantly, several answered, "Water!" "Relaxing in water." "Watching the kids playing with water." Hearing these comments, many of the young mothers smiled and nodded.

Their response reminded me of when my own boys were small. They, too, loved water, especially playing outside in a small plastic pool. Or painting our path with an old brush dipped in water to make the paving change color.

As adults we forget we were born to play, created for curiosity, beauty, and fun. If we focus exclusively on work, or try to substitute shopping and entertainment *for real recreation*, we quickly lose heart.

Because

Play is not the icing on life's cake
or an optional extra if you have time.

Play is your soul breathing
and your spirit laughing.

It's like sending giggles to heaven
as a prayer of gratitude for life.

Two Doors

One sunny morning we wake up and know it's time.

Time to stop analyzing the darkness and begin exploring the light.

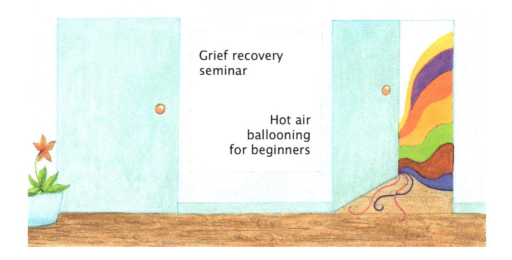

Section 3: The Cocoon

Part 3 Transformation, Integrity, Purpose

In the moonlight, the dewy cocoon glistened with frosted fire. A gentle breeze rocked it gently to and fro and hummed an airy lullaby through its silken strands. All was well, yet the caterpillar could not fall asleep.

Night and day, questions drifted through his mind like silver mist, making him restless, teasing him. Tickling his imagination until his whole being itched to know the answers.

"What's the point of life?" they whispered, "And all these changes?"

The caterpillar made no reply because he simply did not know. Even his body seemed to belong to someone else, and he had no idea why. Some nights the questions coiled around his consciousness and hissed in his ear, "Is this how your story ends?"

But not everything was dark. All his squirming and stretching weakened the cocoon until a tiny crack appeared. Then another. One day, shafts of sunlight began to play along his skin and flicker in his face. Surely something good was going to happen . . .

MAGIC WAND?

Transform me,
oh God,
but please
don't ask me
to change.

The whole idea is irresistible.

It turns peasants into princesses and "frogs" into princes. It turns wrinkled skin to smooth and gray hair to gold. I can see the pictures right here in my glossy magazine where they shine like new-spun fables . . .

So, let's you and I try.

You wave a magic wand over me, then I'll wave one over you.

But before you begin, I have to warn you not to touch some areas of my life. For starters, my habits are out of bounds, as I'm rather attached to them and, of course, my beliefs. And please don't mess with my relationships—I've put a lot of love and thought into getting them this far. I'm sure you understand.

I would enjoy being more fit, so you're free to wave your wand there. But remember, the weather here is either too hot or too cold, so I can't do any jogging. Feel free to make me younger, except I don't want to lose my happy memories or my hard-won experience.

Now, let's begin.

You wave your wand first.

Then I'll wave mine!

Beyond Self

When I reach the limits of myself,
and my magic wand lies splintered
among my shattered dreams,
where on earth can I turn?

I like the idea of "self-help." It suits my independent streak. It also suits my ego.

My touchy, don't-let-anyone-see-you-struggle ego.

My self-protective ego loves to hear the syrupy words that promise, *Don't worry about a thing. You can fix this yourself.* Such smooth-talking words offer me just what I crave: privacy, especially when I feel vulnerable or ashamed, and a sense of autonomy and personal power. They even offer me the seductive illusion that I'm just a bit better than other people who struggle with the same problem, that I can overcome it where others have failed. Self-help provides wonderful ego fuel! All I have to do is splash a little around, paste on a smile, and stride off in pursuit of a golden future.

Really?

In Australia, we are entranced by the idea of self-help; it suits our *me mindset*. But is *self-help* actually a contradiction in terms?

Lately, I've begun to question the whole idea because there's something about the label that doesn't ring true. Firstly, it seems to me that the idea of *helping myself* when I'm *helpless* is a tad absurd. Surely, if I'm out of ideas, *I'm out of ideas*. And if I need help, *I need help from someone other than myself*, someone wiser, stronger, or with more resources.

Another thing which makes me suspicious of the term self-help is my track record. I haven't made a great success of *going it alone!* If you could see the footprints of my life, you would notice there are several places where I have gone around in circles, places where I have tripped over the same tree roots over and over again or had to scramble out of the same hole twice. Three times. You may also notice that when I've toiled up the sand dunes of life, I've slid back almost as much as I've climbed.

It seems to me that the whole self-help movement, including the production of books and seminars, is based not on self-help at all. It's based *on sharing, on helping others*, passing on tips from our own lives in the hope they will benefit someone else.

Perhaps then, we should begin to label self-help as *other-help* in honor of two things: our *precious interdependence* and the wonderful *generosity of spirit* that leads some people to share their life skills with us. Maybe even a hero we can look up to, someone who role models the kind of skills and attitudes we want. Who shows us what's possible. Someone, near or far, who inspires us and helps us grow.

When I was a teenager, an older student invited me to visit her at university for the weekend. I was thrilled *she took the time to notice me and* awed to be among such grown-up students. *Wide-eyed I absorbed everything I saw as I basked in her acceptance all weekend.*

Since then, many folks have mentored me.

Some have role modeled service, then included me in their projects. When they nudged me forward and gave me the chance to help others, they implied I had something of value to offer the world. Others have hugged me and made me feel lovable. And still others have helped me explore ideas and unravel knotty problems.

Even people I have never met have given me a lift, for instance, writers whose insights and skill with words first drew me into reading, and then into writing.

Who would you love to be your mentor? It may scare you witless to approach them, but isn't it worth a try?

And in the meantime, who could you mentor? Who could you help with the skills and wisdom you already possess?

TRANSFORMATION?

A sheen on the outside
may not indicate there's

a light on the inside.

When I was a child, it was my job to polish the family shoes. Each Friday afternoon, I spread some newspaper on the kitchen floor, then wandered from room to room, picking up shoes. Soon they were all in a row: Dad's heavy black work shoes, mom's white "best" shoes, my scuffed school sandals, and my sister's trendy lace-ups.

Pulling out the cardboard box of rags and brushes, I chose some black polish. Prying open the lid, I dipped in the brush, gave it a little wiggle, and slid my hand into my Dad's shoe. As I began to rub polish into the groove near the sole, his big shoe swung from side to side on my small hand. But eventually, I tamed it.

When all the shoes had their coating of wax, I worked along the row again. With a soft brush, I polished each shoe, down one side, around the heel, and back to the front, then briskly across the toe. After an extra rub with an old rag, the shoes began to gleam.

As I carried them upstairs and lined them up carefully under each bed, I felt a real sense of achievement. Even the worn shoes with creased and faded linings looked better.

But they were not transformed.

Only polished.

THE CHATTY CATERPILLAR

Once upon a time in a beautiful garden,
a little caterpillar wiggled to and fro.

On the whole, she was happy, content to chew and loop her way through life, nibble cabbages, and curl up to sleep under fallen leaves.

But one day, she chanced to look a little higher, and there sitting on a swaying leaf was the most graceful creature she had ever seen. It had long delicate legs, antennae as fine as hairs, and the most beautiful wings. The caterpillar stopped chewing and gulped. Wow!

She stared and stared. What was it? Was it a living creature like herself? It was exquisite. Surely it was made of different stuff, a visitor from another world perhaps. Suddenly, with a soft flap of its wings, the creature lifted into the sky. As it rose, its wings shimmered in the warm air with rainbow hues, then glinted like flakes of frosted sapphire.

Seeing it go, the caterpillar cried out in dismay and instantly reared up, trying to catch it. But her stubby legs just thrashed the air, and she flopped down to the ground. All she could do was follow the glorious vision with her eyes, watch it flutter higher and higher, then disappear behind a hibiscus bush.

"No. Oh no!"

Nothing around her looked beautiful anymore, nothing tasted good. Tears welled in her eyes and tumbled down her cheeks. Over and over, in the depths of her heart, she cried out, "Compared to that, I'm just a nobody!"

The Creator of the garden heard her cry, as he hears all such cries, and he came close to comfort her.[1]

"Dear One, why are you crying?"

Unfamiliar with talking to God, she thought, *Now I'm starting to imagine I hear voices!* And she dismissed God's call, thinking it was just the wind whispering secrets to the swaying grasses.[2]

But the voice came again.

"Precious One, why are you crying?"

Surprised, the caterpillar swallowed a sob and looked around. She couldn't see anyone. Finally, she blurted out. "If you were me, you would cry too!"

"Why?"

"Well, I'm not . . ."

"What would you like to be like?"

Her passion made her brave, and she flung back her head. "I want to be like the creature I saw, *the one with everything!*"

"I know. I designed you to desire all that's beautiful and true, to be transformed."

"You did?"

"Yes. Shall we begin?"

"Oh, yes please. Can you give me pretty wings and antennae that wiggle?"

The Creator laughed, and the echoes of his mirth rippled across the garden, making the white daisies nod their heads. "I surely can! But there's something you need to do first."

"Name it. I'll do anything."

"Be fully open to my loving plans and surrender your whole self to me."

"What? Give up who I am? Oh, that's way too hard. Just give me a lesson on growing wings; that will do."

"You could stick a million self-made wings on your back but still be unable to fly."

"This takes far more commitment than I thought. If I can't glue on wings, just teach me a mantra or two so I feel like a butterfly."

The Creator sighed. "You don't need more formulas to remember. You need me."

"Ah, spiritual transformation?"

"No. There's no such thing. You're not just a mind. You're a whole being."

"What then?"

"I want to give you far more than a partial fix. I want to give you a whole-of-life transformation."

"If you do that, can I still eat cabbages? Or burrow into rose buds, nibbling my way to their fragrant heart? So yummy!"

"No. *You can't think like a butterfly and continue to act like a caterpillar.* You won't want to destroy things anymore. Leave a trail of empty holes in your wake. You'll start to relate to life and every other creature in a more kind and healing way."

"That's a lot to consider, so much to give up! So many old habits to grieve. *Will I still be me?*"

The Creator chuckled, and the sun laughed in delight. "Oh yes! The most glorious *Me* you've ever been. Trust me, that's what happens when you yield to my love!"[3]

Baby Steps

We long for instant growth,
but earth's revolving seasons
show that gradual change
can still be change for good.

Small bulbs unfurl their petals,
one by one, and soaring trees
grow ring by ring to reach
the golden sun.

We are not as patient as plants. Our imagination leaps ahead and urges our feet to hurry. We want to outpace plodding nature and achieve instant success.

We want birthdays to come *today*—at least while we're young! We want to fix everything that's broken—right now. Heal every hurt. Stop grief in its tracks with a mantra, a prayer, or a song. We form queues for the gym, hoping to gain muscles yesterday. We trek to the top of mountains before dawn, hoping to become enlightened as soon as the first rays of the rising sun turn the plains to gold.

But this rarely happens.

Most of the time, we find ourselves still plodding through life's lowlands, toiling our way up and down the sand dunes of life, falling behind a step, stumbling forward two, slipping and sliding in the soft sands of reality, and making little spiritual progress.

Apparently. But perhaps, through the journey itself, God is teaching us more than we realize.

Helping us understand patience at a far deeper level. Strengthening the muscles of our resolve and making us a little more wise and kind than yesterday. Giving us daily opportunities to forgive and show heartfelt compassion, to feel and express deep understanding for ourselves and others.

May he, with loving and practiced skill, be shaping us into the person we long to become? The ideal person we pictured way back in the beginning, when we started our spiritual quest?

When we prayed for transformation of body and soul?

AMBIVALENCE

Ambivalence shines a spotlight on our
humanity and the complex nature
of authentic love.

The new mother is pacing up and down in the dark, patting her baby's back,
the baby of her dearest wish and deepest longing.

This downy-haired little human is too young to say, "Thank you," so instead,
he screams into her ear. Hour after hour. She loves him to bits but hates his
screams. She is thinking of giving him back, but there's no return warranty.
He's hers for keeps! No baby card, saying "Congratulations" and no cuddly
teddy bear has prepared her for this. For the primal urge to protect her baby
with her whole being and the primal urge to run away. Go anywhere to escape
his screams.

And this is only the beginning! From the cradle to the grave, ambivalence is our
silent companion. It is the push-pull instinct that drives us nuts, the sneaky,
unmentionable, taboo in every relationship. The inner conflict.

It's there when your darling toddler spills milk all over the floor, then splashes
in it, jumping up and down on the soggy carpet with grinning delight, calling
out in glee, "Look at me!" It's there when you take your scrubbed and shiny
child to school for the first time, then hurry home to sob because your baby
has grown up.

It keeps step with the father as he proudly walks his radiant daughter down
the aisle, then with a silent gulp, places her hand in the hand of another man.

It kneels beside us in the pre-dawn darkness as we linger by the bedside of our
beloved, willing them to live forever, yet hoping they slip away soon. Longing
to spare their suffering, and our own.

Whenever it appears, *ambivalence offers us no script.*

Taken by surprise and plagued by doubts, we say all sorts of sad and silly things
to ourselves like:

"I can't settle my baby, so I must be a bad mother."
"I like my job, but some days it's really tough. Maybe I don't have what it takes."
"I promised to love my partner in sickness and in health, but now I just want a break. I want to flee from this clinical room and join the people walking to and fro in the spring sunshine. I want to forget death and rejoin life!"

Romantic stories and flowery cards teach us to associate love with celebration and warm feelings of adoration. But cards and paperbacks tell only half the story, or perhaps they share only a misleading quarter. Just enough to be emotionally dangerous! They set our dreams ablaze and put stars in our eyes, but at the same time, they twist our expectations out of shape.

Cards rarely mention the push-pull of love. They don't say you can:

Adore your baby, but wish he came with a silencer.
Be a loving father, but still feel mad when your child trashes your bicycle.
Be a good spouse, but still find your partner's habits annoying.

Such information is too messy for a card and too messy for most conversations!

Left without guidance or permission to share how we feel, we can drift into darkness, into believing that *if I have mixed feelings toward a family member, it means I don't love them*. But could the opposite be the case?

Might our days of wondering and nights of wrestling actually show how committed we are? How deeply we care?

For hate and indifference never wrestle with ambivalence.

Only love does.

I don't know how you are traveling, or what your relationships are like, but I've struggled with ambivalence myself and I know how tough it can be. So, just in case you bump into ambivalence yourself one lonely night, here's what I've discovered so far.

We feel ambivalent because we are human. Because, in all relationships, there is a "them" and an "us," and sometimes the needs of the two clash. Sometimes the cultures of two people argue, or our relationship skills are still in training mode.

Ambivalence is woven into all our memories. For instance, we may feel great love for a parent, sibling, or friend, yet at the same time remember with a pang how much they hurt us.

We do not conquer ambivalence by denying its existence or by suppressing all our muddled feelings and our apparent duplicity. If we try, the confusion just settles into our psyche, where it erodes our confidence and hope. Where it casts a shadow of doubt over our most treasured relationships.

So what can we do? We can embrace it!

Ambivalence may not come carrying a script or easy answers, but it comes carrying something even more precious—good questions!

Questions that help us grow.

What values do you treasure?
What's your deepest purpose?
What resources and skills could you develop?
Who do you truly love?
Who do you want to become?

Answering these questions helps us prepare for the final challenge ambivalence poses. The one that shapes all we do, and *who we become.*

What's your next step?

INTEGRITY

For Richer?
For Poorer?
Who knows?

"Please, can we stay just a few more minutes?"

When I was young, my mother and I often walked to the local shops. It was a fair hike down country lanes, and I was always happy to pause halfway. For there, in a scruffy pen, a farmer kept a strutting peacock. One sunny day, the peacock had opened his tail for us, and I had been entranced by the swaying fan of iridescent blue and green feathers. So each time we walked that way, rain or shine, I begged, "Please, can't we stay a few more minutes?"

But my mother lived by adult time, and eventually, she led me away. As we walked on, I often looked over my shoulder, hoping.

Once we were in town, I had to keep my wits about me. The local market thronged with people, and my mother wove in and out among them, hunting for bargains. I trailed after her as she bought onions and potatoes, carrots, and a fat green cabbage. She stuffed these into stretchy string bags until I thought they would burst. Then she pulled out a cloth bag, unfolded it, and filled it with cans of baked beans, a bar of soap, and a loaf of bread wrapped in white paper. At last, as the sky faded, we hurried to the bus stop to catch a ride home.

The lumbering double-decker buses in our area looked striking on the outside with their cheery green paint, and they were fun to ride in the summer. But in winter, they were bitterly cold, even inside. At every stop, the folding doors swished open, and the wind howled in. Sometimes it carried in flakes of snow, and these frosted the metal floor with icy glitter.

The bus was staffed by two people.

The driver was cocooned in a little cubicle at the front. And behind him, all day long, the busy conductor walked up and down the chilly aisle. He collected fares and issued tickets from a small machine strapped to his belt. Sometimes, if the conductor went upstairs, one or two people could slip onto the bus downstairs, ride a few stops, then slip off again without paying.

One evening, as my mother and I huddled together on our faded plush seat, our feet squashed by sagging bags of potatoes and beans, the conductor clattered upstairs without taking our fare. A little whisper of hope echoed in my heart, and I wondered, *will we get a free ride?*

As the bus passed familiar stops, I pressed my nose to the cold window, urging us on. The sky grew darker, and the streetlamps began to glow like candles in the gloom; I had to keep wiping my breath from the glass to see them. When our stop was just ahead, I felt like bouncing on my seat with excitement. The conductor was still busy upstairs, and we were going to get our first free ride!

As the bus wheezed to a stop beside our road, I scrambled to my feet quickly and followed my mother up the aisle. But just as we reached the door, we heard the conductor's big boots thumping down the metal spiral staircase. Urgently, I grabbed my mother's hand and pulled her toward the door. But she let go of my hand and lingered at the bottom of the stairs. "Quick, he's coming!" I hissed. But she didn't move. Instead, she dipped her hand into her worn purse and pulled out a few coins. Then, with a smile, she held them out to the conductor and said, "Here's our fare." He smiled broadly in return and dropped them into his leather pouch; then he thanked her warmly, pleased.

But as I stumbled off the bus, I was far from pleased. I shrugged my mother's hand away and stomped down the path. When a cold gust of wind slapped me in the face, I burst out, "Why did you pay him? We could have ridden for free!"

My mother stopped walking and put down her bags with a sigh. Turning to face me, she asked gently, "Lorna, did we ride on the bus?" Grumpy and frustrated, I could only manage a nod. All I could think of was the missed opportunity to save money, money that was very tight. I had seen how my mother counted every coin *to make ends meet*. I had seen the empty spots on the pantry shelves. My own soul had shrunk a little smaller each time I had pulled a hand-me-down dress over my head.

After a few moments, my mother tried again and softly asked, "So, isn't it fair that we paid for our ride?"

For a while, I could not speak. But finally, I mumbled into my woolly scarf, "I s'pose so."

I was about six years old when my mother and I snuggled deeper into our coats and trudged the last few steps home. But whenever I remember the event, a strange glow warms my heart and I'm still glad my mother refused to sell her integrity that dark night for the price of a bus ticket.

FREE TO BE HUMAN

No one
was designed to be
merely a creator or a

custodian of things.

We were designed to be
living human beings
to whom things bow.

Enough?

In a world stuffed with
More for some people and
Less for others, try playing with
Enough until she yields her secrets.

That is all.

TEN PERCENT TEARS

Gratitude,
like a wide-eyed child,
discovers blessings invisible
to careless eyes.

As I slip and slide through the challenges of life, I have often missed the significant difference between the following two statements:

"My cake is dry" and
"My well is dry."

Please, pause for a moment and read the two statements again. *What does each comment imply?*

When I first thought of the phrases above, I noticed something profound.

I saw that the nature of my complaint actually indicates the level of my blessings.

If I complain about having *a bad hair day*, I have hair!
If I moan about the weeds taking over my garden, I have a garden!
If I fuss over my messy toddler, I have a child!

Could recognizing this change our whole approach to life? Could it help me notice how yummy the picnic is rather than grumble because my partner forgot the salt? Could it set me free to enjoy humming a familiar song and tapping my feet to the beat, even when I've forgotten half the words?

As human beings, we have an astonishing capacity to "see" what's missing and "not see" what's right in front of us. We do this repeatedly in situations and relationships.

Are we crazy?

Why on earth do we set ourselves up for misery? Why do we act like misers, dolling out tiny coins of praise and gratitude as if we'll run short? Why do we allow ourselves to drift into becoming critics? Then congratulate ourselves on being smart?

Why do we act like hound dogs on the trail of flaws? Then howl with horrified delight when we find one? When we manage to track down a mistake in the movie or the meal?

Or in the person we love the most?

Why do we spend a lifetime weeping and wailing over the ten percent we lack when we could be delighting ourselves, *and thanking those we love?*

Swirling, when we get the chance, in grateful joy and doing a "Ninety Percent Dance"?

Do You Like It?

Our "Thank you" is the gift
we give the giver.

One day, a lady handed me an unexpected gift, but before I had time to say a word, she began to apologize.

"I hope you like it. I wasn't sure what color to get . . . and I had to guess your size. You can take it back to the store if you don't like it."

All this tumbled out before I'd even untied the ribbon or pulled open the wrapping.

After the lady left, and I had thanked her for her lovely gift, I realized she had given me two gifts that morning. She had given me an item of clothing *and a lesson in vulnerability*. I saw that, like her, *we put a little bit of our heart into all the genuine gifts we give.*

Whatever they are.

Whether we buy a family member a dress or share a cake we have baked. Whether we help someone weed their garden or fix a glitch on a friend's computer.

Every gift costs the giver more than the price tag. It costs time, attention, and thought. *Because the giver reaches beyond themselves, it also involves risk.*

By the tone of her voice and the rush of her words, this kind lady told me:

"I'm going out on a limb here. I'm scared you won't want what I have to offer. That you'll reject my gift, and in rejecting it, you'll reject me." This is not a trivial fear, something to be dismissed out of hand. Because, *to be accepted* and *to belong* are two of our most basic needs, things we crave deep in our soul.

As human beings, we have an inbuilt need for recognition. By this, I don't mean glory or praise but rather the desire to be seen, to be heard, to be noticed, and therefore valued. Whatever our age, we want to know that we have something to offer, something others want. That we can make a contribution to the marriage, family, or workplace. We want to know that, whatever our talents or our limits, *we are a valued part of the team.*

Little children understand this and pester their parents to let them help. (Even when the parent knows their "help" will be a hindrance!) Old folks understand it and offer us biscuits, pre-loved clothes, and advice.

Looking back to my own childhood, I can see that my mother understood this principle of vulnerability and risk well. When I was a child, after Christmas Day and after every birthday, she sat me down at the kitchen table, then she passed me a pen and some paper. And each time she did this, I grumbled. "Oh Mom, do I have to? Writing thank-you letters will take me ages!"

"Mmm, how long do you think it took Grandma to knit that sweater? Or Aunty Letitia to go shopping for that doll?"

Big sigh. "Okay!"

I wrote a lot of wobbly letters during my childhood, very short letters with some very creative spelling. But write them, I did! Once I got started, I actually had fun embellishing each letter with some crayon flowers, stickers and smiley faces.

Whether my mother planned this or not, noticing people became second nature, and saying "Thank you" became one of my lifelong habits.

Now I understand that *expressing thanks is one side of a social trade*. It's a key part of the give-and-take of a loving life. *As such, it therefore involves more than gratitude. At its very core, it involves having a heart and mind that's open to seeing people, seeing their outstretched hands and acknowledging their worth.*

Conversely, when we do not acknowledge a gift, or someone's effort, the person can feel as if they have cast their heart and their time into a great dark void. Leaving only a hollow, empty, echo ringing in their ears.

Offering genuine thanks involves noticing both others' special gifts and the daily effort they put into the take-it-for-granted stuff; the washed clothes, the mown lawn, and the baked potatoes. The accurate business report delivered on time.

To be effective at thanking, we don't have to go over the top! If we expressed thanks for every little thing, the exchange itself would become meaningless, even irritating. But I wonder, what would happen at work or at home if we chose one small thing each day to acknowledge? One thing to thank a parent, partner, or child for? It may involve saying something as simple as, "Thanks for letting me finish watching my program before you swapped channels." or "That was yummy, thanks for baking it."

I'm not sure if the urge to say "Thank you" can be woven into a child's DNA after birth or into the DNA of an adult.

But, is it worth a try?

THE TEN TO ONE RATIO

When you serve others,
thanks are not guaranteed,
but effort and risk are!

I've combined two ancient tales to form this story. If you are curious about the original stories, you can find the links in the Reference section.[4]

As the group of friends ambled along, their sandals scuffed up puffs of dust and their robes billowed out behind them. Unconcerned by the rough road, they continued to laugh and chat about everything under the sun. Suddenly, out of nowhere, a ragged group of beggars blocked the path ahead. Their tattered clothing hung haphazardly on their gaunt bodies and their missing sleeves revealed running sores and twisted hands.

The friends gulped back in horror when the stench of death wafted around them, and instinctively stumbled to a stop and flung their arms across their faces. Squinting past their sleeves, they eyed the scruffy crew with scornful gaze. No one spoke, but silently, their minds screamed out in disgust, *"How dare they stand in our way?" "Who do they think they are?" "At the very least, they could take a bath!" "What a bunch of sorry messed up rejects! Nobodies!"*

While the friends muttered, and fell over their own feet in a bid to retreat, one man stepped forward.

Alone.

For, he saw something different.

He did not see nobodies, or even just bodies. Instead, he looked past the sores and scars, and saw people. Precious individuals who were hurting in body and soul.

So, he strode forward, and held out his hands. Reaching out across the great gulf chiseled by taboo and fear, he gently touched the sick skin-wrappings of their souls. Without flinching, he braved the mess and stench to embrace each person with his love.

And they were healed.

No one took photos that day to post on social media. No one snapped "before" and "after" pictures of disfigured faces made whole. No one paused to grin in smiling "selfies" with the healer.

But someone did record their story and immortalize the moment and he was eager to hand it down to us through the generations. Thrilled to tell us how Jesus touched the untouchable. *To remind us that he still does.*

The outcasts of society. Those broken by sin and sickened by despair.

Cocooned as we are in modern society, where hospitals stand in most towns and soap lies beside most sinks, I think we miss the gritty rawness of this story.

When Jesus walked the earth, men and women who developed leprosy were considered to be worse than scum. Dirty, grotesque, and stinking, they were required by law to self-isolate. Because they had an infectious disease, they also *had to initiate their own shunning!* Whenever they ventured out to go shopping or scrounge for scraps, they had to warn others they were coming and cry out in agonized self-condemnation, "I'm unclean! Unclean!" So everyone could hold their noses and flee.

This left the person with leprosy standing so very alone.

Only able to find refuge, if at all, in the company of other loners. Misfits.

On that day, when Jesus healed those lepers, he didn't just solve their health crisis; he took a bunch of nobodies, and transformed them into some-bodies again.

As was his lifelong habit.

He welcomed a bunch of outcasts and made them into insiders again, people who belonged.

He took away their labels and gave them back their names. He returned, with interest, their original legacy, destiny, and purpose.

When they cried out in desperate hope, "Lord, if you are willing, you can make me clean."

He answered with warmhearted assurance, "I am willing."

Then he reached out his hand!

As you can imagine, the lepers were overjoyed. Leaping with new life. Elated!

Steady on . . .

Are you sure?

I wish the story ended with a party, a celebration of gratitude. But it doesn't. Instead, it ends with a simple question.

"Weren't ten healed?"

The answer, of course was "Yes."

But of those ten, how many do you think said "Thank you?"

All ten?

About eight?

Five or six?

One!

This story tells me many things about the generosity of God, about the realities of life, and about really seeing people. *It also shows me that service of any kind involves risk.* That we may spend a moment, or a lifetime, healing others and helping them stand tall, but rarely receive a word of thanks.

As God himself knows.

We may cook meals, sweep floors, and care for children. We may build houses, fix leaking pipes, or plant a crop so others can eat, but never receive a medal.

We may give gifts and send cards, only to feel our gladness and kindness has vanished into thin air and wafted away on the wind. But the story of the lepers does not leave us without comfort. Instead it assures us, "You are not alone, for God understands." When nobody responds to all our effort, we can console ourselves with what I've come to call,

The Jesus Ratio.

It's a ratio that most carers already know. Most parents and nurses, teachers, and helpers who take the time to serve or heal, but rarely receive any thanks. These folk live with the 10 to 1 ratio on a daily basis and they know it's not a fair deal. There are no sure winnings here. No 50/50 chance of success.

So, naturally, they sometimes grow weary of serving and ministering to others.

As partners, parents, and workers, we, too, may *grow weary of caring*.

However, when all is said and done, we are faced with a stark choice.

We can *focus on the risk of giving*, as mentioned in the previous topic, and invest only in people and projects where we are likely to be appreciated and applauded. Or *we can choose to serve others anyway*, whether we receive thanks or not. Serve, not as puppets of others' demands, nor in ways that squander or disrespect our own energy or talents, but in ways which honor us, and honor others. Striving to find the rare balance between *someone's need to be served* and their equally important *need to learn self-reliance*. And also striving to balance *our desire to live caring lives* with *our need to be replenished and nurtured*.

Ultimately, we care for others however they respond, *because of who we are* and because we care!

Because, one way or another, we have caught a glimpse of divine love. Of how The Holy One, embraces the hurting ones. And, looking into his face with wide-eyed wonder, our own wounds have been revealed, then healed.

Freely you have received,
freely give.[5]
—Jesus

GRACE

Like summer rain,
your lavish grace refreshes
my parched soul.

Growing up in England, I had scant regard for rain.

Rain ruined my teddy bear picnics and made my dolls' dresses wet. It trapped me inside on long winter afternoons and painted our living room walls in shades of gloom. On cold rainy days, I felt like a trapped sprite. Restless as a caged elf, I pressed my nose to the window and watched icy squalls sweep across the land and bend the specter trees. The walls of our stone cottage seemed to wick up puddled rain until everything felt damp. Even our flannelette sheets smelled musty. In winter, when I crossed the room to stand with my back to the fire, I still shivered.

In my childish opinion, rain was a nuisance. It made winter miserable, spring slow to come, and the canvas of our summer tent sag. It turned playgrounds into soggy marshes and blotted out the friendly sun. It layered the sky with gray clouds and cast shifting shadows across the landscape of my soul.

But in all my complaining, I hardly noticed that it kept our grass green or that the rain made the daisies grow in summer. In childish delight, I simply knelt on the lawn, haloed by sunshine, and with careful fingers, linked the star-white daisies together. Then, with innocent kisses, I draped the floral necklace around my mother's neck.

When I grew up and married, I followed my husband to live in Australia. For the first time, I saw what a rain-starved land looked like and I felt what the unshaded sun could do. I saw flowers bow before its glare and leaves curl up in homage to its heat. I watched the burning earth crack open and tall trees wither and die. I saw shadowy sheep wandering aimlessly, kicking up the drifting dust as brushfire smoke painted the twilight sky an eerie crimson.

Without rain, heat waves shimmered on the horizon, and the roadside ditches filled with dust. As the singeing summer lingered, all my memories of rain evaporated. With each passing day, my whole body began to long for rain. Even my soul felt thirsty. Once, in silent desperation, I dribbled a cup of water over a few scrawny weeds by the back door just to see something green grow. When the tiny green leaves burst from the gritty earth, I felt reassured. Maybe life could return to this sun-created moonscape after all.

At last, one summer evening, dark clouds piled up in the east, and all nature held its breath. One drop fell, then another. Faster and faster they fell, making mini craters in the dust. Suddenly, the drops joined hands for gladness and began to tumble to earth in great cascades. Water gurgled in the gutters and streamed down the roads, filling the ditches with swirling bubbles. Torrents of water surged into the ponds until they overflowed.

All earth was soaking. Washed clean!

Finally, the clouds parted, and we rushed out into the steaming new world. Everywhere there were puddles, glassy puddles, mirroring white scudding clouds and the brilliant blue sky. Shiny, shimmering, gloriously wet puddles.

Barefoot, my sons and I laughed and splashed and danced. We ran down to the local pond and giggled at the ducks paddling in puzzled circles over the submerged park benches.

We opened our arms and opened our hearts.
We soaked up the abundance.
We gloried, body and soul, in grace.[6]

INTERIOR DESIGN

You are your own
interior designer.

Moment by moment, with
every thought and story,
every song and prayer,
you furnish the mind-space,
where your soul lives.

How beautiful
is that?

THE JOURNEY OF A LIFETIME

Why are you still searching
for the perfect place and perfect
time to begin your journey?

The perfect place is here.
The perfect time is now.

Today, you may be deep in winter's snow or soaking up some tropical sun. You may be counting up your coins to catch the bus across town or adding up your frequent flyer points to jet across the globe. But wherever you are planning to go, you still have the same goal:

You want to be somewhere else.

Why?

Only you know.

As humans, we travel around a lot. To work, and home again. To friends and family. To war, and sometimes home again. To love, play, and make peace.

In addition to taking physical journeys, we also take spiritual journeys, journeys of mind and soul.

In our quest for meaning, we may fly to a distant land to sit cross-legged by the sea, climb a snow-capped mountain, or trek across the burning sand. But even then we may still come home empty, never realizing that peace and purpose can be found within, wherever our feet fall.

For it's in our hearts that we take the greatest journeys of all.

Recently, when I wanted to find inspiration for a spiritual trip, I turned to a book I've named The Book of Journeys. I discovered a huge range of story-trips listed there.

Some offered to take me back in time to when Planet Earth was young.

Others showed me the weary earth-grown-old and a glimpse of the earth-made-new.

Some trips invited me to travel from Revenge to Forgiveness. Others showed me the uphill path from Despair to Hope.

Finally, I found a trip, described in just two words, which seemed tailor-made for me.

The two words are so simple that I've often overlooked them, yet so profound that they change the way I see myself and everyone I meet. These two words promise to take me from isolation to being part of a family.

A gloriously complex family, which includes the rich man with his yacht and the poor man sewing his sails. The wealthy woman enjoying a leisurely spa treatment, and the humble woman kneeling at her feet painting her toenails.

The blessed child surrounded by gaudy Christmas presents, and the refugee child fleeing barefoot from staccato machine guns. The teenager on the honor roll at an exclusive school, and the homeless youngster sampling drugs in a dark alley.

So, what are these two life-changing words? The words which invite us to travel from isolation to inclusion?

Which make us all family?

"Our Father."[7]

Our home.

A place rich with belonging and a place full of challenge, because family life is not always easy or smooth sailing!

Just because everyone is "family" we don't have to like what every family member says or does! A devoted mother will not *like it* when her daughter sneaks in and steals her stash of chocolate. A loving father will not *like it* when his son kicks a soccer ball through the kitchen window scattering shards of glass in the salad he's just made. There are times when all parents don't "like" what their children are doing. This means they sometimes set limits, and sometimes dole out consequences. *But they don't disown their children.* Their children, however irritating or grumpy, are still part of the family, whatever their age.

If family members are kind to each other, home is a happy place to be, but if self-interest runs amok, war quickly erupts. War among siblings over who gets to sit in the front seat of the car, or war among neighbors and nations over who gets to sit on a certain piece of land.

We know that war of any kind hurts people and destroys lives. We know war creates crippling fear, devastating havoc and heart breaking grief, sometimes for generations. But we also know that even the most prolonged and blood-soaked war does not stop us from being human beings. Or stop us from being family. (Whether we like each other or not!)

Ultimately, whatever our background, whatever our wounds or opinions, family means we are in this together. If I cut down a forest, you have less oxygen to breathe. If you plant flowers, I enjoy their perfume. Our attitudes and actions affect others, sometimes deeply, but we still have equal status as God's children. And the term "Our Father" reminds me that *he wants and loves each one of us.*

Could this be why God, like a loving parent, chose to wade into earth's mess and mayhem? Why he came in the form of Jesus at great personal cost, to offer us healing, forgiveness and peace?

Many cultures and communities pride themselves
on being inclusive, but the words "Our Father,"
spoken over two thousand years ago,
form the most inclusive statement
I've ever heard.[8]

A Credit to the Family

Every act of brotherhood and
every kindness shown a sister
contributes to our shared identity.

Our family has some "black sheep" in it, members who make us tremble or run and hide. People near and far who make us weep, or shake our heads and feel ashamed of our current surname:

"Humanity."

But, our family has some heroes in it too. People who make us proud to be part of the human race.

I've often been inspired by local family members and also by the stories of people who lived long ago or in countries across the rippling sea.

One "sister" who inspires me lives in Africa. Though I have never heard her name, I treasure a copy of her picture. The newspaper clipping is yellowing now, but I often pull it out to gaze at her in awe. In the photograph, she is carrying a tall stack of handmade mud bricks to build herself and her family a simple shelter. A home of dirt, in that most earthy of places, a refugee camp.

If I was walking in her shoes, or rather, in her bare feet, I would be angry, blinded by resentment and pain. Wandering aimlessly down dusty detours of grief. But she is striding across the page. Head held high. *And she is smiling*. She is grinning from ear to ear as if she's carrying treasure. And she is. She's carrying an armload of hope.

Go sister!

Many brothers inspire me too.

You can see a group of them in a second newspaper clipping, a scrap of paper which has survived many cleaning and decluttering sessions. The picture shows a team of village men inside a deep well, hand-carved in the searing landscape. Attached to the inner rim of the well, you can just glimpse a homemade ladder of withered branches lashed together. Several men are standing on this ladder, one above the other, gripping the twigs with their bare toes. Together they form a human chain. It begins with the man at the bottom. He dips his battered bucket into the water and passes it up to the next man. Finally, the man on the surface pours the water into a trough, and the cattle push forward to slake their thirst.

The water is muddy, but in my imagination, above the sound of splashing, I can hear the men chanting in rhythm, singing as they haul dirty drinking water up for themselves and their livestock.

Did you hear that? They are singing over the gift of dirty water. For this is a *singing well*.[9]

Go, brothers!

Many brothers and sisters unconsciously enrich my life by their example and their courage.

Even when I don't know their names, they inspire me.

Even when they have no idea I exist, they help me stand tall.

I remember the bald teenage girl who, with bright eyes, sings and prays her way through chemotherapy.

I think of the ninety-nine-year-old grandmother who still manages a trembling smile and a kind word for those who visit.

I honor the good man who quietly picks up another's burden and faithfully carries it on his own shoulders, year after year, for love.

These are our family members. Yours and mine. Or to paraphrase a famous statement.

Whenever you do a kindness
to a brother or sister, you are
really doing it for our family,
and for Me.[10]
—Jesus

JOY

Dear God,

as I begin today,
please give me
enough joy for two.

Some for me,
and some to share.

Thank you.

ALCHEMY

Within the base metal of your ordinary life,
there lies the glorious potential to create
spiritual gold.

So, with all my heart,
I hope you create your own unique formula soon
and choose to craft beauty from brokenness.

I pray you discover, slumbering in your heartache,
enough hope and wisdom to bless others,
and be blessed yourself.

Dalmatians

Each pattern of spots is unique,
but spots themselves are universal.

Several years ago, our family visited some friendly older folks who ran a mushroom farm. As I settled into one of their sagging armchairs, I pulled my youngest son onto my lap. Glancing past his ear, I noticed a hand-painted plaque on the wall, faded with time.

There is so much bad in the best of us,
and so much good in the worst of us,
that it hardly becomes any of us
to talk about the rest of us.[11]
—*Unknown*

Like Dalmatian puppies, we are all spotty. Our spots are just in different places. One person has a spot over a deep heart wound. Another hides their shame under a spot of anxiety. Where I stumble, you may be strong, stride through life, muscle-proud. If so, good for you.

Whether we are a child, teenager, or adult, most of us have days when we bounce into life full of optimism and vitality. Days when the sun shines, our eyes sparkle, and hope makes us feel fleet-footed and playful.

But we also have days of defeat, when, trembling, we long to crawl under the nearest couch and hide. Days when we stumble out of bed, weary to the bone, and look in the mirror, lift our eyes to the spot-scattered vision before us, and think, *no one has as many flaws as me. I'm a walking disaster!*

On days when we feel strong, we are tempted to leap past others and think, *How can they be so slow?* Or preening together before life's shiny mirror, look at others and think, *How awful to have a spot there! I'd never let that happen to me. They really should wash it off.*

Noticing another person's spotty sins and secrets may help us feel smug and superior. Telling a neighbor about them may give us a quick thrill, a moment of undivided attention from those who listen. But if we damage another's reputation in the process, if we spoil a friendship, and isolate and condemn a vulnerable soul without the benefit of a fair trial, what has anyone gained? Whatever our age or stage, putting others down is not a way to climb higher, and gossip is not a form of entertainment or self-protection.

Nor are hate and prejudice.

There are times when we need to shield ourselves from dangerous people and warn others who are at risk. Times when we have to stand up to evil, or flee. But most of the time, we just need to be tipped into a tub and, like a grubby puppy, given a good scrub!

In the end, the words we send out into life tend to return to us. Our attitudes and actions boomerang back. What we do matters because, ultimately, how we treat others, we will treat ourselves.

In our strength and in our weakness, on our wobbly, vulnerable days and our bouncy days, you and I are in this together.

Tumbled into life.

A life where we have the glorious opportunity to play, pray, *and be kind*.

Where, by our attitudes and actions, we help to shape the communities that form around us. The places we live out our days. If we wish, we can create communities of snapping, yapping condemnation, where we routinely snarl and "chew each other out." Or families, clubs, and worksites full of playful grace, where each person makes it their business to encourage a colleague. Where young and old cheerfully share food and water.

And, snuggle up safe in the sun to snooze!

One day, there was a conversation in heaven, or so I've heard.

It went something like this . . .

"Well, Son, which one will you adopt?"
"One? But Dad, I love them all! Can we take them all home, please?"
The Father chuckled and replied,
"They will make a lot of mess and leave muddy footprints everywhere.
If you want them all, *you'll have a lot of saving to do.*"
To which the son replied,
"That's okay, Dad, they're worth it."

Or, to liberally paraphrase Paul's words:

While we were still spotty,
busy doing our own thing,
hurting ourselves and
stumbling into trouble.

Oblivious and rebellious,
our minds messed up
by sin and our hearts
distracted by sorrow,

Creator God loved us.

In Jesus, He came
to scoop us up,
hug us to his mighty
heart, and save us.

To free us from
fear's cruel cage,
to play, explore, and
bask in holy awe.[12]

THE BRIDGE

Never underestimate
the power of a simple "Hello!"

It's amazing how much courage it takes to walk across a room, to launch a solo, unassisted, expedition across *The Great Gulf of Silence* between two people.

But when we do, something magical often happens. We begin to *make small talk*. And small talk is not small at all.

During small talk, two people begin to sketch a bridge of friendship in the air with words.

A bridge they may build for a day, a decade, or a lifetime.

When we make small talk, we are really launching a kind of personal low-risk *relationship feasibility study*. This is true whether we are at a party, a pool, or a working lunch.

We often begin this informal interview by talking about safe subjects, like the weather. But in reality, our minds are hoping to answer some deeper questions; for instance: *Is this person interesting? Do we have anything in common?* We may also wonder, *What skills or ideas do they have which I could use?* or, *Would one of my life stories inspire or impress them?*

While our minds are busy making small talk, our gut is doing some research of its own. It asks questions like, *Does this person make me feel physically and emotionally safe?* and *Do they like me?*

Each time we sense a "Yes" to one of our questions, we are likely to share more of ourselves. Risk building a stronger connection to someone else in the hope we have found a new colleague, friend, or soulmate.

All this wealth for a simple "Hello!"
and a smattering of small talk.

The Bridge of Hope

For a bridge to work,
it has to be connected
at both ends.

Be deeply grounded
in the bedrock of
both trial and triumph.

I have a question for you. Is it possible that you have endured both pain and joy, brokenness and healing in your life to equip you to become *a bridge of hope* for someone?

For a wanderer who, even now, is starting to follow in your footsteps?

The Game of God

Just because I hide,
don't assume I don't
want you to find me.

Each spring, when I was a child, our family attended a conference for my father's work at a soaring stone mansion on a sprawling English estate. It was the highlight of my year, and I loved exploring the house and grounds with the other children.

We scrambled through overgrown gardens choked with ferns. We ran down wandering paths and stumbled into hidden glens. We discovered crumbling stone fountains sleeping under blankets of ivy.

On rainy days, we ran amok inside (to the dismay of the maids). We paraded up the grand staircase imagining we owned the place, and scampered down the twisted back stairs reserved for the servants. We opened dusty doors and tip-toed along dimly lit secret passages.

We played hide-and-seek for hours.

My favorite place to hide was curled up on a deep stone windowsill behind the plush crimson velvet curtains. When I heard the countdown, ". . . three, two, one," I was quiet as a mouse. And when the one who was IT shouted, "Coming, ready or not!" I held my breath, pulled my knees up to my chin, and pressed my body against the cold glass.

Even though I took great pains to hide, in my heart, I still longed for one thing, that someone would search long enough to find me.

I also dreaded the opposite outcome.

That the children would give up their search, ignore my absence and move on to the next game. Leaving me to clamber down cramped and alone. Forgotten.

When I grew up, I stopped playing hide-and-seek. But sometimes I still longed to be found, to be noticed, to have someone take the time, and make the effort, to really see me. To know when I was hurting, discover some unsung talent or find beauty in my soul.

I thought others may feel this way too and wondered what I could do. At last, in the spirit of childhood, I decided to invent an adult version of hide-and-seek. *This game involves seeing invisible people.* The beauty is, you can play it anywhere, even if you don't live in an ancient English mansion!

To play, all you need to do is look around for *an invisible person.* They may be in your own kitchen washing the dishes, yet again. They may be sitting by themselves in a corner at a party or sweeping the street as you hurry by busy doing very important things.

Once you have seen the invisible person, the idea is to let them know they have been found, not by springing on them suddenly and shouting, "Ah-ha, caught you!" But with a little more tact and style. Perhaps by making eye contact and smiling. Perhaps by saying "Thank you" or "Would you like a hand?"

Whatever it takes to make the person feel valued and visible again.

As I began to play this game, I had such fun that I decided to expand it. Now I don't just see invisible people; *I also see people who aren't there,* people like the motel cleaner. After I have packed my bag, I leave a little gift on the bed.

When she strips the sheets and a thank-you card and chocolate bar tumble out, I hope it makes her smile.

If it does, that makes two of us.

Playing hide-and-seek was such a natural part of my childhood that I rarely wondered who invented it. But I've discovered the game has a long and illustrious history. According to the ancient book of beginnings, Genesis, the first person to say, "Coming, ready or not!" was God himself. Searching through Eden's glorious garden, he called out to Adam and Eve in a voice full of lonely love and longing,

"Where are you?"[3]

It's a game God's playing
still, with all his heart.

Though he knows
where we are, he still calls
you and me. Invites us
to be seen, and heard,
and real again.

Unlike children at play,
God never gives up,
even for a moment.

Whatever it takes,
he searches day and
night until he finds us.

Until,
beaming from ear to ear,
he can sing out,
Ah ha! There you are!

Ice, Eggs, and Grass

Can the losing of me
be the finding of me?

Many times I've been stirred by an inspiring message or charismatic speaker, and I've desired spiritual transformation. Longed to be made new, and have a fresh start.

But each time, brim full of fervor, I've chosen to ignore the fact that the change will cost me something, and I will always lose something. I don't like the sound of this, but in all settings, that's what transformation requires!

For water to be transformed into ice, it has to give up being a liquid.
For sunshine to be tucked inside a blade of grass and become food, it has to give up being light.
For a raw egg to be turned into a solid and keep its shape, even when all external restraints have been removed, it has to yield to the transforming power of heat.

As you seek spiritual growth and yearn for transformation, what price are you willing to pay for it?

What are you prepared to relinquish, or surrender, to be made new?

What old habits and prejudices will you give up?

What grudges?

Griefs?

And musty fears?

What stubborn independence?

Like me, will you try to clutch the old ways tightly to your chest and simultaneously reach out for a new life with the same hand?

Will you expect to be more loving, but still reserve the right to ridicule your neighbor?

Will you vow to live a kinder life, but still plot to outmaneuver others at work?

Will you decide to be more friendly, but elbow others aside to grab a bargain in a summer sale?

Will you be so attached to your regrets for the past and your fears for the future, so obsessed with self-management and controlling everyone and everything that you become anxious, snappy, and brittle with the effort? When, all along, God is graciously calling you to relax into his joy-filled providence?

And there's more to consider:

It's an annoying irony, that our primary motivation for spiritual enlightenment may not be as altruistic as it seems, instead, it may stem from a twisted form of self-obsession! Because, even if we pride ourselves on being spiritual seekers, in practical terms, we may revel in being self-centered. It's easy to slip into ruminating, or hanker after the attention our quest brings. Indulge and amplify our feelings, or long for the short-term payoffs of our old habits.

We like the attention we get when we're grumpy. Or we enjoy pulling others' strings so they dance to our tune.

We like using the skills we've carefully honed to subtly get our own way. And we enjoy managing others with a raised voice or a raised eyebrow *so they return the power to us*. Hand over the remote control so we can "channel surf," and pick what we want to watch on television.

We may also be addicts of one kind or another, lured by the quick thrill of harmful habits, hoping, meanwhile, that our good intentions are enough to spare us from adverse consequences.

Many of us are good at playing games like this, toying with the idea of transformation as if it were a new hobby, and *pretending that superficial changes are fundamental changes.*

We find it easy to live in a world of make-believe values or buy the idea that a new car, a new house, or a different hair color *is a soul makeover*.

I wonder, who do we think we are kidding?

Who are we fooling?

Others? Ourselves?

God?

While the media holds out gift vouchers for face makeovers and we queue up to be painted as clones of our culture, God takes transformation seriously, sometimes more seriously than we want him to! If I pray to be made kinder, I'm often seeking a simple upgrade of a certain quality I value. A quick fix. A snack-sized change.

But if I do, I'm out of sync with God because he's longing to pour his whole heart into transforming me. Or to paraphrase Paul,

Wherever the Spirit of the Lord is,
there is freedom.
God's freedom transforms us so much,
that even our faces begin to light up
and glow with the glory deep within.[14]
—Paul

GOD'S ERASER

Where on earth can you find
an eraser to match it?

Do you picture God as someone who gets excited? Whose eyes sparkle with delight?

No?

Someone who bubbles over with so much enthusiasm that he wants to tell the story of his love in a million ways? Needs the whole sky and deepest sea to describe his forgiveness?

A person so brimming over with generosity that he chooses to illustrate his point with metaphors like this?

"I'll search all earth's storms for the thickest thundercloud. Then I'll pick it up and use it like a giant eraser to wipe the sky! To clear away even the slightest vapor trail of your sin so my light can shine on you!"

And again,

"I'll stomp on all your mistakes, pound them into the dust with my feet so no one can ever track them down again."

And,

"I'll carry all your sins out to sea, then I'll throw them overboard so they sink beneath the waves without leaving a trace!"[15]

In Deep Water

How far
is far enough?
How loved
is loved enough?

Bending his back with the effort, he drags the small boat down the beach. It's so heavy, the hull makes a deep gouge in the gritty sand. At last, he reaches the water's edge and pushes the boat into the surging waves, then he wades into the water and leaps aboard.

The tide is coming in, and the current is so powerful that his muscles bulge with the effort. But he dips his oars into the choppy waves anyway and steadily rows out toward the open sea.

As he passes the headland, the wind begins to buffet his body without mercy. It whips the hair across his face and fills his eyes with windblown tears. He licks his lips hoping to moisten them but they dry out almost instantly and the cracks fill with stinging salt. He longs to gulp great mouthfuls of water, but the rippling brine only mocks his thirst.

Battling his pain, he rows on. Dips and pulls on the oars in a steady rhythm until he is far from land.

At last, he stops rowing and his boat drifts a little then becomes still. This is the place. Resting his oars in the rowlocks, he stretches his cramped fingers and turns his hands over. Glancing at his palms, he notices that sharp splinters in the coarse wooden oars have created gaping wounds across each hand and the oars are stained blood red.

He looks around.

Glassy ripples flow over the endless sea and fade into a shimmering haze near the horizon. The wind is easing, and the gentle lap, lap, of the waves on the hull is all he can hear, and high above his head, a lonely seabird's call.

He allows himself to sit for a moment to catch his breath, and his heart slowly stops pounding.

He is the Creator of the Sea, and yet, as a man, how vulnerable he is out here. All alone.

So why is he here, so far from safety? So far from land? Sitting in a wooden boat so low in the water that some of the waves splash over the prow and soak his sandals?

He is here for me. As his cargo plainly shows.

For stacked high in the boat are boxes. Scrawled on each one, in my own handwriting, I can see a single word: *Regret, Sin, Failure, Fear, Grief* . . .

Taking a deep breath, Jesus lifts the first box, and muscles straining, he drops it over the side. The boat rocks and sways with the movement, and water splashes up His arms, making his hairs glisten in the evening sun.

The box floats for just a moment, settling into the aquamarine water, then it starts to sink, spinning deeper and deeper down into the darkness until it's out of sight. Gone.

Never to rise again. *Never to rise again!*

Even when cramps grip His side and dark clouds build on the horizon, he continues to unload his cargo. He drops each box overboard until his boat rides high in the water and bounces like a cork on the waves.

Then he picks up the oars, and grasping them in his strong but scarred hands, he turns his boat toward land again.

Though his body bows low between the wooden oars, broken and weary, his soul swells with elation, with unspeakable, divine joy.[16]

His mission is accomplished and he is heading home.

It is finished!

He has lifted every weight from my soul

and set me free!

TRANSFORMING LOVE

This luminous poem has been attributed to various authors, including Roy Croft. However, the most likely author seems to be Mary Carolyn Davies.

I love you,
Not only for who you are,
But for who I am
When I am with you.
I love you,
Not only for what
You have made of yourself,
But for what
You are making of me.
I love you
For the part of me
That you bring out;
I love you
For putting your hand
Into my heaped-up heart
And passing over
All the foolish, weak things
That you can't help
Dimly seeing there,

And for drawing out
Into the light
All the beautiful belongings
That no one else had looked
Quite far enough to find.
I love you because you
Are helping me to make
Of the lumber of my life
Not a tavern
But a temple;
Out of the works
Of every day
Not a reproach
But a song.[17]

—Mary Carolyn Davies

Section 4: The Butterfly

Vision, Significance, Legacy

The caterpillar began to squirm. *I'm sure no one's been tied up as long as me*, he muttered. *If I have to stay in this cocoon one more day, I'll burst! Please God, get me out of here. If you do, I'll be content to crawl for the rest of my life, I promise!*

Wriggling this way and that, he hardly noticed that fragments of his cocoon were flaking off. Soon a tiny crack appeared, then another. He glimpsed green grass and tasty leaves below, just out of reach. As the caterpillar twisted and turned in his fraying cocoon, he began to see flickers of sunlight and shards of blue sky. Sensing his fetters were weakening, the caterpillar poured all his energy into escaping. Suddenly, the cocoon split open, and he scrambled out into the sunshine.

Trembling with shock and excitement, he paused to catch his breath on a shiny leaf. Joy bubbled up inside him, and he began a skittering dance. "I've been set free!" he sang. He leaped into the air, "Free!" But as he landed, his slender legs slipped on the glossy leaf, and he found himself skidding toward the tip. As he tumbled out into thin air, he cried with all his strength, "Help! Help!"

The wind rushed past his cheeks, and he squeezed his eyes shut, waiting for impact. But when the ground did not slap him in the face, he risked opening one eye, then the other.

What he saw amazed him, for he was no longer earthbound.
He was soaring high in the sky on God-given wings of freedom!

NEW YEAR

Today is
New Year's Day.

Today is always
New Year's Day.

Happy New Year!

LAUNCH DAY

Come on, let's make a start,
no matter how small,
lest we never begin at all!

I'm a dreamer, and one day I'll change the world. Make life better for someone, somewhere.

But not today.

Today I'm waiting for the situation to improve, for the time I need, and the money, for the perfect family, and the weather to clear.

And of course, for the shiny new gadget that's being released tomorrow. I just need everything to fall into place, then I'll act—you'll see!

And when Perfection himself arrives, hand in hand with Ease, then I'll launch my boat and set sail for sure.

But until then, I'll linger in the harbor of One Day Soon. It's comfortable here. I can put my feet up—nobody minds—and lick cake crumbs from my fingers. I can even do some good. I can lend my mind to anyone who wants to borrow it, even strangers on the television. All I ask in exchange for my mind is an hour of drama, or a laugh.

Once in a while I get a bit of exercise to keep my spiritual-seeker muscles supple. I follow the still-warm tracks of a guru on a meandering detour to nowhere, so I can say, "Been there. Done that" just in case anyone bothers to ask.

The wind will change soon, and the rigging will hum the right tune. Then I'll leave the harbor. But until then, I'll take things nice and slow.

I'll lean out of my window and wave the early morning joggers on their way.

I'll beam at lovers naively walking hand in hand.

I'll smile at children.

Whenever the urge to do something significant surfaces, I'll turn up the sound on the evening news. That usually kills my creativity.

And if someone tells me they believe in God, on this earth so peopled with questions, I'll admire them, then I'll beckon doubts and invite them to track muddy footprints across my spirit again. Become squatters in my soul, where faith longs to live.

Or maybe, on second thoughts, I won't!
That's taking things too far!

I won't laze my life away in the harbor of One Day Soon.

I won't defer my decision for The Living God.

I won't wait for Perfection to drop by or Ease to smooth life's ocean, for neither have promised to come.

I'm going to get off my sit-upon right now and get moving! Launch my boat. Place Faith in the wheelhouse and unfurl the sails of Hope. I'm going to head into the waves and see what lies beyond the horizon of The Known.

But the ocean's so vast! Do I dare?

Yes, I dare because,

God knows, I was born for adventure!

FREEDOM

Courage today;
Freedom tomorrow.

In the past, I associated the word *freedom* with politics, with mass marches, civil protests, and social activism. Freedom was the word to splash across banners in red paint and across newspapers in bold type. Freedom was an idea for which others lived and sometimes, tragically, died.

But recently, I have come to see freedom in a more personal way and asked myself this confronting question:

How well do I handle freedom?

At first, I didn't think of myself as *free*. I simply saw myself as busy.

But when I paused for a moment to glance through a typical day, I noticed many personal *freedom points* scattered across it. For instance, at breakfast, I can choose what to eat and drink and how fast to chew. At work, I can choose how tall I sit and which tasks I do first. I can choose how long I look out of the window, where my thoughts wander, and how soon I harness them and bring them back.

Of course, I don't have total freedom. No one does.

But *I can cherish the freedom I have*
and take it out for a spin.

MY NORMAL SELF

What is the normal state for a butterfly?

1. An egg
2. A caterpillar
3. A cocoon
4. A butterfly
5. All of the above

What is the normal state for a human being?

1. A baby
2. A child
3. A teenager
4. An adult
5. A mature adult
6. All of the above

As you scanned the first list of multiple choice questions, which butterfly stage most appealed to you? Do you like the idea of being curled up in a cocoon to rest or the idea of flying high in the sky?

And what about the second list? Which stage appealed to you most there? Do you wish you were older? Or younger? When I scanned it, I naturally labeled some stages of life "good" and others "bad." For, of course, they are. But wait a minute, that's my life I'm talking about!

My only life.

Am I really destined to live my life either in "good" or "bad" mode simply because of how many breakfasts I've eaten? Am I destined to experience shame or anticipation simply because of how many moonlit nights I've enjoyed?

Who says?

Where has my selective ageism come from? Such terrible bias? This prejudice I so easily direct toward others, and myself?

While I was considering these questions, I passed a rack of birthday cards. One of them boasted, "Good friends don't count the years." Really? Why? Should I be ashamed of how young or old I am? Is my age such a disgrace that even good friends can't mention the passing years in my presence? *Is living itself something to be ashamed of?*

When we pause long enough to think about each stage of life, doesn't every age have the potential for pleasure or pain?

For instance, we may long to have baby-soft skin again, but do we really want to wail our way through teething once more?

We may wish we could play freely and have the innocence and imagination of a child, but who wants to go back to school or do homework again? Who wants to be sent to bed in the middle of playtime?

We may envy the energy of teenagers and driving a car for the first time. But who wants mental hitchhikers like Loneliness, Insecurity, or Self-Doubt as back seat drivers?

Who started the idea that our lives should be infused with one form of shame or another, however old we are? Who has so befuddled our minds that we forget that *normal itself is magnificent? That being alive is an awesome privilege?* One which links us to all living, breathing creatures on earth and sea and sky?

Oh, that we would remember this core truth,
that, as human beings, *whatever our age,*
we have the amazing capacity to play,
celebrate, and laugh together because
The Creator Himself wove giggles
into our genes with his fingers.

Or, to paraphrase David's song,

You knit me together in my mother's womb
and celebrated the day I was born![1]

—David

And God's promise,

I will stay with you all the days of your life.
Even when you're old and gray,
I will carry you and keep you in my care.[2]
—God

My Normal World

Normal, like mercury, is fluid.
Catch it if you can!

At a rough count, there are 400 silvery moths fluttering against the black square of my kitchen window. With eager wings and urgent feet, they climb up the glass, seeking the light. As I pause to watch this aerial ballet, some moths lose their balance and fall in a gray blur down to the windowsill. I wonder if they are hurt, but no, in a moment, they are up again, climbing, climbing. From where I stand, in bare feet on the warm kitchen floor, it looks as if a silver river is flowing up the glass.

Mesmerized by the moths' tenacity, I move closer. The window is half open, and the window screen is rust-brown, almost clogged by windblown topsoil from our sunburned fields. Slowly, I step forward and gently lay my face against the screen. As I hold my breath, I can hear the whisper of the moths' wings fluttering right against my cheek. I smile into the darkness of the hot summer night. All is well.

A few years ago, when I first encountered the flies and heat of rural Australia, I felt out of place in an alien world. It was a raw world of drought, flood, and fire quite different from my early years in England, where my sense of *normal* was formed. As a child, I walked to school down leafy village lanes and pedaled my blue bicycle along wobbly tracks through a confetti of wildflowers.

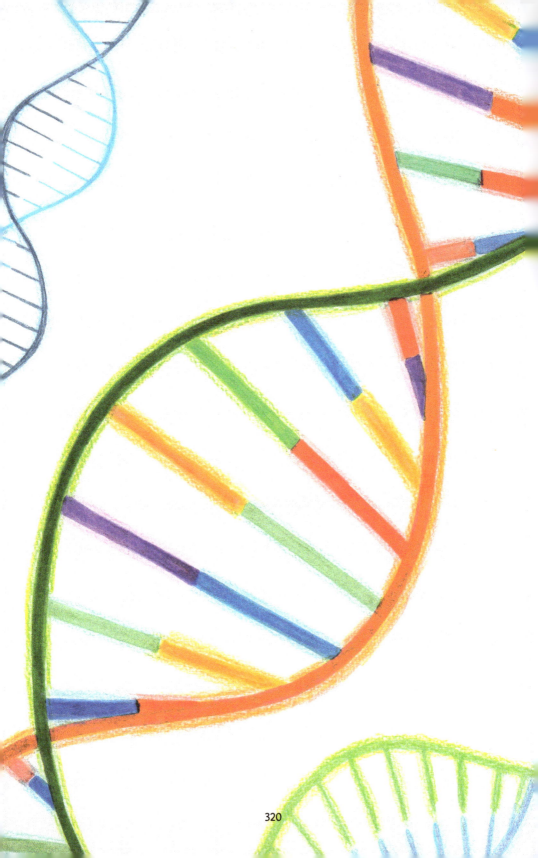

Like my neighbors, our family lived in a stone cottage. On winter evenings, we huddled by flickering coal fires to warm our hands and turned our backs to the windows where rivulets of icy water streamed down the glass. In the nearby fields, mist-shrouded cattle cowered under windblown trees, and damp sheep huddled in soggy clumps in the lee of dripping sheds.

Each night, I shivered up the "wooden hill" to bed, hugging to my trembling chest a freshly filled hot water bottle. Tumbling it into the foot of the bed, I slid under the heavy load of blankets and slowly stretched out full length. As I did, my bare toes probed the arctic folds of the flannelette sheets seeking that warm bottle, longing for it as a traveler longs for buried treasure.

But as Easter approached, the clouds lifted, and the dark earth became rest-less. Buds popped out on *dead* branches. Impatient snowdrops and daffodils burst from the ground to carpet the earth in flowers. And as the glad res-urrection bells rang out from the old village church, life itself seemed to stir and wake, to be reborn.

And as a child, so was I.

Every cell of my body sensed that spring had come, and I bubbled over with joy. Flinging open the kitchen door one morning, I rushed out into the sun-shine. Scorning shoes, I ran through the fields and woods under a canopy of new-furled leaves. I skipped barefoot along the woodland paths and picked armloads of bluebells. Then I sped home like a fairy sprite, hugging my living treasures. Heedless of the glassy loops of sap glistening on my cotton dress. Eyes laughing and hair streaming out behind me, I ran home to my mother.

In summer, wild roses filled the hedgerows along our lane and glowed pink and white in the dappled light beneath the swaying limbs of willow, elder, and oak. On rainy days, the lanes were filled with green and dripping twilight and as I walked to school, the roadside grasses bowed to me in jeweled surrender. In the afternoon, when I hurried home, stray raindrops trickled down my neck and made me shiver. Sometimes I scurried under a spreading tree, bending over a little, hoping to keep my books dry. Peering out through wet lashes, I watched the rain doodle rippling circles on the tadpole pond.

At home, in our cottage garden, the drenching rains soaked deep into the soil, and the thirsty roots of all the green and growing things drank their fill.

Sap surged up each stem. It urged the climbing beans to scramble up their twiggy trellis. It filled the pods with pea-green pearls and inspired the strawberry plants to send out tender tendrils to explore the contours of the earth.

Most summers, we visited my cousins' farm in Cornwall. Their house was over eight hundred years old and the sturdy granite blocks winked at us when the sun kissed the fragments of quartz embedded in them.

After drying the dishes and feeding the hens, we were released from care to wander in the open fields and moors. We clambered over stone styles polished smooth by generations of children and ran free in the tall grasses. Nettles hiding there among the wildflowers stung our bare legs, and itchy pink welts crisscrossed our calves and shins.

In the barn, we played among the fragrant bales of hay for hours. Sometimes we climbed up the stack to crawl on our bellies under the cobwebbed beams of the sun-warmed iron roof. Trying not to sneeze, we elbowed our way forward, hoping to discover secret nests of newborn kittens. Then we silently watched wide-eyed as they mewed blindly for their mother. When my aunt sang out, "Dinner's ready," we slid back down the stack and landed with a bump at the bottom. Springing to our feet we scampered home, carrying wisps of dried grass in our hair like trophies of joy.

As the sun dipped low, we walked "out moor" to find the cows. We quickly scanned the open spaces where wiry grass gyrated to the whim of the whispering wind. Then we searched here and there among the rocky dells where golden gorse bushes hid their prickles under tangles of bracken. Once we found the cows, we herded them back onto the black ribbon of road and sauntered behind them under the vast canvas of crimson sky. Following them home as they ambled to the barn, their swaying udders full of milk.

Since time began, normal has meant something different for every man, woman, and child on earth. *And it always will.*

For you, a normal day may include work or leisure, poverty or play.

Your normal family life may be full of shared hugs and laughter. Or, as you enter your front door, you may brace yourself for a barrage of criticism.

Your normal evenings may involve sinking into a squishy couch to watch television alone and stuff your soul with popcorn. Or it may mean dancing with your family in the garden under a fading sky, while your grandfather strums his guitar.

Normal is so much a part of us that we easily forget how transient it is, that it is unique to each time, person, and place. Sometimes, when normal has been fixed for a long time, life seems boring, and we itch for adventure. At other times, normal life soothes and comforts us. It provides stability in the midst of external chaos and change. It grounds us and provides certainty. It makes life predictable and simple. *It gives us the illusion that we are in control.*

But even the *normal* our family has known for generations, and the habits we have formed for years, may not be as stable as they seem. *Time and world events kindly or brutally show us that normal is transient.* Fluid. That throughout the living world normal naturally changes with each season, stage of life, and relationship.

And whether we like it or not, it always will.

This means that, just as we cannot step into the same river twice because the water is always flowing, we cannot retain *the old normal* once it has slipped away. Nor can we, as we wish in times of loss and grief, or even in times of growth, *just get back to normal.* Even if we long for normal to return, this may be impossible because others have changed or because circumstances have changed. Or perhaps because we ourselves have changed.

If our lives are too full of change, we begin to feel unsettled. We become drained physically, emotionally, and spiritually and experience a kind of adaptation fatigue. We feel all at sea, as if we have been cast adrift without a compass. Depending on our personality, this may make us clumsy, anxious, or afraid, or simply weary and short-fused.

When we experience a significant loss, which changes our sense of normal forever, we may feel deeply grieved and bereft and long desperately, and frequently, for our old normal to return. We feel may feel as if we have been cast into a whirlpool of swirling emotion and dysfunction. That we will never stand on dry ground again.

In a bid to assert some control, we may be tempted to make rash decisions. Lash out at anything that moves to regain a sense of volition or lighten the load somehow. Depending on our personality, we may decide to have a big clear out and give stuff away, then wish we could ask for it back. Or, on a whim, sell up the family home and move house. If we act in such dramatic and reactive ways, we may experience a quick surge of adrenaline, but in the long term, we actually add to the chaos!

Increase our stress at the very time we need at least a few key things to stay still!

Therefore, instead of leaping into random action, our healthiest response may involve staying still ourselves! Seeking refuge. Finding comfort in simple familiar things. The soup bubbling on the stove on Friday nights, sharing homemade spaghetti or taking solitary strolls along the beach at dawn.

After the chaos subsides, whatever our losses, we begin to adapt. We take baby steps forward and accept that normal is not something we can own or buy. Ever. Normal is not something we can tie down, lest it escape.

By and by, as we heal, we realize something profound. Normal is not just something which has been handed to us by others. It's not a gift we passively receive. Rather, *normal is something we help design. It's something we can actively create with each daily decision.*

Buoyed up by this thought, we begin to hope again. We start to take the initiative.

We buy a different breakfast cereal. We listen to a new song. We reach out and make new friends who understand *who we are now*. We dust off our deepest values and give them pride of place once more. Or we install better ones.

Little by little, we establish new habits that serve our current situation better. We regain our former competence or develop a new competence in a different area. As a result, our confidence silently grows. We dare to dream again. We begin to redraw the boundaries of our comfort zone, making it larger than before.

Gradually, we establish a new and vibrant normal, our *unique and dynamic response to what is*. (Even if we don't like *what is!*) We create a normal that more accurately reflects how we want to live and *who we want to become*.

Traditionally, this is called, "making the best of things." But it's more than that, because to succeed, we need to summon all our creativity, ingenuity, and faith. We need to cherish our souls and, in love, choose to *make the best of ourselves*. Suspend self-judgement long enough to explore, experiment, and adapt. To celebrate curiosity and be willing to learn as we go along.

Then, one day, we may pull on fleece-lined boots to splash joyfully up the lane between rain-soaked hedgerows with an umbrella under one arm.

Or we may pause in bare feet by our kitchen window to watch the light fade from the sky. Then listen in awe as an iridescent cloud of papery moths flutters their silvery wings to welcome the summer moon.

Butterflies Can't Eat Cabbage!

Regret is Wisdom
looking over her shoulder.

A butterfly skimming lightly among the flowers appears to have an idyllic life. It sips nectar, rests on roses, and spins daydreams among the daisies. Compared to a caterpillar, it can fly wherever it chooses. It can view the entire garden at a glance. Its fluttering shadow flits to and fro over luscious purple cabbage leaves, tender broccoli, and creamy cauliflower, a veritable feast for body and soul.

For a caterpillar.

The problem is the butterfly is no longer a caterpillar. It's a butterfly, and it cannot eat one bite of the banquet, not even a tiny nibble of cabbage for old time's sake. It's nibbling days are over. Done. Never to return.

Throughout your life, you, too, will pass many milestones from which there is no return.

Perched on these dizzying heights of hindsight, you will view feasts of missed opportunities and banquets of untapped potential. Always.

Why?

Because you are human, and your scope and reach are limited.

Sorry.

So what will you do with the vision before you? Will you become weighed down with regret? Grounded with self-recrimination? Will you choose to believe your days of purpose and joy are gone forever?

You can if you like.

But before you plunge headlong into self-pity, remember this: just as it was physically impossible for a caterpillar to have a butterfly's eye view of the garden, it was also physically impossible for you to see everything *then* that you can see so clearly *now*.

Now you can see how things turned out.
Now you understand life better.
Now you know who you are, and what you can, and cannot, do.
Now you know whom to trust and whom to avoid.

But you did not know all these things then.

So, if your mind fills with *if onlys* on a regular basis, try filling your soul with forgiveness instead, forgiveness for your own immature self and forgiveness for all the other immature people who made foolish mistakes alongside you.

And one more thing: Please remember that regret is not just about missed opportunities. *It's a stunning chance to recognize your own growth, because the very presence of regret indicates how much your vision and wisdom have expanded.* It reveals the new skills and insights you have acquired through days of sunshine and shadow.

Congratulations.

Here's to your future.

Enjoy!

SHY

Most people are too busy flapping their
own wings to notice how well we fly.

Yet we may ground ourselves for a lifetime
because one gossip doubts we can try.

Okay, let's be honest, as you close your front door and step into the street, a few people will see you. This is because, in spite of childhood fantasies, you cannot swallow a magic potion to make yourself invisible, though sometimes it would be nice!

When people see you, they may have a fleeting opinion about what they see. A few will notice your flaws, and one or two may see your scars. Others will focus on your friendly smile or sparkling eyes. But whatever your age and however you look, *what others focus on is always up to them.*

Being visible is risky. For all of us.

Sometimes being visible can even be life-threatening, but most of the time, we face a more routine *visibility dilemma*, which goes something like this:

On the one hand, I want people to notice me. When I enter a room, I want people to see me, not ignore me. I want people to love me, include me in what they are doing, and make me feel welcome. But on the other hand, especially on days when I feel weary or fragile, I want to be invisible. I want to slip unnoticed into life's day without thought of fashion or fear of criticism. I want some breathing space, some *invisible time* to regroup. I want some space to glue my smile back on before anyone sees it has slipped.

What about you?

Are you considering the advantages of being invisible? Wondering if you should stay in the shadows to be safe? Perhaps at work, when blame is drifting around? Perhaps at home, when a more talented sibling is boasting to your parents?

If you're too scared to publicly honor your highest values. If you're too shy to live your most authentic life. Or if you feel too broken and lonely to dust off your dreams, I suggest you check out the reference section and the special song I have listed there. I think it was written for you![3]

I also want to lift your heart with a quick story.

One sunny morning two azure butterflies emerge from their cocoons. Trembling with joy, they shake out their gossamer wings and prepare to fly. Looking into the sky, they see it's full of splendid butterflies. How beautiful they are. How confident. The two butterflies are all a-shiver with excitement.

"How wonderful," one whispers, "that's where we belong!"

But as they give their wings a final shake, the two butterflies chance to look down. And in unison, they exclaim in horror, "Oh no! My legs are so hairy!"

Quaking with despair, the first one whispers, "What can I do? If I lift my wings in flight, everyone will see my hairy legs. They'll laugh at me for sure. And if they laugh, I'll die!" And then, even though it crushes her soul, she hangs her head, folds her beautiful wings, and crawls back into her tattered cocoon. She cowers there, trembling, waiting for circumstances to change, for someone to search for her and rescue her . . . *for someone to love her more than she loves herself.*

The second butterfly also sees her hairy legs. She stares at them for a long moment, then she looks up, and with a burst of determined bravado, she launches herself into the sky. High in the blue air, she pirouettes. She dips and dives and soars. She joins the other butterflies in their gloriously imper- fect aerial symphony to life.

She lives joy.

Precious One,

How long will you be content to crawl
through life in timid fear,
resigned to being earthbound
when I have poured my divine heart
into offering you the sky?

Yours faithfully,
God

TALL POPPY

It takes courage to be creative
and let your soul be seen.

To be a tall poppy shining in
the sun above a field of grass.

You may live in a high-rise apartment or in a cottage where lace curtains waft in the breeze. But wherever you live, when you discover a new idea or create something unique, a voice within you urges, *Go on, share it. Tell someone!* But often, another fearful voice whispers, *What if no one likes it? What if they laugh at your idea?*

And so you dither and dally and wonder . . . which voice will I believe?

Will I share my idea? Or won't I?

Some nights the voice of fear sounds the most persuasive. It hammers your heart with doubts, and you decide to forget the whole thing. Turning from the open door, you slump in a chair and watch television to numb your grief.

There's always tomorrow . . . until there isn't.

Right now, the world needs brave people who are willing to ask new questions in science, faith, and life, people with creative minds who can find fresh solutions to lingering problems. Paint bright canvases of hope in full view of a world-weary humanity.

And deep within, you and I also need to be that kind of person. We need to feel inspired, to find causes that set our souls on fire, and to have a purpose that gets us out of bed in the morning—rain, hail, or shine.

So, how can we encourage each other? Help faith and passion win?

Perhaps, for a start, we need to be open about our struggles. Acknowledge the tension between *blending in to be safe* and *taking the initiative and standing out*.

We can also give ourselves permission to start small. Take one step at a time. We don't have to push ourselves relentlessly or leap off an emotional or physical cliff to demonstrate our courage. We can begin with one idea and share our vision with one friend who is likely to understand. Suggest a simple solution to a supportive colleague at work, then ask for their ideas in return.

We can take our time and learn as we go along. Play with possibilities until our ideas take shape and our courage blossoms.

We can gather with others who have similar ideas and gradually form a mini tribe of like-minded souls.

So together we can reach for the sky.

Just in case you haven't heard . . .
In Australia, a "tall poppy" is a person who dares to raise his or her head above the crowd, someone who has the initiative and courage to use their talents to the max. Unfortunately, in a land where equality and humility are valued, a tall poppy tends to be the target of mocking jokes. Especially if the tall poppy is too "full of themselves" and people itch to bring them down a peg. For no one here likes someone who promotes themselves, or boasts.

But, if the talented person keeps their feet on the ground. If they laugh once in a while at their own foibles, and most of all, if they use their skills to help other people shine, then Australians begin to call them by a different name. Instead of mocking them as a tall poppy and trying to cut them down to size, they call them, with great affection, "A Living Treasure"

And proudly embrace them as one of their own.

Good Company

Together,
we are one.

Today you may feel very alone as you ponder great mysteries and plan small miracles, as you create.

But one day, I hope you realize a greater truth. That when you decide to do something noble and kind, you are in the good company of a vast throng of brave souls, people who, since time began, have been willing to initiate rather than imitate. People who, even now, in every culture and country, are looking at life with new eyes and solving problems in unique ways. Men and women, and teenagers and children who rise above fear to live their lives inspired by curiosity and love.

People who don't strive to be tall poppies, but aspire instead to bless others. Creating, as they do, vast "meadows" of beauty for everyone to enjoy.

And suddenly, you know your tribe
and where you belong.

Welcome!

WING WARDROBE

When the seasons change,
we naturally change our clothes
and shop for the things we need.

But when our lives change,
do we shop as freely for advice?
Seek new skills without shame?

Pour as much passion into
finding faith, hope, and
love to clothe our souls?

Recently, I visited an unfamiliar town and decided to go shopping. As the layout of each store was new to me, I sometimes asked for help to find things. This saved me a lot of time.

In one large store, I approached a sales assistant and asked, "Where's the sock counter, please?" She smiled and pointed down one of the aisles. Following her directions, I quickly found my way to a bright array of snuggly socks.

How normal is that? How easy!

Yet, sometimes we act as if asking for advice is shameful, *as if we should know everything about life already, and we are dumb because we don't.*

Why have we made asking for advice so taboo?

How much smoother life would be if we could ask for life-directions as easily as we ask for socks. Ask for good advice freely, whatever our age or situation, *without hesitation or shame.*

WING WARDROBE

Treasure Hunt

The glitter we seek may distract us
from the treasure we truly crave.

Early one morning, when I was a young adult, I came down the winding stairs of my aunt's cottage and saw her sitting at her kitchen table. She smiled at me, then resumed flipping through her Greek lexicon. She was searching for a deeper understanding of a Middle Eastern story. And breakfast could wait.

Did she pride herself on getting up early and being a scholar? No.

Was she trying to set an example for me? Not at all.

She was simply having fun. You could see it by the sparkle in her eyes. Even though she was over ninety years old, she was like a girl on a treasure hunt, aglow with delight, her whole being alive with boundless curiosity.

Later, as we sat across the breakfast table, my aunt shared some of the wisdom she had found. As she described her discoveries, some of her enthusiasm rubbed off on me. And as I buttered my toast, I sensed that *the love of learning is caught more than taught.*

Inspired, more than compelled.

However old we are.

Vocation

In *being,* we find meaning
and in helping others *be,*
we discover significance.

It sounded as if a herd of elephants was thundering up the stairs. Emma and I looked at each other, smiled, and took a deep breath. Moments later, a busload of teenagers surged into our career advice center. They tossed their school bags in a heap and scrambled to find chairs.

Their teachers hoped their students would sit still for five minutes and listen to our career talk. But we hoped for something more. We wanted to inspire the students to live lives of meaning and significance and discover careers they could enjoy. Jobs where they could pour their energy, skills, and talents into earning a living and also into being a blessing.

For three years, I worked in a community career center, where I offered support and advice to students and job seekers. Teenage boys sauntered in and asked about apprenticeships. Mothers bustled in to ask about returning to work after rearing their children. Migrants asked, with hesitant smiles, "Are my qualifications recognized in Australia?"

Whatever each person's age or qualification, there lingered in the air three deeper questions:

Can I make enough money to live on?
Can I live a life of purpose?
Can I use my skills and talents to make a difference in the lives of others?

I don't know what fills your day, or if you have ever sought career advice. But if you are able to provide the basics of life for yourself, and those you love, you are well on your way. And if you are living the answer to the above three questions, in a paid role or as a volunteer, you don't just have a job, you have a career.

You have a sacred vocation, and your daily life is already a blessing.

Thank you.

THE BOX OF SCALES

Each person on earth has
a box of scales that they use
to weigh every experience and
action in the world.

Imagine finding a great wooden chest in the attic of your home. The box looks familiar, but you can't quite remember what it holds. So you brush off some cobwebs, lift the heavy lid just a little, and peer inside. You glimpse an ancient set of brass scales and, behind them, a metal measuring jug.

Curious, you bend down, and with a mighty heave, you flip the lid wide open. The chest is crammed full of measuring tools: scales, rulers, jugs, pressure gauges, and thermometers. Some of the tools are half-buried under a tangle of dusty tape measures.

You pick up one of the tools, a long wooden spirit level, and wipe off the dust with your sleeve. The brass plaque reads, "From Dad with love. Get building!" Good old Dad!

You carefully place the spirit level back in the box and reach for a small alarm clock. The label says, "Rise and shine! Love you, Mom x." You smile ruefully and yawn. After rummaging for a while, you let the heavy lid drop. A puff of dust tickles your nose, and you sneeze. What on earth are all those tools for?

I think you know,

Because each scale in the box is a gift from one of your ancestors, and you carry their messages with you wherever you go. Each time you travel, you put these heirlooms in the backpack of your mind. And when you move to a new house, they are the first items you carry over the threshold of your new home.

So, what are they? These "measuring tools" are your core values and beliefs, your expectations, assumptions, prejudices, and standards. Each one tests your thoughts and behaviors. *Your performance*. If you pick up any tool in your box, it will tell you whether *you measure up* or whether *you have failed*.

For instance, you may pick up a scale from your mother marked, "Birthday Expectations." The fine print below lists all the attention your mother expects on her birthday. (In some families, the list of expectations on each scale is very long. In some families, it is mercifully short!)

As you scan the list of birthday expectations, you begin to wonder, *Did I do enough for Mom's birthday last month?* After a few minutes of self-examination and weighing up your actions, you decide, *Yes, I think I met her expectations. I gave her a hug and a kiss. I told her that I loved her, and I baked her favorite cake!*

Phew. Relief washes over you. It's as if you have just passed an exam.

And, in a very real way, you have.

Most of the time, these inherited scales prove useful, just as your parents intended. They save you from making a fool of yourself, gambling your way into debt, or marrying a risk-prone spouse. They help you discern between "right" and "wrong."

But sometimes the scales you and I use to measure ourselves and our world become unbalanced, distorted. Then our scales get us into all sorts of trouble.

How?

For a start, yesterday's scales may not fit today's circumstances, or the values which some of your ancestors ignored may be very important to you. For instance, the way they viewed certain cultural groups may make you cringe. Therefore, as you mature and grow, you will need to sort through your box of scales to decide which ones to discard and which ones to keep.

Another problem is that each person on the planet has inherited a unique set of scales *with different calibrations*. This is a big deal!

Using his own set of scales, one man may decide that his behavior is good, and his ideas have great value. But his neighbor, using a set of scales with different calibrations, may decide that his ideas are stupid, or even bad.

These *scale discrepancies* cause all sorts of kitchen table *debates*.

Social and religious muddles.

Wars and tears.

But there is hope.

Not because we will always agree. Nor because our value systems will always match. But because we have ears to hear, if we choose to use them. We have the capacity to listen to others' stories if we are willing to take the time. And we have eyes to see beyond a person's actions to the beliefs and values that prompted them.

And in seeing, discern.

And in discerning, learn.

Learn where we need to humbly adjust our own scales and graciously accept another's calibrations as valid. And where we need to protect our own calibrations, in dignity and grace, in intelligent, faithful homage to one or more overarching, eternal truth.

Each day we choose
which scales to discard
and which to live by.

Which scales of others
to ignore or challenge,
tolerate or embrace,

And which scales to pass
on to our own children
with judgment, or with joy.

If you want to simplify your life, you may enjoy exploring some of the world's more basic "universal scales." I've found some that really stir my soul, so I've paraphrased three for you below.[4]

Treat others as you would like to be treated.
—The Golden Rule

If you listen to your heart,
you already know what to do.

You don't have to
make dramatic sacrifices
to atone for your past
or make lavish donations
to gain status with others.

Simply,
Act with integrity and treat people fairly.
Look out for folks, and love being kind.

Above all,
Remember what a sacred honor it is
to walk through life holding God's hand.
—Micah

Today I am giving you the most
finely calibrated scale that heaven
and humanity have ever known:
"Love each other!"
—Jesus

SHOULDS

Your inherited and selected *shoulds*
shape every aspect of your life.

They are your treasured values
out walking in the world.

Tied onto one hinge of your Box of Scales is a threadbare cotton bag. If you untie the frayed ribbon and open the bag, you will see it is stuffed with small handwritten cards.

The cards near the top are easy to read. Their ink is bright and clear. But if you delve a little deeper into the bag, you will soon discover a few worn cards. As you pick one up and tilt it toward the light, you will notice the writing has faded and the words are almost invisible. But that doesn't matter because you know what's written on each card, by heart.

You have carried these *should cards* with you for a long time. Since childhood, they have been your blueprint for living. Each one tells you:

How you *should* behave or
How the world *should* work.

What others *should* think and do
and even how God *should* run the universe!

Often, the further we are from a situation, and the less we understand, the more convinced we are of the way others should manage it!

If you and I meet one day and spread our cards on the table between us, some of our cards may begin like this:

When a man courts a woman, he should . . .
A good wife should . . .
A good husband should . . .
A mother with a newborn baby should . . .
A student should . . .
A politician should . . .
To keep world peace, we should . . .
To live a good life, I should . . .
To care for our planet, we should . . .

Some of your *should cards* may match mine, and some may not. This partial match is true of everyone you meet, including relatives and friends, co-workers and grown children. In every relationship, especially marriage, there can be much shuffling of cards!

You may be tempted to dismiss the whole idea of having cards and say, "I don't go around pouring bags of cards out onto the table each time I meet someone!" Of course, you don't, and yet, in effect, you do. When you meet someone new, don't you pull out a few of your most cherished ideas, then see if any of their ideas and values match yours? Isn't this part of "small talk"?

Don't you feel an instant bond with one person because they think like you? But feel puzzled, irritated, or enraged by someone else because they don't?

But do these *should cards* really matter? Can't we just toss them out of the window, watch them waft away in the wind, and just get on with living?

Yes, and no.

We can toss away the metaphor but not the ideas themselves. Because our shoulds affect every aspect of our behavior and guide all our choices. They affect what we buy and where we live. They influence who we befriend and who we shun. Who we accept, and who we reject and judge. They shape our conscience and what we feel compelled to do, or not do. Our shoulds even affect what we take pride in, or feel guilty for. (Many of our internal dialogues begin with, "I should have . . .")

Depending on the type of shoulds we have, and how rigidly we follow them, they may form a framework for a healthy life, or a cage which traps us.

A healthy *should* often involves regulating our own behavior to achieve an outcome we value. For instance, *I really should get out of bed and go to work, even though it's freezing outside*. Or *I should leave this party; I don't feel comfortable with what my friends are doing*.

In contrast, an unhealthy should often oozes with fear or judgment. For instance, *She really should know better. How stupid can you get?*

If we live with a lot of unexamined shoulds, they tend to form a *should cage*, which constrains every behavior and locks us into cultural or familial patterns that no longer serve us.

At first our creativity tries to escape this cage, but each time it makes a bid for freedom, it bumps into one *should bar* or another until, bruised and defeated, it languishes. For instance, if a person believes *good manners dictate that an adult should always eat with a knife and fork while seated at a table*, they will not plan a finger-food picnic, even on a sunny day.

If we have influence of any kind, we may also make should cages for others. Cages that imprison, instead of using our skills to build foundations and frameworks that empower.

Though joy and creativity wither in a *should cage*, some things flex their muscles. These include:

Arrogance—it loves knowing the rules and *what everyone should do*. It thrives on having the right answers to all life's questions, even before anyone asks. It can never admit it's wrong, so it argues readily. It's convinced its own values equate to The Truth, so it wears an air of moral superiority and acts like a mobile conscience policing others' behavior. (There's a lot of fear and pain in arrogance. The arrogant person feels much safer when they can control things and people. When they can strengthen their brittle sense of stability and status with external props.)

Jealousy—tied up in legal knots, the trapped person hates gazing out of the bars and seeing others play so it scorns their delight and mocks their freedom.

Judgment—this is often jealously hiding behind a stern mask of offended values.

Resentment—this gains traction if a person simultaneously takes pride in their knowledge and rigid shoulds, but also hates being trapped by them.

Unhealthy shoulds damage the heart.
They are like rules without soul.

If *unhealthy* shoulds are driving behavior, the mental dialogue sounds something like this: *I know I'm supposed to buy her red roses to say I love her, so I guess I should, or I will be in big trouble . . . Wow, they're expensive. What a con! I'll just get a few and smile lots; that should do the trick. She had better appreciate them. There's no way I'm buying her roses again!* How would this man's internal dialogue change if the primary driver in his heart was love for the lady concerned?

Because God did not design us to live trapped lives, we are free to examine our shoulds with curiosity and intelligence. When we do, several wonderful things happen.

For a start, we begin to lose our fear of the unknown, of questions. We enjoy playing with them. Like explorers, we begin to track down motives to their source and understand at a deeper level what drives our thoughts and behavior. We also discover, hiding within our hearts, all sorts of unspoken cultural assumptions about how life should be lived.

When we start to understand ourselves better, we are also less motivated by fear in our relationships and careers, especially fear of getting it wrong, failing, or making a mistake. We are more motivated by a living sense of purpose and a growing nobility of soul. So we make more informed decisions. More discerning moral and lifestyle choices based on foundational principles, on liberating values like kindness, love, and respect.

As our hearts relax and open up to new possibilities, our creativity is no longer trapped and it springs to life. We have fun with color, poetry, and good music. We try new sports and feel free to mix with people of different beliefs and backgrounds. We volunteer more. We design our garden to suit the age of our children rather than copy the way our parents landscaped their turf. We decide to hike in the mountains instead of spending our summers sitting by the sea, even if everyone else is going to the beach. We start new Christmas traditions full of faith and laughter.

Finally, we don't treat others with respect *because we should* but *because we want to*. We begin to judge less and understand more. Intrigued by their value systems, we listen to their stories. We ask them more open questions, like, "What do you think about this idea?" or "What potential do you see there?"

One summer, I had an ideal opportunity to explore my own shoulds when I was the brief guest of three very different families.

The first family believed that each person should make the most of their talents to bless others. So to free-up time to do this, they employed part-time staff to care for their children, house, and garden. As a result, they excelled in their careers and made a great contribution to the health and welfare of others.

The second family believed you should live in the city, have a rich social life, and serve meals in lavish style. When entertaining, you should maintain proper etiquette. Each guest should know which fork to use for the entree and main meal and which glass to use for water or wine.

The third family believed you should shun the city and live simply off the land. You should gain practical skills, put your children to work rather than send them to school. And, with tenacity and teamwork, you should grow your own food.

Each time I entered a different home, I carried my own shoulds with me. This meant I was more comfortable in some settings than in others. But in each home, whenever I sensed dissonance arising between their shoulds and my own, I purposely checked myself. I paused to listen and learn. To see life from their point of view rather than impose my own views on them. As a result, the summer proved to be a brilliant opportunity to explore new ideas and others' values. It was an experience that expanded my understanding, enhanced my level of tolerance and enriched my life.

I also noticed that all three families had something in common.

Whatever cutlery I used, or whatever the culinary beliefs of the family, each family welcomed me with open arms. They loved me, and gave me the best they had to offer. One couple even gave me their own double bed to sleep on. (I did not discover their quiet gift until the last morning, when I saw them hastily packing up a folding bed as I entered a hallway.)

In each family, I found their *warmhearted acceptance of who I was* very humbling.

Throughout our lives we will encounter shoulds, in ourselves and in others. Sometimes we will decide to explore different ways of thinking. Sometimes we will need to flee from unsafe encounters. But generally speaking, when we notice our own shoulds and try to understand the shoulds that drive others, we will become more authentic and kind.

Eventually the day comes when our values become crystal clear and we can "lay our cards on the table" with a steady hand. When this happens we are free to be both honest *and* warmhearted, free to befriend others *and* preserve our own unique values and personal beliefs.

We know *who we are*, and *who we are not*. We know why we do the things we do. We feel secure, grounded, and whole so we are free to say with genuine warmth, "Pleased to meet you."

Once, long ago, a discussion broke out among some local scholars who liked to show off.

In an effort to gain status with their students and their audience, they began a serious and dignified debate. The theme was, "Which is the greatest *should* of all?" The debate started out well, but it soon turned into a shouting match between puffed-up egos. At last, in frustration, one of the scholars turned to Jesus and said, "So, what's your opinion?"

Calmly, Jesus replied (paraphrase mine):

If you want to sum up all the *shoulds* in the world, here they are in short form:

Love God with all your mind, your heart and your soul
and love your neighbor as yourself.[5]

That's it!

IN A FLAP?

We soar together,
or we all stay grounded.

We talk about *rights* a lot—the rights of one group or another. We carry banners and use militant language. We stride into the present, hoping to change the future and make history.

But what if *rights* alone are not enough?

What if both rights and responsibility are essential for living a fulfilled life? What if they are like two wings, and both are required to carry freedom into the sky?

Picture for a moment, a one-winged bird standing on a patch of dirt. It flaps its wing. It flaps harder. It flaps until the feathers form a blur. You watch, mesmerized. You identify with its struggle to fly and urge it to succeed. You hope its effort and bravado will be rewarded. But with all its striving, and all your goodwill, will the bird fly?

Whatever our background. Whatever our story. Is it possible that we could contribute to our own downward spiral if we spend our lives striving and straining like one-winged birds? Pushing either rights or responsibilities too hard?

For instance, suppose you feel wronged, and you decide to go all out to fix things. Grab whatever you can. Flap the wing of your "rights" and wrest what's owed to you from another's grasp. Correct, by force of words, will, or weapons the inequity of generations.

If you take this all very seriously, *will you have time to live?* Or will you be so busy flapping in others' faces that you forget to care for yourself? Develop your own talents? Use your own skills?

What a tragedy it would be if, at the end of your life, you found that you had actually *perpetuated inequity by neglecting your own potential!* Made yourself less than you could have been. Busy blaming others for the past and holding still others responsible for the present, you had given away some of your greatest God-given assets, including your time and your energy? Your ability to respond to life with creativity and purpose, and be "response-able?"

In every life, there are tipping points, times when you decide to push harder for a just cause or let one or more causes go. Because, as farmers here say, "You can't chase every rabbit down its hole!"

There are so many layers to this topic. So many wounds, feelings, and stories to consider.

In contrast to the person above, you may not spend your days flapping on and on about your rights. Instead, you may be busy flapping and flapping the wing of responsibility, beating it day and night to the point of exhaustion.

If you are, what prompts you? Family commitments? Others' expectations? Or were you told something like this growing up, "It's your job to make a difference, to change the world. You were put on this earth to help people"?

Eager to be of use, you believed everything you were told. You claimed *helping* as your life purpose and *serving* as your primary motivation. Therefore, since you were *knee-high to a grasshopper*, you have tried to shoulder the woes and ills of humanity. You have taken on extra jobs and worked all hours of the day and night. *You have tried to save everybody and every situation. You have made it your lifework to please, appease and serve.*

But once in a while you pause to ask yourself, *does anyone see me as a person anymore? Or am I just a resource? Good only for work?* Then, with a sigh, you silently ask, *Where have all MY dreams gone?* Weary beyond reason, you feel your soul is sliding toward silent or seething resentment.

Surely there is a better way to honor your humanity.

Our humanity.

Balance the *rights* we claim and the *responsibilities* we shoulder. Share things around a bit. Know the relief of forgiving and the fun of fostering each other's dreams.

Maybe if we are too old to change our polarised patterns, we can at least start with the young! We can role model the joy of give and take to our children. Lead them into situations where they experience for themselves the deep satisfaction of contributing to the common good *and* reaping the benefits of community.

Ideally, we can do things that build body and soul. Practical, real stuff, like cleaning up a beach with friends, then swimming together in the sparkling surf. Baking cakes for lonely folks, then staying to chat and share a slice.

Perhaps, if we consciously weave the experience of being a contributor and a consumer into our children's lives, we will help them soar in life. Naturally give them the skills to make the most of who they are, and help others do the same.

Beat the wings of their "rights" and their "responsibilities" in balance.

Maybe then one bright day we can soar together and claim the whole sky as our playground!

Scorn Power?

When a person does not live by my values and they
have more power than me, my fear distrusts them.

When a person does not live by my values and they
have less power than me, my ego scorns them.

But when my personal value is anchored in God's
love for us both, my heart honors them as family.

THE STORE OF THE WORLD

Bringing our deepest desires in
the coins of our personality
and cultural currency, we rush
into the store of the world,
hunting for bargains.

We search at stalls of pride and
status seeking significance.
We rummage among remnants of
lycra craving prowess and silk
seeking beauty of heart.

Then, clamoring for attention
in a thousand voices, we queue
for junk food, hungry for hope
and thirsty for love, longing to
belong and be healed.

THE GAP

The greatest chasm ever bridged
was never spanned with stone or steel.

But bridged at last, when day was done,
by those who linked ideal with real.

If we drive from our farm to the city, it takes us about three hours. The road
passes through farmland and small towns. It rises and falls with each hill and
valley. It also crosses several bridges.

Some of the bridges span deep gullies where glittering streams trace their
wandering way to the sea. Other bridges cross minor roads or gleaming
railway tracks. Each bridge whatever its length makes our journey possible.

I have no idea who built those bridges, the strategies they used, or the weather
they endured. But I am grateful for each person who stayed with the job

until it was done, for the squint-eyed surveyors and the hot-tar-pourers, for the gravel scatterers and the white-line painters. Because each one of these people contributed their skills and resources, I am free to drive to the city in safety.

On the road of life, we also encounter many gullies and gaps, ravines, and chasms we want to bridge. One of the widest chasms we face is the gap between The Real and The Ideal, the gap between *what is* and what we think life *should be like.*

If we have strong beliefs and values, perhaps about the importance of equity or kindness, these physical or social gaps may irritate us. Or they may grieve us so deeply that we become passionate about bridging them.

Some gaps are too big for us to cross. We can only navigate them as best we can and hope someone else has the skills and resources to bridge them.

But one day a small gap may call your name. It woos you. It stirs your conscience and keeps you awake at night. It pesters you and bothers you. You begin to tell your friends about it. You catch yourself saying, "Someone really should do something." Then, one day, you know for sure deep in your heart, *I am that Someone. This is my gap to bridge! My problem to solve. My wound to heal.*

And you begin to think, *What on earth can I do?*

As soon as you ask this question your brain leaps to attention. It dreams up a thousand solutions. It stirs your imagination, and your fingers itch to sketch plans on scraps of paper.

You gather resources from far and wide.

Finally you roll up your sleeves and begin. Even when success is not guaranteed, even if you have to start with something very small.

You feed one stray cat a saucer of milk.

You plant herbs in a community garden.

You tidy up your spare room and welcome one foster child.

You telephone your estranged brother and invite him for tea, then bake his favorite cake.

You stay after school and mentor one struggling student.

Most of all, you learn to pace yourself, to rest and regroup, to nurture your own spirit, and to care for your own health and family. You manage your energy so that, when opportunities naturally arise, you have some strength in reserve to make the most of them.

These opportunities to build bridges or heal wounds slip into our lives in various shapes and sizes, often unannounced.

For instance, one day after a good night's sleep you meet a friend for coffee. You chat about the weather and the cute baby on her lap for a while, but suddenly she hangs her head and whispers, "I don't know what's wrong with me. Everyone expects me to be excited about our new baby. All my friends bring cards and want to celebrate." Her eyes well with tears. "I'm supposed to be happy, but I just feel numb. Exhausted. What if I don't love my baby? What if I'm not meant to be a mother?"

In response, you reach your hand across the table past the empty cups and take her hand. And without a word, you listen as she pours out her heart. When she pauses to wipe her eyes, you tell her very softly about your own struggles with postnatal depression. You reassure her that she's normal and a good person. Before you part, you scribble a phone number on a slip of paper and give her a hug. And as you wave goodbye, you see a glimmer of a smile in her eyes as she silently mouths the words, "Thank you."

Another day, you flip through a magazine at the dentist and notice a story about young girls missing school by spending hours hauling drinking water from the river near their village. Sitting there in the dentist's chair, mouth agape, the story swirls around in your mind. You shrug and think, *But what can I do?* As you emerge into the sunshine, nursing your numb cheek, you ask yourself again, *what can I do?* Suddenly you sense the answer, *I can hold a garage sale.*

By dinnertime you are really fired up, as your family soon discovers as they slurp their soup. Filled with a passionate vision of being a bridge-builder, you wax eloquent, "Come on everyone. We can do it! Let's all pitch in and have a clear-out!"

A few weeks later, you are raring to go. The kids print out a few wobbly signs declaring your aim. You fill your driveway with pots and pans and prop a too-small bicycle against the front fence. You borrow a clothes rack from next door and hang up last year's fashions. And the people come.

That evening, as you gather around the kitchen table to add up your little stacks of coins, you find there's just enough to give a small community their own fresh water. Wow. Leaning back in your chair, you smile at your own precious daughter and say, "Now a teenage girl just like you can have fresh water to drink and even attend school." In response your daughter smiles, then glances at her stack of homework and groans!

One step at a time you make a difference. You take who you are and what you have, and you summon all the love in your heart and you begin.

You build a bridge from
The Land of What Is
all the way across to
The Land of What Can Be.

Thank you so very much!

THE VISIONARY

For better or worse,
visionaries change the world.

From earliest times, history has been illuminated by Bright Sparks, visionary people who change the world for the better. Men, women and teenagers who see into the future and imagine what a wonderful place it could be.

But there is a dark side to idealism, and some of our greatest visionaries are, unfortunately, *blind*. Blind to how they are affecting their nearest and dearest. Blind to how much they are risking their own physical and mental health for their precious cause.

Often, as an idealist's vision grows, their workload also increases. When this happens their resources begin to peter out. In an effort to cope, some visionaries are tempted to kick aside a value here and there to smooth the road. Or they bully a family member into helping, using various versions of the loaded phrase, "If you loved me, you would help me with . . ."

In their zeal, the idealist may not realize what they are doing or the effect their passion is having on those whom they profess to love. For instance, to stamp out slavery, an idealist may press-gang his family members into working long past their bedtime filling out petitions or stuffing envelopes. Or he may urge them to wave placards in windblown city streets. Hardly caring if his "volunteers" are hungry, thirsty or elbowed in the ribs, as long as they support his protest march.

Another idealist may walk day after day past the litter and tangled weeds in his own front yard, then stomp off with self-righteous tread to save a distant rainforest. While down the street, a busy idealist may be snacking on junk food as she drives from school to school, lobbying for more vegetables to be included on the canteen menus.

Some idealists become so passionate about their cause that they begin to act like Robin Hood. They tell themselves it is okay to *steal* attention and resources from one person or group. Then they bestow it with a benevolent flourish on another *more worthy* group. Desperate to pursue equality for strangers in a global setting, they unwittingly trample equity into the dust in their personal lives.

They become oblivious to the fact that they are *exploiting* vulnerable people in an effort to *help* vulnerable people.

Gradually, obsession may swamp discernment until health and common sense wither and die. This makes no sense at all!

If two idealists marry and share a common cause, they may help and encourage each other. But if their goals lie in different directions, each person may draw on the energy bank of their marriage until it teeters on the brink of bankruptcy. Sensing this is happening, one or both may ease off on their workload to replenish it. Or they may struggle on regardless, thinking as they do, *why can't my partner see how important my work is? Why can't they support me more?*

Many of us are driven by multiple goals, busy beyond reason. So perhaps it's time to press pause and ask ourselves, *How can I be more savvy?*

When we do this, the first step forward may actually involve *stepping back*. Stepping back from all we are doing so we can gain perspective. See what's really happening in our lives and where we are spending our energy. Pause to notice where our money and time are going. See how we are affecting our partners and children. Or at the most basic level, notice where we are letting weeds of resentment or weariness grow unchecked in our own souls.

The next step may be to have an open conversation and ask for family feedback. (This is not for the fainthearted.) Hopefully, if everyone is not too burned out, this will pave the way for creating a more sane, sustainable, and equitable future for all concerned.

As part of this process, we may choose to ask ourselves a few hard questions like:

Am I so obsessed with this project that I'm ruining my own health and neglecting the people I profess to love?
Am I leaving the dirty work of running a home to others, so I can ride out into the world as a hero? Do I secretly love applause and standing in the limelight? Am I really *the one who is needy* because I have an insatiable hunger for compliments?
Will I go to a great deal of effort to convince other people I'm a good person? To convince myself?
Do I meddle in others' lives, under the guise of helping, to avoid facing uncomfortable truths about my own life? Or because I'm procrastinating? Ignoring issues I need to address?
Is it safe for people to give me considered feedback on my performance or attitude, or am I too reactive and defensive to listen and learn?
Who could I turn to for objective advice?
Are other people more qualified or better placed than me to carry this project forward? And if they are, am I willing to release control to them and let go? (Or could we work together to double our impact?)
Do the people I'm serving really need to be helped, or am I only helping them to make myself feel good? May I, in fact, be teaching them learned helplessness?

For me, how we handle idealism isn't just about principles or even fairness. It's personal.

When I was a child, I saw my parents quietly give their lives to various noble causes.

I sat in the cold car while they spoke warmly to struggling strangers. I saw them bring foster babies in by the fire and rock them to sleep. I watched my mother knit shawls for women shivering in nearby tenements and my dad sharing his books and garden vegetables. Their whole lives were colored by sacrificial devotion.

I knew they loved me, but some days there were simply not enough resources to go around. Their attention, money, and time were spread too thin. Eventually, my mother's health faded, and I watched her energy ebb away. She had emptied herself for others for so long that, before my eyes, she became a shadow of herself, almost translucent with self-denial and weary beyond saving.

I wonder what caused her slow decline.

Was it her years as a young midwife carrying her bag through the London slums? Was it nursing civilians and soldiers during the war and helping some survive, but watching others slip away? Was it the strain of taking in sick foster babies or giving up our family room to lonely old ladies? Was it trying to make financial "ends meet"? I don't know.

All I know is that when I was about eight years old, my mother was often in the hospital and too sick to care for me. As my faithful but equally weary father worked shifts I was eventually sent to live with friends.

I lived with a kind family in Cheddar for several months. I loved playing with their daughter and cycling to school with her, but when it was clear my mother needed more permanent care, my parents sent me to a distant boarding school. Although it had a good reputation, I was only nine years old, and all the others started at eleven years old. Most then stayed until they finished school at eighteen.

My father drove for several hours to take me to my new school. By the time we arrived, the sun had already set across the sweeping lawns and shady woodland, and all we could make out was the large building looming above us in the gloom. It had a scattering of shining windows on the upper floors, so we knew someone was home. Not sure what else to do, we pushed open the red metal swinging doors, and my father carried my suitcase up four flights of stairs to my room. I trailed behind him, hugging my teddy bear, eyes wide. Wondering.

The lady in charge welcomed us and introduced us to my roommate. She was about fourteen and had enjoyed the rare privilege of a room to herself, so she greeted the arrival of a tousle-haired child with muted enthusiasm!

After my father had settled me in and hugged me goodbye, he turned and headed back down the creaking stairs.

I walked over to the window, a black square under the eaves, and stared out into the darkness, patiently waiting. A few minutes later I saw a shadowy figure emerge from the school doors. Then I heard a car door slam and an engine purr into life. Bright taillights pierced the night as my father drove out from under the tall fir trees guarding the school. I fixed my eyes on those red lights, tracing their progress down the sweeping driveway. As they grew smaller, I pressed my nose to the cool glass, willing the car to pause, then turn around. But the lights moved steadily on until they were only tiny pinpricks of red in the dark. Then the car passed a curve in the drive, and my father disappeared.

Later that night, I awoke and looked around, confused, trying to make sense of the vague shapes of beds and drawers. Then I remembered.

I needed to go to the bathroom, so I felt my way to the door and slipped out into the dimly lit hallway. I had been given a quick tour the night before and seen the bathroom was divided into cubicles. Some had baths and some had toilets, but I wasn't sure which ones. So, I fumbled around for the light switch. No luck. I would have to explore the room, stall by stall, in the dark.

At last I found a toilet and sat down. But within seconds, I was introduced to schoolgirl humor, for someone, no doubt giggling with mischief, had liberally covered the toilet seat with thick honey. Alone, in that huge dark building in the middle of the night, all I wanted was my Mommy!

After a few weeks I began to feel at home. I saw that boarding school life had plenty of benefits. For instance, I met new friends, tried yummy food, and gained a new sense of freedom. One day after school I ran outside in my socks. A day student noticed and said, "Won't your mother tell you off for walking outside in your socks?" Blithely I replied, "No! I don't have to wear shoes if I don't want to. I can just wear sock wherever I like."

The weekends were the most fun. I joined the church choir and sang Christmas carols by candlelight. On Saturday nights, we played games in the hall or watched movies. Near the end of each term, when we turned plastic bottles into water pistols, I even learned how to play a little mischief myself.

I wonder, sometimes, how my life would have been different if I had stayed with my parents. Would I have been more serious? Probably. Would I have done as well at school? Made such good friends? Studied later at a wonderful university full of international students? I doubt it.

Looking back, I can see many gains and losses in the choices my parents made, in how they managed their lives, resources, and time. I am achingly aware that I lost many things, and maybe even my mother, because of their sacrificial choices. But I recognize now that I also gained many valuable things. I gained a deep respect for kindness, an awareness of other customs and cultures, and a lingering sense of curiosity about spiritual things.

And these are precious gifts.

My parents are no longer here now, and they cannot make any more choices. But you and I are here, and we can. We can choose to make a difference in this world.

In fact, we need to.

But as we consider our resources and skills and the needs that surround us, let's determine to make a difference in sane and sensible ways. Let's live balanced lives and explore creative and cooperative ways to be *help-smart* and to practice *sustainable giving*. Let's be visionaries who have good *near sight*, so we can see those closest to us and good *far sight* so we can see the untapped possibilities of tomorrow.

When we master this visionary balance, we will be less tempted to shirk the tough, boring stuff at home. We will care as much about one little kid in pajamas who climbs on our knee and asks, "Will you read me a story?" as we care about the literacy campaign in our town. We will pause before flipping on our hero cape to remember that each person in our family needs time and attention. Especially the one whom we promised to "love, honor, and cherish." The one who is, even now, mowing the lawn or washing up our dinner dishes!

We will also pause to recognize that each person in our family or workplace, in our charity or church, *has a conscience of their own, goals of their own, dreams of what they want to achieve.* Creative and unique ways they want to use their skills to serve others. When we recognize this, we are less likely to use other people as resources, or expect family members to *drop everything* to help us. Instead, we will honor their boundaries, just as we honor our own.

We will become warmhearted
visionaries who bless the world.

People who care for others with
wisdom, kindness, and self-respect.

CAPACITY?

When you live with all your heart,
you will always:

Love more children than
you can raise.

See more sick folks than
you can heal.

Picture more goals than
you can achieve.

Smell more flowers than
you can grow.

View more mountains than
you can climb.

Discern more truth than
you can live.

For even when you stand
on tiptoe, your arms
are too short to embrace then share
the full scope of God's love!

Gap Fatigue

If you are an idealist,
you will experience
gap fatigue.

The syndrome goes something like this . . . Little by little, you develop a personal vision of what life can be like. Everywhere you look, you see possibilities. Vast potential.

One day, the tipping point comes. You read another book, attend another seminar, or listen to a series of workshops, and you feel inspired, thrilled to the tips of your toes. You are desperate to begin NOW!

For a week, you talk nonstop about all your ideas; you burn the ears of family and friends with your passion. For a month, you try very hard to put it all into practice. You walk more, pray more or eat more leafy green vegetables.

But after a while, all this striving takes its toll. It depletes your energy reserves, and robs time and attention from all other areas of your life, especially your relationships. As your energy wanes, you feel as if you are wading through treacle. Privately, you are discouraged and wish you had not advertised your splendid goals so widely. You begin to mutter when no one's looking, *What's wrong with me?*

The answer is, *Probably not much!*

Welcome to *gap fatigue!*

In many ways gap fatigue is the result of mathematics that has gone awry. For instance, if your vision has grown by ten percent but your performance has only improved by three percent, you have a deficit of seven percent. This means the gap between your *real* and *ideal* selves has not narrowed; it has widened, even with all your extra effort. No wonder you feel thwarted and frustrated!

But take heart! You are not alone. This post-seminar slump is a natural part of life for most earnest seekers. For perfectionists in any arena.

So what can you do?

With a few variations, when you are in the throes of gap fatigue, you face three basic options. You can wade through options 1 and 2 if you like, but you're likely to enjoy life more if you skip straight to option 3!

Option 1) Try harder
Get up earlier. Push yourself and everyone else to the limit. Become more serious, earnest, and desperate. Draw on every drop of your raw courage until the well is empty. When things don't move fast enough in the direction you want, cry, or yell, depending on your personality. Clutch life with white-knuckled desperation, determined to be in control and wrest each situation to your will. Slide into manipulating others, (for the good of your cause, of course).

When control still eludes you, lose hope. Collapse in a burnt-out heap wondering wearily, *What on earth happened? Where did I go wrong? I tried so hard!*

Then increasingly mock or shun the cause you once loved, because it appears to have been your downfall.

This often leads into Option 2.

Option 2) Give up and get mad!
Throw your hands in the air and moan, "It's all too hard!" Then turn your back on your ideals and dreams and stomp off. Shouting over your shoulder

to those you love as you plod up the road, "If you lot had helped me more, I could have done it!"

Wearied by Option 1, you decide to forget *significant* and settle for *mediocre*. But, as the aimless days drift by, you grow to loathe both your dull life, and yourself. You also try to stifle the sneaking suspicion that you're a coward. Even a failure. In an attempt to smother such thoughts, you make a lot of noise, or seek a lot of noise. Anything to drown out both the voice of your conscience and the groans of your dying dreams.

Hoping to silence your inner critics, you turn your pain outward and become a vocal critic of everyone else. You scorn the whole *impossible idea you previously considered to be precious. Mock the apparently crazy system* that led you into failure, and shun the *deluded people* who espouse it. You laugh at those who still hope and dream. Especially if they succeed, because their triumphs rub salt into the wounds of your failure. You become jealous of the lucky insiders who belong, but fear asking for forgiveness or advice so much that you linger in your pain, unhealed. You, cloak yourself in bravado, then pretend you like the independence of being an outsider.

This can lead to a compelling need for Option 3!

Option 3) Understanding
First of all, if you are already tired from over-work and over-rescuing; rest!

Or, if you are a beginner and you have just noticed a twinkling, glittering, prize of perfection up ahead, *take a deep breath before you rush to grab it. Become very still, relax your shoulders and consciously step back from all demands, oughts and shoulds. All the rhetoric and hype.*

If idealism continues to pound on the door, ask it to take a chill pill. You need some time and space to think. For this is a pivotal moment fraught with risk! (Like all calls to valiant action!)

On the one hand, if you silence your conscience, suppress compassion and ignore God's prompting, you may be taking the first step on a slippery slope. One that spirals down into selfish irresponsibility and nihilism.

On the other hand, if you thoughtlessly leap into action to save the world, you may find yourself trapped in the no-win desperation of Option 1, either for the first time, or repeatedly!

So, what can you do?

How can you be a visionary, and sane?

Inspired, but also practical?

Focussed, but not obstinate or obsessive?

A person who is passionate about worthy goals, but also nice to live with? Relaxed, balanced and kind?

Ah, these are tough questions, and idealists have wrestled with them for generations! Half the time, I'm still playing with the questions, rather than finding answers, but this is what I've found so far.

Sustaining life and health comes first. You're no good to yourself or anyone else if, in your passionate pursuit of your goals you end up half dead! Or worse yet, pushing up daisies. So, open your heart to being (not just doing). Honor the Life Giver who created you by caring for your own life. If you are driving for a long distance, you need to stop frequently to fill your car with fuel. This both delays your journey, and enables it. When you serve others, rest and recreation, are your fuel stops. Along with nutrition and nurture. Enjoy them, guilt-free—no one apologizes for refueling their car!

Love your nearest and dearest, and make your home a secure refuge. A place of belonging, laughter and hope. Relationships matter. Honor your commitments. What's the point of neglecting the precious kids you have been given, to care for someone else's neglected kids?

Decide to let impossible ideals and unrealistic expectations go. This is so tough to do! Big dreams are far more inspiring than ordinary, daily, small steps! But, if you have one hour, give one hour. If you have two, give two. This may not feel magnificent, or world-changing, but it may just be enough. You don't have to be a hero to make a difference. The job of Savior has already been filled, but it's within your scope to take your glorious, yet limited, humanity out for a spin!

Distinguish between care, grief and response-ability. This is one of the hardest to practice! Oh, how it grieves us to see someone hurting. Oh, how we want, with our whole heart and soul to help them. To lift, encourage and heal folk, or make grand sweeping reforms. But most of the time, this is beyond our means. To arrive at any kind of peace, we will need to distinguish between what we can control, what we can influence, and what we can only observe. In some settings, all we can do is share a kind word or a hug and a smile. Several years ago I saw a teenage girl weeping at a train station. I barely had time to speak to her, rush to the platform kiosk and buy a few snacks, and push them into her hand, before the train whisked her away, and she was gone. I never knew her name, but as her train disappeared around a bend, my prayers and best wishes swept along the tracks in her wake.

Be teachable, but not gullible. Scattered liberally among the indifferent folk, the arrogant know-it-alls and the fools, there are many wise people waiting to be found. Befriend them! Rustle up a team. Going solo may be simpler, and it may feed your ego more, but collaborating together with others who are smart, motivated and experienced may yield greater success.

Live lightly. An intense flame uses more fuel. A rigid structure cracks under pressure. You don't have to take everything seriously to show how committed you are. Fear is brittle and insecurity is rigid. But love? Love is secure enough to freely bend, adapt and dance!

Explore faith. When someone says, "You're on your own there mate!" I feel cut off. Set adrift. As if all responsibility for the task has suddenly fallen on my shoulders. In contrast, I thrive best and hope more, when I trust that God is sovereign. That he has both a saving plan for me and my life, and the capacity to follow through. That he can bring good out of evil for all of us. Be our Redeemer.

Your personality and your opportunities are unique. Why copy a guru? Why compare yourself with your neighbor who has different skills and talents? Why try to imitate someone who is more rich in resources, or at a different life-stage? *Love yourself, and be yourself.* The world does not need duplicates, or clones! *Glory in the gifts God has given YOU!*

Have fun! Let your joy and purpose be replenished from God's inexhaustible supply! When you glimpse all the possibilities for serving spread out before your eyes, instead of panicking, or feeling overwhelmed by responsibility, chuckle with delight!

Imagine for a moment that you you are a small-town jeweler summoned to the royal palace of a great king. When you step into the throne room trembling, you have no idea what to expect. Silently you wonder, *will the king tell me off? Send me to a dark dungeon? Commission me to undertake a secret mission? Why on earth has he called me?*

Confused, and wary, you look around for a way of escape, just in case.

But all self-conscious thoughts flee when you see the king and his whole face lights up in welcome. Stepping down from his glittering throne he wraps you in a big hug, then says, his voice full of musical delight, "Follow me." Bemused, and in awe at such a personal welcome, you trip along behind him as he strides deep into the castle down labyrinthine hallways. At last, he stops before a huge door and hands you a golden key. "Go on, open it." You slip the key into the lock, and give it a hefty turn. When the door doesn't yield at once, you lean your shoulder against the door until it swings wide.

When you look up, your jaw drops. Stunned and speechless you turn to the king, your mind full of questions. He chuckles and says, "All these treasures are for you." His hand sweeps in a wide arc across boxes overflowing with glittering diamonds, bowls of sapphires and chests of rubies. "All the wealth of my kingdom is now yours. All, my peace, all my joy and all my hope. The treasures of eternity, adventure and an abundant life. I have been saving them for you. Enjoy!"

Stammering your thanks, you shake your head and whisper, "But what do I do with it all? Where do I begin?"

The king puts his arm around your shoulders and says, "We begin together!"

Dear One,
whatever your calling,
when you live motivated by love,
you serve others by Royal Command.

So remember,
whatever the hour, or your feelings,
all heaven stands ready to cheer you on,
eager to guide, encourage and bless you.

THE FEAR–LOVE CONTINUUM

What drives you,
drives you.

Two emotions compete to dominate my life.

Fear and Love.

Fear whispers his miserable propaganda in my ears. He tells me in fiendish delight, "You'll fail!" or "Others will laugh at you. They'll think you and your ideas are crazy. So forget your dreams and goals."

Sometimes Fear's warnings come true, but not always. Most of the time, Fear has no real evidence. No prophetic insight. Fear just plays spiteful games to keep me guessing and sabotage my peace. Given half a chance, Fear banishes Hope from my mind and shoves Anxiety onto the throne in his place.

In contrast, Love tells me that being alive is an adventure. She spreads all nature's beauty before me in lavish color. She invites me to explore the earth, the sea, and the sky. She assures me that sooner or later good will win. That my life is richer and happier when I care for others as well as for myself. She urges me to live my best life and take my dreams on a journey of discovery.

Why are these two forces of Fear and Love so powerful?

Only God knows for sure.

Some of our deepest fears stem from our own unruly imagination or life experience. Some come from the stories or actions of others.

I've also found hints here and there in sacred writings about a great war between good and evil, a battle for our minds.

I don't like the sound of this.

I long to live in a world of flowers, hot chocolate, and fluffy slippers, a world of peace. But I also want to be a realist. If there's a war going on, I want to survive it! I want to be guided by accurate and timely intelligence, *the best there is*. I want the God-given power to repel Fear's attacks and move along the continuum toward the safe haven of Love—one thought, one hug, and one prayer at a time.

I'm tired of having my dreams delayed by superficial irritations. I'm sick of being tripped up by Insecurity, blocked by Swamps of Regret or lost in Deserts of Self-blame. Weary of being derailed by the dread trio of Distraction, Discouragement and Doubt.

So, over and over, I return to a few lines in John's memoir of Jesus. They help me understand what's really going on and find the path of purpose, because John describes both the cause of all my distress and the route to healing in vivid detail. He places the blame and the hope where they belong.

The masked thief, known as Satan, is the one who
plots to wreck your life and derail your dreams.
He schemes to steal your confidence, health, and hope.
With diabolical cunning he aims to saturate
each thought with fear, lay you low and
make you shake until you fall to bits.

But don't give his malevolent whispers
a megaphone. Nor let his ideas
gain a foothold and destroy you!

Instead, come to Me

Because I'm here to welcome and heal you.
To weave My peace into your mind and
pour my love into your heart.
I alone can restore your vision
and help you create
a life full of purpose and joy.
One rich in passionate vitality.

Even in the darkness, I have the capacity
to light your way. To bless you with
an eternal hallelujah and an ever-echoing,
triumphant *Yes!*[6]

—Jesus (paraphrase mine)

EXPECTATIONS

Expectations are feral things.
Unruly, wild with power.

They shout in our soul's silence
and snicker at our success.

They push us to do more,
then more again.

To demand more of others until
we all collapse, exhausted.

Unless we boldly tame them
and use their power for good.

The expectations we have of life, self, and others are so much a part of us that we rarely notice they exist. *We just assume that what we think and feel are normal.*

Because our expectations seem so normal to us, we may assume that everyone has the same expectations. That the people we love or work beside are all reading from the same script.

But this is rarely the case.

Knowing this discrepancy exists makes all the difference, because if we expect someone to act in a certain way and they don't we can be deeply hurt. We can take their indifference or actions personally. Be grumpy and upset. But they may have no idea what we are feeling or what silent expectations they have *failed* to meet.

What on earth can we do?

I'm not sure. Maybe we can begin by acknowledging our expectations to ourselves, then communicating them more clearly to others. (Or maybe it would be kinder and more productive to listen to others' expectations first!)

In an attempt to manage some of my own expectations, I've asked myself a few questions, which I've listed below. You're welcome to play with them too if you wish and see what you discover.

Life:
When I was young, what did I expect things to be like when I grew up? In what ways have my expectations been met, or shattered? As a result, do I see life as fair or unfair? What criteria am I using to determine my answer, for instance, am I considering my health, wealth, or status? How can I create more realistic, authentic expectations of life in the future?

Self:
What do I expect of myself in each area of my life—physical, mental, social, financial, and spiritual? How realistic are these expectations? How may I need to modify them to reflect my family life, work and health? My energy levels, age, and the demands I face?

From Others:
What do I expect others to do for me in each area of my life? Why? Have I slipped into taking their kindness for granted? Do I turn their acts of grace into a form of obligation? Preoccupied with my own needs and stresses, am I drifting toward seeing others as *resources* more than as *people*?

To Others:
What do I expect to give others, for instance, in terms of resources like time, money, and attention? Where have these expectations come from? How realistic and healthy are they for me and for the people around me at home, at work, or in my community?

From God:
What do I understand by the phrase "God is love"? What am I expecting God to do for me? What selective evidence may I be gathering with regard to his provision, care, or love? What picture of his personality am I painting?

To God:
What do I believe God wants from me? Why? Am I basing this on things like tradition, habit, and gut feeling? Or on personal research, prayer and the records of Jesus' ministry? On an honest desire for truth?

When I began to explore some of these questions, I realized I had assumed many things about what my life would, and should, be like. I had also taken the kindness of many people for granted, and I was deeply sorry.

Although my answers to these questions were sometimes painful, I found the quest itself liberating. Exploring each area helped me to see life in new ways, relax a little more, and let others be themselves.

I also saw how much I had to be grateful for! How many expectations had been *more than met*.

And, when all is said and done,
gratitude, in itself, is healing!

BREAD

Please pass me the bread.

Here you are.

Hey, that's just an empty plate. I asked for bread!

I'm sorry, I haven't got any bread.

But I'm hungry; you need to give me bread.

As I said, I haven't got any bread,
but I've got a whole packet of cookies that
I'm happy to share. Would you like some?

We place so many demands on our relationships and on each other. We expect, and desire, many things. We long for understanding and romance, for time together and time apart, for shared hobbies, leafy trees, and space to run a dog. We want others to spend their energy and resources supporting our projects. If possible, we even want people to think like us, or at least reach the conclusion that our opinions and plans are right!

Busy with all this *wanting*, we tend to forget that the other person is only human, that they were not put on this earth solely for our benefit, or even just to smooth the path to our goals. Like us, they have limited strength and resources, which means that *they may not be able to help us even if they want to*.

Unless we realize this *and respect others' lives and boundaries*, we can slide into using various manipulative tactics to get our own way, to corner, push, and bully people.

When we were children, we used the raw "want energy" of toddler tantrums, and with some parents, this worked for a while. But as we aged, we developed more advanced strategies. This was not only to look more reasonable and civilized, but also with the hope that we would get our own way more often!

Sometimes we opted to speak very slowly. Or we implied with a patronizing sneer that only an idiot would disagree with us. Sometimes we acted like a person traveling in a foreign country and turned up the volume of our voices, hoping to push home our point. Or we managed people using emotions like anger or impatience rather than truth. Sometimes we richly embellished our demands with a sob story or two, begging for a pity vote.

Throughout history, one of the most insidious and manipulative ploys humans have tried is to use someone's virtue against them. For instance, even a very weak person can say, "I knew I could count on you to help me. Everyone else has abandoned me, but the whole street knows you're the kindest person here. Now, how soon can you start?"

Whether we nag people half to death, hoping they will eventually give in, or we choose another tactic, *we may lose even if we win*. Lose ground and love in our relationship with someone else. Lose the fun of collaborating over shared goals. Lose respect for our own integrity.

Focused on trying to get our own way, we forget *who we really want to be. Determined to win, we lose sight of how we really want to treat others.*

We miss seeing that the other person has

limits and needs, hopes and dreams too.

Deeply held desires as valid as our own
worthy of consideration, respect and support.

EXPECTATION TRAINING

We are all trainers.
By our words and actions,
we teach others what
to expect from us.

If people routinely expect too much of you, it may be all their fault. They may be heartless, manipulative, and demanding.

Or not.

Like you, in a bid to survive, they may simply be trying to make sense of life. To work out who will do a task and who will not then use historical data to estimate their best course of action. For instance, if one parent routinely helps a child with their homework, and the other does not, what expectations and behaviors will the child develop?

Recently, a friend told me the following story and gave me permission to share it with you. She said it had been handed down in her family from mother to daughter.

One day, a lady was invited to her friend's house for dinner. She decided to roast a chicken and take it along as a gift to share. Her friends were thrilled and gave it pride of place on the table. Throughout the meal, they commented on how tasty it was. When she left, they smiled and thanked her once again for her gift.

The next time she was invited for dinner, she remembered what had happened, and brought a roast chicken again. This time, her hosts were busy and distracted, and they simply cleared a place on the table without a word.

A while later, she was invited a third time. Tired and worn out with work, she looked forward to dinner all day and relaxing with her friends. When she knocked on their door, a tumble of children came to open it with eager smiles. But when they saw she only carried her purse, one of them demanded, "Where's the roast chicken you always bring?"

Later, when they all sat down to eat, the hostess apologized that the meal was "a little light on" and cast a meaningful glance her way. When all the family turned to stare at her with reproachful eyes, her hand began to tremble, and the peas rolled off her fork. As soon as the meal was over, she made a polite excuse, and fled.

As I thought about this story, I realized that, for better or worse, all of us are in *training relationships*. That is, whenever we interact with others, we are engaged in expectation training! And unless abuse is involved, we are choosing the role we will play.

Every day we teach others what to expect of us.

If this is the case, and we are all *expectation trainers or teachers*, can we re-shape what others expect or demand of us?

Yes. But . . .
If we have repeatedly thought in a certain way, it may take us a while to master a new curriculum.

If we have trained our *students* for many years to have certain expectations, it may take a lot of effort to convince them that things are about to change, especially if they are used to having an easy ride at our expense!

So what can we do? We can make a dramatic statement of intent and throw our relationships into chaos. Or we can take things slowly and make small changes that gradually edge us toward more balanced relationships.

We can:
Be reliable, without being taken for granted.
Be trustworthy, without becoming a resource.
Be loyal, without being stepped on.
Be kind, without being used.

When we create healthy boundaries around what we will do, and what we will not do, we begin to feel less used. We start to release the hurt and resentment that's been stuffed deep in our hearts. This makes space for our own sense of volition to grow. We begin to feel that, once more, or for the first time, we are in control of our own lives.

This, in turn, gives us the stability, desire, and capacity to support others freely and generously whenever we can. It helps us create more flexible and resilient relationships based on mutual honesty and respect.

So integrity and love can flourish.

AMORE

Loathe to goad animals,
we goad ourselves instead!

When my fear-based ego drives, that's all it does. It goads me relentlessly and whips me into believing I must work harder and faster to be *somebody*. It tricks me into believing that the cowshed of perfection is my only refuge.

Cowshed?
Yes.

Because we only seek perfection when we are afraid. When, like wild-eyed, horn-tossing cattle, we are on the run, on the run from failure, shame, and rejection.

But *I don't want to live my life on the run*. I don't want to seek perfection at the cost of sanity and peace. Instead, I want to be *an amateur*, a person who is inspired by amore, by love. A person who explores, learns, and grows for the sheer joy of it.

Whatever my role.

And whoever is watching.

A TO B

Every detour teaches
us something.

I would like to suggest that the person who coined the phrase "as straight as the crow flies" did not spend much time watching crows fly, or butterflies, for that matter. At least not butterflies, which fly in windy weather.

Whatever their destination, butterflies have to share the garden with other creatures and other objects. If they plan to live, they have to dodge predators, watch out for unyielding brick walls, and skim over wire fences.

The irony is that, to avoid all these obstacles, the butterfly may actually *choose to go off course briefly in order to ultimately stay on course*. If, one blustery day, the butterfly finds itself veering off course whether by choice or circumstance, what does it do?

Does it flop to the ground and weep over its own weakness and stupidity?

No.

Does it land on a swaying stem and scream insults at the wind?

No.

Does it abandon its flight and crawl, quivering, into a deep, dark hole?

No.

It simply gets back on course again, as soon as it can, without wasting energy on drama, rage, or self-criticism.

Yes. Yes. Yes!

SYNTHESIS, PART 1

After analysis,

chaos. Always.

After chaos,
a new creation.
Sometimes!

I tried; honestly, I did. But how can anyone focus on writing an English essay in class when Spring herself is breathing in at the window? When sunbeams quiver on my paper and pen? Teasing me? Calling me to come outside and play where all the wild things dance?

And there was something else distracting me.

Every few minutes, a deep boom rattled the classroom windows. With each rattle, my eyes wandered to the other side of the school lawn where an elegant old hospital was being demolished. As it crumbled, I sat glued to my chair, mesmerized.

A tall crane was swinging a large metal ball to and fro on a long chain. The steel ball pounded against the walls. It smashed into the soaring hospital windows, and fragments of glass rained down in a sparkling shower. It thudded against a tall white pillar once, and the pillar stood firm. Twice, and the pillar trembled. Three times, and the pillar gave way and collapsed in a cloud of chalk-white dust.

As the elegant mansion fell to her knees, I felt like weeping.

I did not know it then, but on that balmy spring afternoon, *analysis* was literally happening right before my eyes. For something big was being broken into smaller pieces. Shattered.

Whenever we break up something big—whether it's an old building, a value system, a family, or a creed, we end up with fragments, a pile of physical or emotional rubble.

Always.

Whatever the cause, the result is always the same.

Rubble.

Where order and certainty once reigned, we have instead a kind of jumbled chaos, a whole heap of mess. And usually, *a whole heap of lonely, bewildered pain*.

Nothing seems stable anymore. Nothing makes sense. Beliefs of a lifetime suddenly develop fault lines and tremble under the impact. Friendships shatter. Habits disintegrate. And the shock waves leave us reeling. We wander around, our heads spinning, asking ourselves questions like, *What just happened?* and *What on earth can I do now?*

Nothing adequately prepares us for these life-quakes, and no belief-structure, relationship or assumption is quake-proof. At any time, we can be thrown off-balance. Perhaps because we are dismissed from a job we considered to be secure. Or we find a throbbing lump where no lump should be. Perhaps because we face unexpected divorce or sudden bereavement.

But it's not just *bad* things that shatter our carefully constructed beliefs. Good things can shatter us too. A scientist may make a wonderful discovery one evening and hardly sleep for excitement. Then, at the breakfast table, suddenly realize that the new piece of evidence changes everything, every cherished belief and scientific theory he or she has held dear.

When life's foundations tremble like this, what can we do?

We can do whatever we like.

But usually, we end up in one form of grief or another.

We rage.

We sit in life's ruins and weep.

We try to bargain with the universe.

But sooner or later, we use the last tissue. We feel around the bottom of the box with damp fingers, nothing. And we realize we cannot cry forever. But what other options are there? Red-eyed, we look around.

At first glance, we see what we have always seen: a mess. And we turn away. But as we do, something catches our eyes. Among the rubble, one tiny fragment glitters in the sun. We reach out and pick it up. We turn it this way and that in our fingers, thinking.

Looking again, we see another small fragment. And we line up the two broken pieces and discover they fit together. A tiny glimmer of hope begins to grow. We scramble to our feet and begin to search in earnest. Using every waking moment, we salvage all we can.

Soon a pile of useful pieces begins to grow. We unearth talents, long forgotten, rediscover dusty skills and brush them off. We remember resources lying in the long grass of memory and scrub off the spots of rust.

Then, in the dark, *we become once more architects of dreams.* We make lists of things we still need. We rally friends. We pray for divine inspiration, for wisdom and courage. Then, little by little, we pick up each piece of rubble, and gluing them all together with hope, we begin to rebuild.

Gradually, we create something stronger, more beautiful, and more enduring than ever before.

And we revel, body and soul,
in the beauty of synthesis.

If you spared a thought for that stately old hospital, you may be wondering, *Where is it now?*

It has gone.

Each scrap of plaster has been swept up. Each shard of broken glass has been picked out of the grass and carried away.

Nothing is left.

But wait, the land itself remains. And firmly anchored to the earth, stand the ancient trees. Season by season, they wait. They grow taller and sink their roots deeper. One day, under those stately trees, men begin to build. Brick by brick and window by window, a new elementary school takes shape. The teachers arrive, then truckloads of chairs and books.

Today, in the very place where pale hospital patients once shuffled, bright-eyed children play. Little girls build cubby houses among the trees' sturdy roots.

They stir mud pies in dented pans to feed their dolls under the cedar's dappled shade. Older boys and girls play hide-and-seek among the whispering firs.

Every spring, when the sap of new life flows in their veins, one or two brave children slip away from their friends. They scramble silently up into the spreading branches of an ancient oak tree, where they search for a nook to call their very own. A secret place where they can hide among the new-furled leaves and lean back against the great warm trunk.

To look out upon the restless world below
and dream.

SYNTHESIS, PART 2

A bricklayer is a practical optimist.
He sees a home in a humble brick
and a city in a single wall.

As a child gleefully pulls apart a toy to see what's inside, we pull apart big ideas. We call this process analysis, but that's just a grown-up name for curiosity. Being curious is lots of fun. Fueled by curiosity, we solve problems, explore continents, and discover spiritual truth. But curiosity and analysis come with risks.

If we pull something big apart, whether it's a kitchen gadget, a lawnmower, or an idea, we want to be able to put it all back together again. But sometimes we can't. And that scares many of us out of meddling, even exploring. We want adventure, solutions, and deeper understanding, not chaos.

But sometimes the urge to tinker is irresistible. And we pull things apart anyway and get ourselves into a big mess. Then we are tempted to mutter, "Why didn't I just leave it alone?"

Things may get so bad that we may feel like running away.

Or pretending our mental chaos is someone else's fault.

But if we can quell our panic long enough, we begin to see that the very chaos we have created with our questions actually has potential. Each piece of rubble, each fragment of an idea whispers, "See what you can make of me. Go on, pick me up!"

Every day, in science, medicine, and technology, wise explorers do just that. They pick up the pieces of their broken ideas, beliefs, and dreams and play with them. They look at each piece of information from every angle. Slowly at first, then with growing delight, they catch a fresh vision. They feel a shiver of sheer joy as they build, create, and synthesize.

They discover how to write a new story
or build a more buoyant boat.

They see a cure for cancer in a petri dish
or a thriving business in a soy candle.

They dispel community prejudice and
promote friendship and understanding.

Some even send kites of questions into the
sky of hope and discover the Living God.

All these people have something in common.

Unbowed by despair and untarnished by cynicism, they have the *courage to remain curious,* to search, discover, and build. They have the tenacity to out-ride life's chaos and create unique solutions.

To explore humanity's farthest horizons
in the holy quest for wisdom and
The Source of All Life.

The Mirror of Truth

When you stand before the Mirror of Truth,
What are you afraid you will see?
What are you longing to see?

When I was a teenager, I visited a Hall of Mirrors in a fairground tent. As I mentioned earlier, all the mirrors in that tent were intentionally distorted. Some made my friends and I look silly, some made us look grotesque. But whatever we looked like, we were not afraid of the images we saw because of four key things:

We already knew what we looked like.
We knew the images were false.
We knew the images had been designed to make us giggle.
We knew we could walk away from the mirrors at any time so they held no power over us.

These four factors made all the difference to how we felt.

In my earlier story, I briefly explored the fact that we all live in a *human hall of mirrors*, a world where we are constantly being given feedback—both negative and positive—by the people around us. I focused on *false feedback*, where others distort the truth for their own ends or because of their own pain. Now I would like to briefly explore *true feedback*.

Feedback that tells it like it is. That conceals nothing. Feedback that tells me the unvarnished, untarnished truth. This kind of feedback makes me tremble. What if I'm not ready to hear the truth about who I really am? What if the truth hurts? What if it shows me, and everyone else, that I'm not as nice as I think I am?

What if it shows me that:

I'm a coward?
Unkind?
Lazy?

I'm not scared of glass mirrors, (particularly in very dim candlelight), as long as they only show me minor flaws I can easily fix: one hair out of place or a slightly crooked collar.

But if a *human mirror* tells me to my face, "You're bossy" or "You haven't a clue what you're talking about" or more bluntly, "You're wrong!" Can I stomach that? Maybe from someone who loves me. Or from a manager, if I have to. But what if the feedback comes from *a person I see as inferior*? A person *below* me in life's pecking order? A person society deems to be *less than*? A child, an employee, or a person with less education or less spiritual experience?

Can my pride listen then? Can my self-esteem humble itself enough to hear; and hearing, understand, and understanding, change? I'm not sure.

But what about you? How well do you handle feedback? Do you welcome *constructive criticism?* Do you thank people for taking the time and effort to *point out your mistakes?*

For instance, do you thank your son for piping up in front of visitors, "Dad, this afternoon you said, 'I don't want our boring neighbors coming over for tea.' But a minute ago, you told them, 'It's a pleasure having you in our home.'"

Do you thank your daughter for pointing out your moral duplicity when she says, "Mom, why do I have to forgive Mary for stealing my snack bar? You don't forgive. You've refused to speak to Aunt Margaret since the picnic, and you ignore Sam down the road. And they haven't stolen anything from you!"

Do you smile when your grandson says, "Grandpa, why do you comb your hair over your bald spot like that? It looks funny." Or when your granddaughter giggles and whispers, "Grandma, when you dyed your hair, you missed a bit. There's a big white streak at the back!"

Do you thank all these people for helping you become more honest? More authentic? Or do you shut them down? Pull rank and tell them, "That's enough from you! Don't be cheeky!"?

As most adults soon discover, living in a human hall of mirrors is not easy on the ego!

Because feedback can be wrapped in rudeness, or love, it's sometimes hard to decide if the feedback is false or true. And whatever its motive, we can never escape it, because it can come from any direction! It can come from the tangle-haired street beggar sitting on a flattened cardboard box who yells, "You lot don't care about me. You only care about yourselves!"

It can come from a work colleague who mutters in frustration after a meeting, "Why do you always show off and take the credit? We worked on that project together!" Or from your toddler who climbs up onto your lap, places chubby hands on your cheeks, and pressing his nose to yours, says, "Here I am. Can you see me now? Or are you still too busy?"

When truth comes calling like this, it literally tells us to our face that living with integrity is not child's play. It exposes our glib boasting and philosophizing and reveals that what we say is mostly hot air. Oh my, we don't like this one bit! We don't like it when someone calls our bluff or exposes us as phonies.

When a friend or family member challenges me about some of my idiosyncrasies, if I'm feeling hurt or fragile, my immediate instinct is to flee or cry. But if they have offended me and I feel strong, I'm likely to argue my point, to launch a verbal war. (Anything to avoid having to admit blame. Or worse still, having to change!)

If I choose to launch a verbal war, I have several weapons at my disposal, and so do you!

We can *mock the other person's opinion and discredit them*. Try to convince ourselves, and everyone else, that the person is unreliable and misinformed, that they have devious motives.

We can do our best to mute them, even send them to bed if they are young enough! We can shout them down *with our version of truth*.

We can *blame the human mirror*, subtly or overtly, while still polishing our own haloes. Seek out a gossip and, with straight and earnest faces, say how *concerned* we are about the other person's flaws. How we are praying *they will change!*

We can *engage in open war*. Seek to smash the living mirror before their truth can destroy us, our business, or our reputation.

The scary thing is, *we may pride ourselves on doing all these things.*

Think we are managing situations and people well because we are avoiding fallout and keeping things under control. If we have been duped into thinking duplicity is in our best interest, we may actually *drift into defending lies and denying the truth*, something which, in our saner moments, we abhor. We may routinely weaken our integrity until we hardly know who we are anymore, except that we are getting really good at lying!

But truth takes no prisoners.

Either we listen and grow, or we deny the truth and slowly wither. Either we live by our values and trust ourselves and become trustworthy, or we discard our values and begin to distrust ourselves. *We cannot lie our way through life and expect to have greater self-esteem! We cannot live in sneaky ways, and love ourselves more. We cannot smother our values and have greater self-respect!*

If we routinely play lie-making games, we can fool ourselves into believing that no one notices what we are doing. But our defensive, reactive, even volatile attitude soon dispels that myth!

So, what can we do to remain authentic?

We can take our courage and integrity in both hands and face the truth while it's still small enough to manage.

We can silence our uppity ego long enough to listen.

We can apologize where we have wronged someone.

We can sift through others' comments and decide, in our calmer moments, *which ones to take on board and which to let slide by.*

And one more thing.

We may need to admit to ourselves a startling idea, that *we have some ambivalence where truth is concerned*. On the one hand, we love *the idea of truth as a philosophy*. We love to don a hero's cape and defend truth's honor in debates, *but we rarely want truth up close and personal*.

As spiritual seekers, it takes a lot of courage to see, and name, our own ambivalence. To own that we may have spent a lifetime seeking truth and loving the daring nature of the quest, but also spent a lifetime fleeing it. It takes real integrity to see that when truth has knocked on our own front door and pulled up a chair for a chat, we have rapidly bluffed and blustered our way out of the room, then fallen over our own feet in a headlong scramble for the back door!

I wonder why.

Is it because truth confronts our hypocrisy? Lays bare our motives? Do we fear being vulnerable and facing who we really are because we may despise the person we find? Are we scared we will fall apart? Fatally unravel? Or lose status and social leverage?

Ultimately,
We decide how we respond to truth.[7]

Whatever others say or do.
Whatever their motives or status.

We can choose to retaliate or grow.
Stay the same or be transformed.

THE DOOR

If I barricade the door of my heart
against Truth, I trap my soul
in a House of Lies.

But when I dare to welcome
God's good truth, he frees my soul.

Then curiosity, liberated,

springs to life and full of wonder,
love and holy awe,
I explore with eager eyes
the reaches of infinity.

TRUE ACCOUNTABILITY

We all face pivotal moments in life
when taking responsibility
is key to healing.

This is not because it's soothing
or easy, but because it opens the door
to regaining our power.

I had been dodging the idea for weeks. Trying every mental trick I knew to cast the blame elsewhere. I had created self-pity stories in my head, sobbed out my story to sympathetic listeners, and even started to create a ragged *following* for my side of the story.

But one night I knew the game was up. I knew I needed to face a few home truths about myself and my life, about the choices I had made. I could either slide deeper and deeper into the blame game or take responsibility for my part of the mess. I could make excuses and become a perennial, perhaps even a permanent victim. Or I could live with integrity and grow.

I could not do both.

I think many of us face this dilemma, especially after a time of great loss. If we are already in pain, perhaps even awash in shame, we are terrified we will drown if we have to shoulder the blame as well. So, like many an overloaded manager, we try to delegate the blame to someone else and get them to carry it.

This may ease things in the short term and let us play the role of The Innocent One. But if we habitually off-load responsibility onto someone else, by default, we also contract out our response-ability, that is, our power to respond intelligently to life.

If we label another person The Cause, we imply that they were the ones with the power in the past. We also cast ourselves in the role of The Victim. Sometimes this is true; sometimes it isn't. But whichever is the case, if we get used to thinking of ourselves as weak and powerless, we inadvertently extend the other person's power over us. We let what happened yesterday or years ago cast a shadow over our present, and our future.

Grieving still, or smug in our conviction that
we hold a valid grudge, we voluntarily
disempower ourselves and stumble into
each new day soul-crippled and limping.

Unless we relinquish revenge,
grasp our power to forgive, and
boldly reclaim our vision and volition.

Although such an attitude can be truly liberating, we don't need to take responsibility for everything that goes wrong or shoulder the blame for everyone's mistakes, *even to keep the peace*. Nor do we need to play the role of a Martyr because, in the end, this doesn't help anyone grow up. Besides, *true accountability does not grovel*. It is, first and foremost, concerned with *truth*. With what's just and fair, with achieving an outcome that offers everyone the best chance of healing and transformation.

Ultimately, truth is simply *what is*.
Reality.

The most secure foundation of all
on which to build a life.

The launchpad for all adventure.
Luminous with possibility.

DEMANDING TRUTH

When Truth holds
hands with Mercy,
Justice and Joy

skip in their wake.

One of the most confronting questions someone can ask us is:

"Are you telling the truth?"

The question itself is easy to answer, for there are only two options, "Yes" or "No." But the implications of saying yes or no can leave us trembling with indecision. So we hesitate.

Because the most primal force in all creation is the instinct to survive, if telling the truth threatens our physical, mental, or social survival, we hurry to deflect its approach. We try to change the subject. We squirm. We create an elaborate dance around the facts.

Whether we are five or fifty, we dread incriminating ourselves and avoid it like the plague. This is true whether we are snuggling up on the couch at home or standing in solitary fear before a judge in the local courthouse. The higher the stakes, the more our instinct urges us to lie, especially when shame and blame hover in the air, seeking a place to land. At times like this, we may have an acute inner knowledge of the truth but still deny it. *Consciously seek refuge in a house of lies.*

How does such duplicity begin, and become such a familiar coping mechanism that it *feels normal* I have been wrestling with this idea for a while now and gradually, two stories formed in my mind.

Story 1

Crash.
The mother knew without leaving the couch that her platter was wrecked. She tossed aside her magazine, leapt to her feet, and rushed into the kitchen. The first thing she saw was the shattered pottery scattered across the floor. "You idiot!" she screamed.
"Don't you know that was my mother's plate? I never should have let you use it. I knew you were clumsy and stupid. Get out of my sight. Now!"
The child scrambled for the door and fled down the garden, plunging behind a leafy bush for refuge. Hugging her knees, she squeezed her eyes shut then stuck her fingers into her ears, but she could still hear the tornado in the

kitchen, the sound of her mother fuming. Cursing her. She winced each time a shard of broken pottery scraped across the floor. She pictured her mother sweeping it all into a jagged pile of evidence to show her father later.

Two against one.

Story 2

Crash.
The mother knew without leaving the couch that her platter was wrecked. She tossed aside her magazine, leapt to her feet, and rushed into the kitchen. The first thing she saw was the shattered pottery scattered across the floor. The mother gulped.
She took a deep breath and looked a little higher. Instantly, her eyes locked with her son's eyes. *Reading them, even as he read hers.*
Before he dropped his gaze, she saw shame there, and fear.
As he hung his head, she stepped carefully across the floor toward him.
Suddenly, he flung his head up and, in desperation, cried, "I didn't mean to drop it. I was trying to be careful."
Unsure what to say, she only nodded.
"Grandma gave it to you, didn't she?"
She nodded again, "Yes."
Gathering her wits, the mother tried to move beyond her anger and sadness. Be practical for her son's sake.
"Come on, I'll give you a hand to clear it up."
Quickly, he responded, "I can help. I can get the dustpan and brush."
"Smart idea."
Side by side, they worked on the floor, sweeping up shards of pottery.
Picking up one of the larger pieces, her son looked at it, as if for the first time. "It's very pretty. If I fetch the glue, can you fix it?"
His mother rocked back on her heels and looked at him sadly, "No, it's too badly broken, which is a shame, as I rather liked it."
"I'm really sorry, Mom."
"I know." Instinctively, she reached out and gave him a quick hug. "Somewhere we have another plate you can use."
"Really?"
"Sure. Then we can finish making the dinner together. I'm proud of the way you're starting to help around the house. I can see you're growing up. Dad's noticed it too, he mentioned it just last night!"

Two, cheering one on!

When someone near you makes a mistake, you are faced with two silent questions:

Will I highlight the flaw and diminish the person?

Or

Will I diminish the flaw and empower the person?

The choice is yours.

You can tell the truth wrapped in love, or just the bitter truth. The consequences of your choice, though they fall more heavily on one person than the other, are always shared. *For how you treat a colleague, friend, or family member when they are vulnerable always affects your relationship from that moment on.* It influences how much they come to trust and respect you. How willing they are to try new things when you are around. How willing they are to be learners and show initiative.

The way you respond to others' mistakes, *will also be the way you respond to your own mistakes.*

What if someone near you has lived for years without experiencing the liberating power of your forgiveness?

What if that precious someone
is you?

TRANSFORMING TRUTH

In God's plan,
Truth never travels alone.
It flies swiftly to our aid
on healing wings
of mercy and love.

If we are in a position of power, and we make it our business to value truth, we may be standing on shaky ground.

How come? Surely not! Doesn't truth provide a secure foundation?

Yes. And yet . . .

What if, in our zeal, we take pride in being right? *In knowing we know the truth?* What if we gradually change from being humble, curious, truth-seekers into arrogant know-it-alls? What if we use information like a cudgel to batter those who are wrong? Or, with studied finesse, we use truth like a scalpel to cut others down to size?

If we do, may we be right and yet also terribly wrong?

In our quest for truth, if we forget our own humanity and crush the humanity of others, what have we gained? If we imply that taking any kind of initiative on our patch is risky, who dares try? And if we flare into anger when someone makes a mistake, if we mock beginners and punish honesty, *don't we teach people to lie to us?* Pressure the adults, teens, and children under our rule into finding cunning ways to survive? Perhaps by blaming others or concealing evidence?

Don't we limit the options of vulnerable people in our care? Push them into pleasing, appeasing, and blindly obeying whatever we say? Make them do whatever we command, or even hint, for fear of our scorn or wrath?

If we routinely react to genuine errors and mistakes by pointing out another's flaws, we may pride ourselves on upholding a certain standard. But our victory is surely hollow if the reward and punishment system we develop actually trains our dependents and subordinates to be devious! To hide truth and send it underground. If this happens, won't it have a disastrous effect on trust and on our family and business relationships?

Hardly the outcome we desire!

As parents, leaders, or employers, can't we maintain high standards of work, or behavior, while still remaining civil? Can't we see, and honor, the person before seeing and magnifying the mistake? Or do we have to go to the opposite extreme and allow sloppy work or behavior just to be nice?

When I face a dilemma like this, I repeatedly return to an ancient story. The story helps me balance accountability and kindness without compromising the integrity of either. It highlights the fact that *the integrity and character of the one in power is paramount* and that a leader can shape, for better or worse, the characters of those who live under their power.

This story also reminds me that justice and mercy are both *regal* and *redemptive*.

Long ago, when the people of Israel were nomadic, they carried with them a large and elaborate chest covered in gold. Each time they stopped to seek pasture and set up camp, they quickly erected a beautiful tent to keep the chest safe. They always placed this sacred tent in the center of their camp, with all the family tents radiating out from it, to symbolize the fact that wherever they traveled, The Living God was *pitched there with them*.

Within the tent, priests carefully tended a seven-branched oil lamp. The flames shone brightly and made the gorgeous red, blue, and purple tapestries glow. The steady lights picked out, here and there, the soft outlines of angels where skilled craftsmen had woven them into the cloth with golden thread.

Inside the chest, there were several carefully preserved items of spiritual significance. These included two slabs of stone inscribed with God's enduring Law of Truth.

On the lid of the chest, two exquisite angels skillfully wrought out of pure gold faced each other. These angels spread their wings over the chest in worship and blessing.

Between the two angels and above the Law of Truth preserved in the chest below was the most sacred space of all. The most holy place where God's luminous presence quivered like living light. Where, wrapped in shimmering glory, his love reigned.

This place was called
"The Mercy Seat."[8]

Good Question?

I have nothing to fear from questions
if I am already living the answers.

"What's for dinner?" I've been asked this question a million times. Well, almost.

And each time I'm asked I feel a different emotion.

If I'm running late and haven't a clue what's for dinner, I feel fear rising. I know I'm unprepared, and my *incompetence* is about to be exposed. So, I bluff and bluster and send the questioner out to play (if they are young enough!).

But when I've planned a splendid meal, I'm eager for someone ask, "What's for dinner?" because I can't wait to tell them!

Same question; different response.

In a similar way, how I answer questions about work, faith, and family depends, to a large extent, on how competent and authentic I feel. How secure I am in my knowledge or my role. In myself, and my ability to cope.

So, what about you?

What questions do you dread, at home or at work?

What questions are you eager for someone to ask?

Why?

Loitering with Intent!

Every step of our lives,
questions will be our
companions.

Questions perennially loiter at the edge of our knowledge. They never sleep. As we grow up and explore further afield, we discover new questions waiting for us around every bend.

People react to these questions in different ways.

Some people resent questions and try to escape them, as a man seeks to elude a pursuer. Some pretend questions do not exist. Others distract themselves from uncertainty with overwork, worry, or with mind-numbing entertainment.

Some people have such a terror of questions that they mentally block their ears and close their eyes. Like young children, they believe that if they cannot see the questions, they do not exist. They may do this physically, emotionally, or spiritually. For instance, they may move to remote places in an attempt to limit their exposure to a world of complex uncertainty. They may shield their children from the pain of wrestling with ideas and try to turn them into temporary mimics of themselves. Clones.

Shielded from the invasion of uncertainty, these people turn into devotees of certainty. As they kneel at the shrine of the past, they place a small hand-written sign by their feet, which pleads, "Do not disturb."

But fleeing or hiding are not our only options.

When questions come calling, we can choose to be brave. We can welcome them as guests. Give them a seat by the fire, ask them why they have called, and unwrap the gifts they bring.

Gifts of understanding,

Humility,

Compassion,

And wisdom.

Even the awe-inspiring mystery of faith.

CIRCLES OF KNOWLEDGE

We reward a child
for the right answer

But as adults, we live
in a world of questions.

Where, then, do we
find our reward?

When I was a teenager and moved back home, I had a bunk bed in my room. I enjoyed sleeping on the top bed, next to the open window. Although I was sometimes cold with my pillow pressed against the glass, I loved waking up to see the sun rising over our garden. As the sun climbed higher in the sky, I watched it paint the tops of the trees with morning light, scatter flecks of sunshine along the grape vine, and finally tip each blade of grass with gold.

At the end of our small garden, there was an elementary school with a large playground. The playground was usually empty when I was at home, but sometimes I had a break from school to study for exams. Then I could spread my books on the bed and watch the children playing below. Playing the games that I had played more than ten years earlier, when I was a little kid.

As I sat there, surrounded by books, the children had no idea what my teenage world was like or even that I even existed. They didn't have to study for final exams, worry if a boy liked them, or stress over an essay due the next morning. Each day I faced challenges and wrestled with questions that hadn't yet entered their heads. Some days, when study weighed me down, I longed to return to the simplicity of childhood. But on other bright and glorious days, my heart throbbed with excitement as I realized, "I'm almost an adult!"

I knew being an adult would be wonderful. I would be free, free to do as I pleased, free to drive a car. I would finally understand life and know everything, like adults did. (I knew they understood everything because whenever I asked one of my teachers or an older member of my family a question, they always came up with an answer as quickly as they could).

But sitting on my bed by the window, I knew I wasn't there yet, so I rolled over onto my tummy and opened another book. Maybe this one would make me wise enough to be a grown-up.

It didn't.

I left school and celebrated my eighteenth birthday. But still, wisdom eluded me. Was there a trick to all this? Was I missing something? Time after time, I dangled a question, like a baited hook, into the vast sea of knowledge and waited, hoping for an answer. Ah-ha, a bite! I reeled in my hook with great joy, and there it was, the quivering, shiny answer! But then I would notice another problem: Every time I reeled in an answer, it came to shore, dragging more questions in its wake, like a fish entangled in seaweed.

Was there no end to the questions? Maybe when I entered university, I would finally understand everything.

In my first year, I worked for a few hours a week re-stacking books in the university library. One day, as I pushed my loaded trolley through the swinging door, I looked along the endless rows of shelves. What a lot of books there were! Thousands of them. Maybe even millions. As I stood there in the brooding silence, the weight of all that slumbering knowledge seemed to press down on my soul. With a sigh, I realized, *I could read day and night for the rest of my life and never finish all these books!* For a dewy-eyed first-year university student, this was a real shock. Then, I thought, *Even if I study hard for years, I will never know everything.* In that moment, a childhood illusion died.

No one warned me about this in school. Perhaps all the adults had formed a conspiracy. Made a pact together that they would never, ever let down their guard and admit to a child or a teenager their terrible secret. Say out loud, "I don't know!" No one tells us when we graduate from school that, beyond our little world of wisdom and experience, there lies the vast universe of the unknown, *an unknown we will never conquer.*

For several years, I lived in a state of quiet frustration, always hoping I would be able to tie wisdom down, capture it, corner and control it, and *know how to do life.* Then, one evening, I stumbled upon these words:

The greater the circle of knowledge,

the larger the circumference of ignorance.

I'm not sure who first said this. Some say it was Albert Einstein, and others think it was Thomas Edison. But whoever it was, I'm very grateful because as soon as I heard the idea, I felt an inner *wow!*

Suddenly, all my frustration made sense. For the first time, I could picture what was happening. Day by day, my knowledge was growing, which was great. But this also meant that the circumference of my *circle of knowledge* was also increasing. Each time my circle of knowledge grew, the border where the *known* and the *unknown* met became longer and longer.

In practical terms, I think it works something like this:

A young child, playing with the bright blocks of kindergarten, knows very little, much less than they will as a teenager. They look at picture books and maybe watch television, but they have no experience beyond their own home and family. While their joys and sorrows can be just as intense, they only have a small circle of knowledge.

A teenager knows a lot more. They have thumbed through hefty textbooks and studied science. They have even discovered where babies come from. Most have made friends, then lost them. They have seen pets die and know they do not come back. They have also taken brief excursions into the world of adults. Therefore, their circle of knowledge and life experience is bigger than a child's.

A mature adult has the biggest circle of all. It's stuffed with wisdom, stories, and life experience. An adult knows what it feels like to be loved and to grieve love's loss. What it feels like to be powerful and competent one minute, and helpless in the face of circumstance and others' choices the next minute. Most adults have met people from different cultures and listened to their stories. They have witnessed tragic wars play out on the world stage. They have also seen joyful celebrations liberally laced with lilting music and bright balloons. Therefore, in addition to their own life experience, they have a wide awareness of life on earth.

Once I became aware of the circles of knowledge, I saw that people deal with what I call their *knowledge boundary* in different ways.

Some people notice the vast *unknown* beyond their perimeter of understanding, and they begin to panic. With urgent haste, they build a fortress-style wall against the threat of questions. And as the years pass, they dig in deeper behind this perimeter fence and clutch their views ever-more-tightly to their chest. When they encounter people with different views, they act defensively, as if they are under permanent siege. Sadly, these people fail to see that the walls of *pre-judged-ness* they so ardently defend are also imprisoning them and stifling their own growth. Unaware they have allowed fear to assume the role of gatekeeper, they are becoming increasingly trapped in a self-made citadel of the fossilized. Brittle. Vulnerable. Lonely.

Other people go to the opposite extreme. They glimpse the vast unknown out there, and their fear takes on a different shape. Overwhelmed by information, they abandon their God-given ability to reason and avoid tough decisions. Unsure what they believe, they refuse to stand for anything, and by default, they languidly decide, *Nothing can really be known. Truth is always relative.* They mock the very idea of boundaries and become drifters, windblown waifs, wafted about by current opinions. They abandon their early idealism, labeling it naive, and become cynics. They lose sight of their youthful dreams. Then, to wile away the time, they amuse themselves as best they can, hardly noticing that life is passing them by. That they are losing momentum and purpose and joy are floating away.

A third group know who they are and what they stand for, but they also have the capacity to be comfortable with uncertainty and live with spiritual mystery. They are practical, grounded in reality, and open to new ideas. They are able to live with joy and purpose because they shelter under a kind of divine grace. A grace that helps them forgive themselves and others and embrace the glory and the flaws of being human. This liberates them. Frees them to honor their own experience *and* listen with warmth and respect to others' stories.

Because they love learning, they see questions as invitations to adventure, not as threats to their identity. Therefore, each day they grow in wisdom and understanding, yet, paradoxically, they do not act like know-it-alls. In fact, they are often humble.

Why?

Perhaps because they hold their wisdom lightly, conscious that there is an even greater amount they do not know. Somehow, *in accepting both sides of the circle, the known and the unknown, they find equilibrium, self-acceptance, and peace.*

This helps them relax and frees them
to become lifelong learners, people
who can listen as well as teach.

Individuals who can act decisively,
yet also maintain a humble
fluidity of spirit.

Human beings who are alive with
curiosity and wonder well
into old age, who are open

To divine mystery and holy
awe for a lifetime and,
by God's grace, for all eternity.

WILLINGLY IGNORANT!

Smart explorers
avoid quicksand.

I love playing with new ideas and tossing bright questions to and fro with friends. But there are some games I refuse to play, some places I won't go and some things I choose not to see.

I'm not planning to *turn a blind eye* to suffering, but where possible, I turn my back on evil and walk past books that glorify crime. I shun horror stories and scroll quickly out of all forms of aggressive or polarizing media. Why on earth would I choose to dwell on things that are ugly? Why would I soak my soul in bloodthirsty news and stain it with misery?

Does setting such moral boundaries make me naive? Perhaps.

But does a smart traveller purposely wade into quicksand? Voluntarily seek destruction and a slow death when there's a sunlit upland path to explore?

Besides, why would I dull my mind with darkness in any form?

My one and only mind.

Significance

Life experience gives us
a healing story to share
then love and wisdom
help us tell it.

As we get older, our physical strength tends to wane.

We may become so conscious of this, and so desperate to claw back some status or control, that we miss seeing something precious. Something vital. *That our spiritual wisdom and strength may actually be increasing.*

This gives us a splendid opportunity to help others shine!

Softened by suffering and made mellow by a lifetime of experience, our capacity to listen, understand, and encourage others may be greater than ever before.

If we can still speak, pray, and smile, we have a sacred purpose to fulfill.

We have blessings to pass on.

As our gift to the next generation.

Our legacy of grace.

Twelve Legacies to Leave

In this section, I explore a dozen ways of making a difference. To me, each one echoes an aspect of the river story, which introduces this section. (Which means I have sneaked in an extra story, providing a veritable *baker's dozen* of thirteen!)

Gifted

Once upon a time, there was a sparkling river.

It ran like a silver ribbon through a dry and dusty land. In winter, it carried dancing ice crystals on its back as it shivered and tingled its way to the sea. In spring, it rose quickly, fueled by melting mountain snow. Pulsing with energy, it reached high up the banks, catching in its glistening arms winter's broken twigs, sweeping away the clogged brown leaves of fall. Great sinews of surging water sped down the rapids and threw themselves in foaming delight over plunging waterfalls.

Wherever it flowed, the river brought life to the land. Green grass flourished on its banks, and shady trees sent their roots deep into the moist soil by its side. In summer, gauze-winged dragonflies played in the shimmering air above the shallows where shy animals came to sip fresh water.

People came too. They gathered from far and near to enjoy picnics on its banks, to lie on homespun blankets and snooze in the sun or watch the idle clouds drift by.

One sunny day, the river saw a group of children wade into the water with muddy feet. Usually, he loved to see them play, but today he noticed that, with each step, they swirled up silt. The river had never noticed this before, and he felt bubbles of irritation rise in his breast. As he surged by, he muttered under his breath, *They're making my nice clean water all dirty!* Some of the children climbed into a spreading tree and tied a rope to a sturdy branch. They swung out across the river, and with joyful cries of courage, let go. As they plunged into the river, water flew high into the air. It shattered into a million diamonds and rained down onto their streaming hair.

Grumbling at their carefree play and apparent disrespect, the river went around the bend. But there he saw something far worse. A local farmer was setting up an irrigation pump. *How dare he*, the river fumed. *Bold as brass, he's stealing my precious water, and I'll never see it again!*

Once he was on a roll, the river noticed *everybody was taking something from him, using him!* Bubbling with bitter resentment, he resolved to stop it.

In a fit of temper, he decided to stop flowing altogether. That would show them. He would keep all the water for himself. Hoard it.

Gloating in greedy delight, he pulled all the water into a secluded pond and hid it from the people and animals in a deserted rocky gully.

Soon, the grass where the river once flowed began to wither, and the animals panted from thirst. The children untied their rope from the tree and hung it on a broken fence post. Then they dragged themselves home to do their schoolwork, their bare feet leaving hazy trails in the drifting dust.

But what did the river care? *Serves them all right*, he muttered. *I'll teach them to appreciate me. Show some respect.*

For a while the river lay smug and sluggish in his hideaway. But as the days stretched into weeks, his gut began to ache. Puzzled, he looked around and noticed he was literally turning green. Alarmed, he saw scum had formed on his surface, and slime was drifting below it in stagnant strands. In the shallows, mosquitos buzzed in hazy clouds and drove him half-crazy with their humming. One dull morning he watched in horror as gasping fish floundered and floated to the surface, then lay belly-up, still.

The river hated to admit it, even to himself, but he was stinking and miserable, sick at heart and *so very lonely*.

One day, moping in his misery, the river looked up and saw great clouds forming above the misty blue hills. The clouds billowed high into the sky, rumbling and tumbling. Like grey-black towers of warning, they flashed with icy fire.

While he watched, fascinated, a smaller storm began to rage in the river's heart as, out of the breathless sky, God spoke to his rebel river.

"Hello there, Precious One. How are you?"

"I'm fine, just fine."

"Looks like you're having a bit of bother. Is there anything I can do?"

"Oh, no. It's nothing. I can handle everything myself. I don't need your help. Thanks, all the same."

"The land I gave you to water seems pretty thirsty. And the children don't play anymore. What's up?"

"Oh, I used to share my water, but they're such a greedy lot . . . plants, animals, people; *all they do is take*. And not a word of thanks, day after day. Besides, the water's all mine, and I'm going to keep it."

"Really? Has hoarding it made you happy?"

"That's not the point. It's mine!"

"Did you make it yourself?"

"Of course not. I can't make water. I received it from the rain, run-off from those hills over there."

"I see, so you were originally *given the water?*"

"Well, yes, if you want to put it that way."

"Looks like more water's coming. Where will you store it?"

"Oh, someplace 'round here."

"Why don't you let your stinking water go? All your hoarded grumbles and gripes, your griefs and sorrows, then welcome my good clean rain to wash it away? Start fresh? It would be wonderful to see clear water flowing through you again. Watch the children playing, and the land turning green."

"Ah ha, so you only care about others? I'm just a resource to you."

"Oh no! I gave you my living water for the pure joy of it. *I love to see you shine.*"

Legacy 1: Hospitality

Plus One

We may only add one,
but to that one,
we add everything.

I was grumpy and bored, slumped in a self-pity-party-for-one on my bed.

All my school friends had left boarding school and gone home for Christmas, and so had I. It was good to have a break from school, but I was surrounded by *old folks*: my father, my aunt, and my ancient grandmother! Sigh!

In contrast, I was sure all my school friends were having a wonderful time, for hadn't they said they would?

In the final days of school, we'd dreamed of the holidays and what we would do. One girl described all the yummy food her mother would cook. Another girl said she was eager to explore the snowy woods with her father in search of a Christmas tree. It all sounded great.

The next day, as the girls stuffed their unwashed clothes in their bags for their mothers to find, they laughingly boasted of all the presents they would bring back to show off next term.

As I pictured them all having fun, the gulf between us widened. And my holidays, with no party in sight, no friends nearby, and no television to watch, seemed to stretch before me forever. Boorrriing!

Suddenly, the telephone rang. It was for me. Our youth pastor, Dalbert, was on the line. He had family visiting, he said, and a full house, but he wondered, "Would you like to join us for lunch? I can come and pick you up if you like." I was thrilled. I forgot my folks (to my shame now) and scrambled to change.

When we arrived at his home, the house was alive with chatter, and laughter spilled out of the kitchen. His wife welcomed me with a friendly smile and invited me to make myself at home. I found a spare corner of carpet and squatted down to join the circle of cousins and aunts. Underneath the tree, there were piles of presents, and one of the children began to play Father Christmas and pass them around. Soon the floor was scattered with discarded paper. The youngest children, buzzing with excitement, zoomed their toy cars back and forth around my feet. I smiled at them a lot, but my heart was growing sadder. There were no presents for me.

Then I heard my name, and I lifted my head. A young child was carefully carrying a brightly wrapped box toward me, and he placed it with great ceremony in my hands. I opened the festive paper to find a box of chocolates nestled there. With a warm smile, one of the grandmas leaned over and told me, "I wrapped those especially for you."

Now it was Christmas, and I belonged.

The wrapping paper has all been cleared away now, and I have eaten all the chocolates. But the memory of that grandmother's face creased with a million smiles lingers still. Lingers to remind me that, with a little juggling, I can often find room for one more around our table or share a bar of chocolate from my own little stash.

And pass the kindness on.

LEGACY 2: KINDNESS

The Snow Dome

Kindness sees beyond itself
to recognize the potential
for wonder slumbering
in another's need.

One of my most treasured memories comes from when I was about nine years old. At that time, I was the youngest of about sixty boarding students living above the classrooms in an old school building.

The winter was unusually cold that year, even for England, and we eagerly watched the pale sky for signs of snow. We even passed around a rumor that classes would be canceled if it became very cold. One Sunday morning, we awoke to find ourselves in a magical world. It had finally snowed! We scrambled into our clothes and raced each other down the long flights of stairs, two at a time. Bursting through the school's swinging doors, we tumbled outside.

Everything was transformed.

Gasping in the cold air, we gazed up at the Christmas-card fir trees in front of the school, then across to the spiky half-buried bushes. Even the dented tin rubbish bins had been included in the bounty and wore sparkling caps of fresh snow.

After breakfast, we pulled on our mittens and ran outside again, eager to make tracks across the pristine expanse of lawn. One of the older girls showed me how to lie full-length in the snow, then wave my arms up and down to form wings. It was great fun. Within minutes my friends and I had edged a corner of the school lawn with a glittering crescent of snow angels.

As the other children drifted off to explore, or gathered in straggly teams for snowball fights, one of the older teenage boys turned to me and asked, "Would you like me to make you an igloo?" Eyes wide with delight, I managed to breathe, "Oh yes!"

We chose a spot in the center of the large expanse of lawn. He scooped up some soft snow and showed me how to squeeze it into a hard ball, then roll it over and over on the ground. Bent almost double, we rolled ball after ball until our fingers were numb and a pile of soccer-sized snowballs lay in a heap.

While I continued rolling, he began to build, forming an open ring of snowballs on the ground. As he lifted each one onto the one below and patted it into place, the round walls of a miniature igloo gradually took shape. When it was almost done, he left a skylight open at the top to let in light and air. Then he added a little tunnel, and with a flourish, he invited me to crawl inside.

I was enchanted. Sitting there in the glassy light, I was reborn as an Eskimo maiden. In my imagination, I was transported to a glittering land of ice, where I lived in a sparkling world of fleecy polar bears and moonlit glaciers.

For several days, the igloo remained on the school's front lawn even when all the snow around it had melted, leaving it sailing alone in a sea of green. If I overheard students talking about it, I eagerly told them how we had made it. Told them in glowing tones about the kind boy who had inspired the idea and given it to me.

All the snow on the lawn has melted now, silently soaked away into the grass. But the little igloo still stands in my memory like a white-domed testament to kindness, a tribute to a teenager called Morris and his generosity to a young girl.

LEGACY 3: TEACH

When you have learned to fly,

Introduce others to the sky.

Listen to their dreams and

Encourage them to try.

LEGACY 4: CREATING BEAUTY FROM BROKENNESS

Shards of shattered glass,
frail fragments in life's dust,
form soaring jewelled windows
in the Master's hand.

We sprawled on our beds or sat cross-legged on the carpet, a bunch of teenage girls, nibbling cookies, chatting, and wondering in a thousand words who we were. With time on our hands, we meandered through teenage topics, trying to guess where life would lead us and who we would become.

Our door was firmly shut against wandering children, for what did they know of teenage angst? Of mirrors, exams, and boys?

Adults were banned too, for adults were aliens, another species all together. They had never been teenagers like us—a curious blend of insecurities, fears, and dreams.

Adults were fixed. Solid. Already formed. Fossilized.

But our identities were still in pieces, and we needed time and space to rummage among the fragments, to work out what to do with it all—the remnants of childish memory, the shards of academic success, and the glittering slithers of hope.

We were still people-in-the-making, and we wanted to make good. To avoid the mistakes of our parents' generation and save the natural world and all the people in it. And most of all, we wanted to be saved and loved ourselves.

And this was a big ask.

So, day by day, as we walked between classes or stared in lonely vigil at the starry sky, we gave it our best shot. We tried to form our own unique identities and create from the scattered pieces of ourselves an adult who would be both credible and incredible.

One day, during these years of teen formation, we were introduced to a song, and it became a kind of anthem. Something we sang together at dusk, or hummed it alone at dawn.

Something beautiful,
something good,
all my confusion
He understood.
All I had to offer Him
was brokenness and strife,
but He's making something
beautiful of my life.[9]

We had no idea, then, who wrote the song.
It never crossed our minds. We were too self-absorbed to care. What we wanted was hope and a bit of gentle direction, someone to really see us and say, "You're on the right track. You'll turn out okay."

I'm all grown up now. Well, most of me is, and I've discovered the song we sang as teenagers was a slight adaptation of the first verse of a song sung by Gloria and Bill Gaither. Where Gloria had penned "made," we sang "making," for we definitely felt unfinished, like sketches of the Divine artist. His work in progress.

I still find the words of this song both soothing and inspiring. They help me remember that it's not all up to me. God has a creative hand in how I turn out too. In how beautiful I become, even now!

So, today, I want to say,

Thank you, Bill and Gloria, for your songs, and for shaping your wonderful, warm-hearted lyrics. I want to honor you for blessing at least one shy teenager and her friends. For giving us hope that one day, through God's grace, we would grow up into beautiful, loveable women.

And even more, I want to affirm you for your lives of generous, joyful ministry, which bless and inspire so many of us. Thank you for your holy and wholehearted legacy.

Legacy 5: Sowing Seed

Throughout your life,
you are free, at any time
and in any relationship
to lay land mines
or scatter seeds
of kindness.

Whichever you choose,
you will change lives,
including your own.

LEGACY 6: LIGHT RELIEF

Youth fills her arms with priceless stuff
that Midlife pays for and protects.
Then Old Age ambles in
and with reluctant sigh,
gives all the price-less stuff away!

"Come on in . . . sorry about the mess . . . mind that table, the corner's sharp
. . . this way . . ."

Grey bun bobbing, the frail lady led us into her home in the Aged Care complex. We were used to the open air of youth and entered the gloom-hushed labyrinth with reluctant steps. Both sides of the hall were lined with furniture of different sizes, and the walls of every room we passed. Eventually, she led us into the living room where she placed us on two dining room chairs upholstered in threadbare tapestry.

As she bustled off to get us tea, she sang out, "Make yourselves at home." Overwhelmed by all the stuff, we stared at each other in numb silence. How could anyone live like this? Even the air was weary. Stale. Like it had been squished and squeezed for so long that its cramped lungs had given up breathing.

With glazed young eyes, I looked around in bewildered and judgmental awe.

Along one wall, I noticed several cabinets. One was full of dusty china figurines. Another was crammed with rose-covered plates flaunting frilled gold edges. Wherever I looked, my gaze stumbled over more furniture. It tripped over sets of drawers and small stools or bumped into large chairs brimming with fat cushions. Cowering behind all this, I glimpsed the edge of a tall piano buried under stacks of sheet music. Even the walls seemed to sag under the weight of fading certificates and sepia pictures.

A few minutes later, she returned balancing a tray stacked with delicate china cups, fancy plates, and chocolate biscuits. With one arm, she swept aside some magazines and deposited the tray with a trembling clatter on a low table between us. Then she smiled warmly, "Help yourselves."

So we did.

Not sure what to say, I nibbled on the edge of a biscuit and listened. Then I listened some more. Within minutes, I discovered that every object in the room had an invisible story hiding in it. The stories were like golden chains of thought that linked her to people she loved. To a man, long gone, who once courted and adored her.

Where I saw only *stuff*, even clutter, she saw *friends*, companions keeping her company and easing her final, lonely vigil. Where I saw wrinkles and wispy grey hair, she felt surrounded by tangible proof of her prowess, of her identity and power, and of all she had done, and been, in her prime.

Before I was born.

Her home has been emptied and refilled many times since then. Repainted. Dusted. Rearranged. The house has been borrowed, then released, by a succession of old folks seeking temporary shelter.

Though I'm still in my prime (or so I like to think), I remember her sometimes when I look around at all my life stuff and survey the story-things I cherish. I think of her in quiet moments, when I pause to stroke with whimsical fingers the soft memory-things where my history slumbers.

None of my things have much earthly value now, but they have plenty of soul value. So, when blossom bursts out on the branches each year, and the urge to spring clean surges, I wave some objects on their way. But I keep a few friendly things for old times' sake.

For love.

Then I fling open the windows to let in God's good sunshine and breathe easy!

LEGACY 7: GALLANT HAPPINESS

Joy is the child of
Courage and Love,
The grandchild of

Faithful Service.

After several hours of being squished together in the car, we were eager to get out and move. Like children, we wanted to nag repeatedly, "Are we there yet?" but we were almost grown up, so we contented ourselves with peering out of the steamy car windows. Staring through the swirling sea mist, and hoping for a glimpse of the cottage that would be our home for the long weekend.

Finally, we rounded a bend and saw the cottage sprawled out before us on the moor. At first glance, it didn't look like a typical house, more like a chaotic pile of stones, as if a giant had casually flung rocks to earth, scattering them in all directions. But as the golden sun sank over the sea in a misty haze, we had just enough light to piece together some form of order, to notice one wing of the cottage stretched east and another west. To see glints of quartz in the rough-hewn granite blocks and a sheen of fading sunlight on the glistening slate roof.

When other cars pulled up behind us on the driveway and more teenagers tumbled out, we scrambled to find our bags and beat our friends to the front door. To grab the best beds and boast of being first.

As we milled around in the gathering twilight, retrieving jackets and shoes, the front door of the cottage was flung open. It cast a square of golden lamplight over the gravel and framed a plump lady who cheerfully sang out, "Welcome to my home. Come on in by the fire!"

Jostling each other, we hurried toward her, only to discover we had to ease back to walk single file down the hallway, bumping our bags either side as we went. We barely had a chance to glimpse the whitewashed walls and the slate floor before we found ourselves in a cozy sitting room.

As there were more than a dozen of us, some of our group were stuck in the luggage-clogged hallway. So, they craned their necks and shushed each other as our hostess explained how to find our rooms. Eager to get settled, we hardly heard what Mabel said, and the moment she finished speaking, we were off.

But finding our rooms was more challenging than we expected. Little lamp-lit corridors led off in all directions, and we charged down them eagerly. Full of blind bravado, we dragged our bags up twisted stairways, only to end up at tiny windows that peered out over the inky sea. Several times we made stumbling U-turns and retraced our steps to try again. We opened creaking wooden doors and found only dusty closets. We jiggled and jostled each other and squeezed past friends going in the opposite direction, equally convinced they knew where they were going. Laughing and sighing, we wished we had listened a little more and hurried a little less.

Finally, I found my room and dumped my bags by one of the three iron beds. When I straightened up, I had to tilt my head to avoid colliding with the oak beams of the sloping ceiling. After the other two girls arrived and dropped their bags, we turned as one to retrace our steps. We heard others doing the same thing, little groups of young people cascading down the winding stairways like living waterfalls eager to converge at the bottom in a pool of lamp light.

Within minutes we were settled around the open fire. Sprawled on flowery sofas, with our socked feet stretched out to toast our wriggling toes. As we nibbled homemade biscuits and sipped hot chocolate, our youth leader guided our wandering ideas and urged us to explore deeper questions of life and faith. While the old clock ticked on in the corner, we sang a few familiar songs and shared laughter and stories. Then we watched the flames silently subside until only glowing coals remained. When the room began to cool, we reluctantly wished each other a sleepy "Good night" and shivered our way up the crooked stairs to bed.

When we lifted the cold metal latch of our bedroom door, we discovered someone had entered while we were away. At first, we suspected the boys of sabotage because in the center of each white coverlet, there was a fat round lump. But when we warily pulled back the layers of blankets, we were surprised to find big earthenware bottles. Puzzled, we reached out our hands and discovered they were deliciously warm!

The next morning, we sauntered into the steamy kitchen for a relaxed breakfast. While Mabel made toast, she chatted with us. Then she slipped on two padded oven-mitts and turned toward her large solid-fuel range. Opening the oven door, she pulled out a big tray of simple oat porridge. I had never seen porridge being made in the oven before and asked her about it. "Oh, it's easier this way. I put it in the oven before I go to bed, and it cooks slowly all night."

Later, as we helped with the dishes, I asked her about our unusual hot water bottles. With a grin, she replied, "I can't afford to heat the rooms upstairs, and they're freezing in winter. At first, I used to give all my guests rubber hot water bottles, but many of the bottles 'walked.' Now I use the big earthenware bottles." With a chuckle, she continued, "They're much harder for folks to slip into an overnight bag!"

After breakfast, we bundled up in boots, coats, and scarves and pushed out into the wind. For several hours, we explored the estuary where the River Thames meets the sea. We walked in huddled groups over the lumpy winter grasses and ran along the sandy beaches, snatching up shells here and there beside the choppy waves. Above our heads, gulls rode the howling wind and screamed at us from the glowering clouds.

When we had proved our great bravery beyond all personal doubt, we hurried back to the cottage and blew in through the front door, rose-cheeked and tingling.

Once more, we settled down by the fire. Soon, Mabel wheeled in a gleaming trolly and served us morning tea. As we cupped our hands around the steaming mugs of hot chocolate, we felt the sweet warmth seeping into our chilled bones. Then, feeling we deserved a reward after our recent adventure, we reached for a second fluffy scone oozing with strawberry jam and cream.

Mabel never intruded on our teenage time or tried to imitate us to belong, but there was something comforting about her presence. Like the sprawling cottage, with all its rustic charm, I sensed she knew who she was and had a solid sense of *self* that I could depend on.

One afternoon, when we had free time, I wandered off alone to explore the cottage. On one of the whitewashed walls, nestled among the fading seascapes, I found a scrap of parchment. Stepping closer, I saw that someone had carefully written out a prayer in flowing cursive script, and I paused to read it. In the silence of the lamplit hallway, the words of the prayer really spoke to my soul. So I scurried up to my room to search for the pen and paper I had stashed in my bag.

What I copied down that day, line by line, was an extract from a version of the Toc H Prayer:

O God,
Teach us to live together
in love and joy and peace,
to check all bitterness,
to disown discouragement,
to practice thanksgiving,
and to leap with joy to any task for others.
Strengthen the good thing thus begun,
that with gallant and high-hearted happiness
we may work for thy kingdom in the wills of men
through Jesus Christ our Lord,
Amen.[10]

I wonder now how many times Mabel read that prayer. How often she chose to *disown discouragement* as she heated vast pots of water, then trudged up and down the stairs with her heavy hot water bottles.

How often she chose to forgive others and *check bitterness* when guests trampled all over her flowerbeds or peered too closely into her private spaces. How often she stifled the hurt when guests gobbled up her scones, then left without a smile or a word of thanks. (Did I do that?)

I wonder how many times she consciously decided to *leap with joy* to serve others, even when her own legs ached. Or took strength from prayer as she washed countless sheets and pegged them to writhe on the long lines where wild winds blew.

I've never been back to that teenage haven or met Mabel since. But, in honor of her faithfulness, I want to acknowledge all the Mabels of the world, both men and women.

I want to thank all the folks who choose to work with *gallant and high-hearted happiness,* where the seas run rough and the stormy winds of life howl.

I want to honor the people who serve others,
in His name,
for love.

I have a *whimsical wondering* to add to this story.

I've heard the streets in heaven are paved with gold, but when the pearly gates swing open, will we see lying there a luxurious length of red carpet? One the angels roll out with a flourish so God can personally welcome home all the Mabels of the world? The men, women, and children who notice others? Who see, and care, and do?

Will it become a scarlet tribute, not to the big people with self-pasted glittery crowns, but to all the little people? The ones with warm smiles and big hearts who serve the food and sweep the floor? Who pick the children up and wipe their runny noses, yet again? The ones who chop the wood in wintery forests and carry it to their cold and crippled neighbors? The ones who clean the cloying mud from farm machinery when the harvest has poured, like a golden river, into the granary of another?

Unlike here on earth, in the Kingdom of Heaven, will the band play and the angels cheer for all the *invisible precious people* who have kept the world turning? The ones who, with faithful joy, routinely volunteered to carry the heavy end of life's burdens, so their loved ones, or even strangers, could bear the lighter end? The ones who gallantly took the late shift, so others could rest?[11]

LEGACY 8: A GREATER VISION

"What's in
your hand?"[12]
—God

One day, a dusty shepherd was doing his usual thing; keeping solitary watch on his wandering sheep. He had done the same thing the day before, and the day before that.

His eyes idly followed a ewe nibbling a tuft of grass, but his mind drifted to the past. His past, though it seemed to belong to someone else. Back then he had dreams. He had youthful energy and high hopes. He was bursting with idealism and gallant ambitions; but now? Now he simply kept sheep. . .

Until he saw the fire. The gold and crimson flames leaping high into the quivering mountain air. The plume of white smoke pulsing with flashes of sapphire. He stepped closer, mesmerized.

Then came the voice. . .

"Moses, what's in your hand?"

Moses looked down, perplexed. All he *saw* in his hand that day was a staff, a wooden pole he used to navigate the mountain's rough terrain or herd his shaggy sheep on the steep slopes. All he *felt* clutched in his calloused palm was his old familiar walking stick.

But God saw something more than Moses, because God had a greater vision. And, in his holy heart there beat a liberating passion. For, he saw that, with his blessing, Moses could use his old walking stick to lead people out of slavery to freedom . . .

Today,

God still interrupts our ordinary days, our soul-numbing, predictable routines, to whisper with passion and purpose,

"What's in your hand?"

It's a beautifully simple question. To answer it, you don't have to gain more resources, gather more stuff, or build more strength. You don't have to sneak a look at what's in your neighbor's hand, because God only asks,

"What's in your hand?"

LEGACY 9: STILL VALID

You are a
ripple-maker.

We met in a drafty hall our hands cupped around mugs of steaming soup, hungry for warmth.

After we had chatted about the weather and glanced with a shiver at the streaming windows, she told me about the last few weeks.

"I've had to resign. I couldn't do it anymore."

I looked at her knotted fingers, blue veins throbbing beneath translucent skin.

"What did you do?"

"I ran a charity shop, mostly alone."

"Had you worked there long?"

"Oh, I volunteered there for many years, perhaps twenty, and often worked five days a week."

I must have gasped because she looked at me more closely.

"It's okay. I didn't mind. With my husband busy at work, I felt it was something I could do to help folks. But I wonder now, *was it worth it?* All the sorting of clothes. The washing and mending. The hours standing behind the counter and watching folk rummaging through the neat piles of clothes, then tidying it all up again before I went home to cook dinner."

I murmured something reassuring, and she chatted on, not really seeing me, looking out at the rain-soaked land.

"There are still so many poor folks. I wonder sometimes if I made any real difference."

I was very moved by her faithful service, and a few days later, I discovered her address and sent her a card, a tiny paper acknowledgment of her great gift to her community. A testament to all she had done for others in God's name. As I wrote, I thought of all the other old folks or those with ebbing strength who feel the same way. The ones who wonder as the sun fades, *Did my life make any real difference?*

This poem is for them.

It's also for you and I.

For the day when a job we love ends, and we are made redundant. For the day our sage advice is dismissed, or our status is diminished. For when a caring role finishes or a cherished child leaves home. For when someone bright and boisterous sweeps through our world and repaints all the walls we have built. For nights when we look back and remember. When we wonder and hope.

Each kindness remains valid and
each smile you've given.
Each hug you've shared and
each healthy meal you've made.
Each encouraging word and prayer.
Each child nurtured till they're grown.

Even when your role changes
or your memory fades,
each act of good lingers on.
Its ripples of grace are relayed
through countless generations
to strengthen, heal, and bless.

Thank you!

LEGACY 10: IF YOU'RE WILLING

When all is said and done,
writing a Will may be your
most enduring act of
courage and of kindness.

Your way to face reality
with dignity and sign out
of parenting, and life,
with a gracious flourish!

One day I visited an old man whom I had known all my life. He greeted me warmly and offered me a chair. As we began to chat, I noticed the voice that had dominated my childhood had a tremor in it now. I saw his previously ramrod straight back now sagged when he leaned closer to the fire and spread out his bony fingers.

As I sat there with him, glad of the feeble warmth in the chilly room, he talked of his faith and his family. While I listened, he wandered through years of stories. At last, he meandered to a stop and wistfully said, "I don't seem to have much say in my family anymore. They decide what happens around here. What happens to me."

I was moved by his vulnerability and the fading light in his eyes. So I took his hands in mine and gently replied, "Your family still loves you and you are more powerful than you think." He looked at me, puzzled. Unconvinced.

"They still watch how you live, hear your stories, and listen to you sing and pray." A smile slowly spread across his face, and a little gleam of the old light returned to his eyes.

"And there's another thing. You have the power to leave a legacy of blessing."

He looked doubtful, "But what can I do?"

Taking a deep breath, I stepped across an invisible taboo and said, "Have you thought of writing letters to each member of your family telling them how much you love them? Saying goodbye?" I knew he often wrote things down, so I thought he may enjoy doing this.

When he lifted his head and gave me a half smile, I took another deep breath and said softly, "Have you written a Will? Asked for expert advice?"

He turned away and stared at the fire, seeing people I could not see . . . but his back straightened a little.

"You'll make such a difference to your family if you do."

A few months later, I received a letter. "We've been to a solicitor and made our Wills. Thank you."

Bravo!

If you have the courage to sow
a fair succession plan today,
whatever the intervening weather,
your heirs can hope to reap a harvest
of peace and harmony tomorrow.

LEGACY 11: BUILDING HOPE

Youth is blessed with near sight,
and old age with far sight,
to help one another.

It's wonderful to be young, but it's also scary.

Many young people are bursting with energy, but they lack the skills to pick themselves up when life knocks them down. As a result, they tend to feel that every failure is permanent, that a relatively minor setback is a disaster. Adults can also feel this way when they are faced with an unfamiliar twist in life's path.

If they lack a listening ear, or life experience, a person of any age or background can tell themselves a story like this.

There's no point in faking it anymore. I'm done for.

I'm sick of smiling and saying, "I'm fine!" when I'm not. Who am I kidding? I'll never make it through this. I can't cope anymore. If only someone cared, but they don't. They don't even see me, not the real me. Anyway, I give up!

Stories like this are mostly told at night when things literally and figuratively seem the most dark. When we are alone, and hope slumbers.

If you are an adult you may have told yourself stories like this *repeatedly!*

And that's the point.

By the time we hit mid-life, most of us have gone through this cycle again and again. Wailed and despaired. Been tempted to give in and give up, and then summoning what little breath and bravery we had left to re-group and recover. *We discovered that the event was not the end, and it did not finish us, even if we felt sure it would!* Even if, at the time, we whispered in heartbroken solitude, "I can't go on!"

We did go on.

Little by little, we rebuilt. We coped. We prayed. We asked for help and found it. Or, lacking help, we just muddled on through. When we were broke, we added more water to the soup. When we were rejected, we wept. When we failed, we tried once more. When we lost old friends, we mourned, and little by little, we found new friends.

We adapted, then adapted again.

We surprised ourselves and others with our resilience. We grew stronger, wiser, and so much kinder.

We realized that *the end of the world* usually isn't.

But not all young folks have discovered this yet.

So if you and I can help one teenager say silently to themselves phrases like, *someone cares about me! Someone actually understands me! I'm not stupid after all.*

I'm normal! I can do it! We may literally have given them several life-changing gifts. Including the ability to see opportunities where before they saw only humiliation and defeat. Believe in their own future and their own potential. Have the courage and vision to step out of life's shadows and into the sun.

If we can help them develop the skills and find resources to bridge the *impossible* chasm in front of them we may yet contribute to a vision that lasts a lifetime.

Theirs and ours.

LEGACY 12: LOVE

You may pass on your knowledge
by the way you teach.

But you pass on life's meaning
by the *way you live your life*.

By the warmth of your smile and
the touch of your hand.

By the faith in your heart
and the hope in your eyes.

And most of all,
by your generous love.

"Ah," you may say, "but I'm empty. I have nothing to give. I'm looking for someone to love me!"

So am I.

So are we all!

But what if you only have a grain or two of love at the bottom of your empty soul? Then share that. Pass it on, and somehow, by a miracle of nature, like a seed planted in good soil, it will blossom and grow.

A couple of years ago, I boarded a plane and strapped myself into the aisle seat. Sitting next to me was a lady with a pile of beautiful fabric squares spread out on her lap. As the plane took off and the sun glinted on the rainbow of colors in her hands, I asked what she was sewing. "I make quilts for service personnel and their families," she said. I was fascinated by her work and her stories. She spoke warmly of each person's sacrifice and told me, "I especially want to comfort those who are suffering from post-traumatic stress."

I was touched to discover that over the years, she had spent thousands of hours piecing together compassion with her fingers, continuing to sew, even when it was harder for her to see.

After we had explored her work for a while, she asked me, "What do you do?" "Oh, I've just started writing a small book about butterflies," I said. "I have a few paintings in my bag; would you like to see them?"

"Oh yes."

So I reached up into the overhead locker and brought a few of my original paintings down. I told her I wanted to share my story about overcoming heartbreak and loss. That I wanted to share the love I had found from others, and from God.

Somewhat wistfully, she replied, "I don't really believe in God."

I didn't know what to say for a moment, so I looked down at her hands as she stitched the glowing fabric. I was inspired by her creativity, her dedication, and the selfless love she poured into her quilts.

Turning to her in awe, I whispered, "Perhaps you know God after all." She looked up, puzzled. So I explained,

"You may not realize it. But I already see God in you.

Because God Himself tells us that *He is love*, and people who love others *already know Him*.[13]

And His love shines through everything you do."

LEGACY 13: EXTRA

You've probably noticed that I promised you twelve legacy topics . . . so why have I added one more?

Ah, this one's quite different.

This is not a legacy you leave for someone else. *This legacy's for you.*

It's one you can claim any time.

In the morning of your life, or when your body clock is winding down. But the sooner the better as the benefits start immediately. Once you've claimed your legacy no one on earth can steal it.

Just thinking about this legacy makes my heart melt, and my mind fill with awe and I often struggle to find words to describe it. So today I'm not even going to try. Instead, I'm leaving the last word on creating legacies to their inventor, Jesus. The One who in a million ways says to you and me . . .

You've no idea how thrilled I am to present my most cherished prize to a legacy-maker like you. How delighted I am to honor you for the way you've cared for others.

Do you realize that you're my Treasure and my Father heartily agrees? We're certainly of the same mind where you're concerned!

One day we decided to put our heads together to create a surprise for you. The idea thrilled us so much that we started designing your legacy right away, even before you were born. In fact, we started ages before we'd created one atom of the world on which you stand! The Spirit was in on the plan from the very beginning and full of enthusiasm. His wise and creative counsel helped us weave joy and compassion into every part of our plan.

When the plan was ready, we shared it with our royal court. The whole place buzzed with excitement and the angels rushed forward to offer their help.

Together we poured all we had into creating your legacy. Ultimately we decided, "whatever it costs us personally, we'll go ahead. We'll even put our lives on the line. We'll do everything we can to bless you". We also decided to make your legacy as beautiful as we could. Wrap it in so much love that, even if you just caught a glimpse of our gift, it would thrill your soul.

As you can imagine, we've waited a long time for the chance to tell you all about it. Eagerly anticipated the day when we could present our legacy to you with smiles, tears and hugs.

We hope you like it!

We've called our exquisite and priceless gift—Eternal Life.

So, please, won't you come forward today and claim your inheritance? Enter the glorious kingdom we've prepared for you?

Then give us the great pleasure of embracing you as one of us? Welcoming you into our royal family with great celebration?[14]

Oh yes!

Section 5: Interlude

Security, Rest, Hope

As I face my own mortality and wait with curious hope for the culmination of all things, I'm aware of a growing sense of humility.

I feel that anything good, beautiful, or wise in my life is just a reflection of something greater and more magnificent than myself. As if I have tiptoed to the keyhole of eternity and glimpsed a glorious mystery which is yet to unfold.

And a little of its light has been transferred to my eyes.

SURVIVAL STRATEGY?

One question shimmers in earth's air.

It whispers in the waving grass where fox cubs play and tracks the hooves of mountain goats to glacial heights. It pads with pounding paw where panthers strike and trembles in the lion's claw. It glints in eagle eye and far below, it slips with sleek and netted haste through sun-splashed seas.

This restless question never sleeps . . .

What is the most endangered creature on this earth?

In every land and language, the answer is the same. It quivers in dawn's silence and thunders from noon's cloudless sky to roar with voiceless power,

You are!

For you are the last one of yourself on earth.

Knowing this changes everything. What you value and dismiss. What you fight for and ignore. Who you spend time with and who you neglect. What you eat and drink and how you work and play. For the greatest motivation in every creature's life is survival.

Or is it?

CONSERVATION?

We plead the cause of whales,
of forests, reefs, and seas,
but most of all,
we plead the cause of *self*.

There was a time, long ago, when all you knew was life. Full of childish innocence, you had no knowledge of death. But then, suddenly, a favorite goldfish
floated to the surface of the tank. Or a beloved pet curled up its paws and died.

Or worse yet, your world shattered into a million pieces when you realized,
My Dad's never coming back!

Since then, your knowledge of death has colored all your thoughts in subtle
ways. It's cast a shadow over sunny days and made you tremble when you've
heard noises in the night.[1]

Even your language has changed.

Instead of saying, "See you soon," as you wave goodbye to your family, now
you say, "Take care, travel safe." You ask your friends, "How are you? I hope
you're well."

Like you, parents in every culture under the sun teach their children how to
play survival games. How to look left and right before they cross each road.
How to eat up their vegetables so they grow big and strong. How to avoid
cliff edges where gravity lingers to lure their childish feet lower.

In many ways, *death, and loss of one kind or another, is the elephant in humanity's room.*

We fear dying socially and laugh at jokes we don't understand. We wear fashions we will soon scorn, to be accepted. We go into debt for lavish gifts rather
than appear stingy. Sometimes we even compromise our values rather than
make a fuss and *die of embarrassment.*

We fear dying physically and build fences, take pills, and visit hospitals in a bid to live forever. We fear dying mentally and hush up any hint of mental illness, in ourselves or members of our family.

We fear dying financially and sacrifice our loved ones and our sleep to work late into the night. We may even participate in a variety of morally compromising games to gain more money, or preserve our cash.

And though we may not name it, we fear dying spiritually unless, God-willing, we don't.

Because we know, beyond
all self-doubt, all fading
self-reliance, and all applause,
that God has promised us
eternal life.[2]

THE PEACEMAKER

At great cost,
we send peacekeepers
to far-off shores, yet we often
neglect the urgent heart cry
for a peacekeeper within.

But there comes a time

When we need to forgive
all we have been, and all we have not been;
all others have been, and all they have not been.
Either because we are dying,
or because we are planning to live.

PREPARATION?

Coming,
ready, or not?

Where dying is concerned, I'm a beginner. We all are, because none of get to practice dying! But this doesn't mean we need to be ignorant about death or even feel powerless when we face it.

For a start, while we live we can pack each day with significance and stay engaged and curious.

We can also gather wisdom from people whose lives are fading, or talk to professionals who are experienced in palliative care. Although there's no way to avoid death, we can still voice our fears, receive reassurance and share our hugs and stories.

By our attitude, we can choose to make saying *goodbye* easier on our own emotions, and on the hearts and minds of those we love.

A SECURE HOPE

Hope sees beyond what's seen.
Linking arms with trust and faith
it steps boldly into the unknown.

When I browsed in a hospital gift shop recently, I noticed several flowery cards bearing the word "hope." Later I saw a collection of "get well" cards jostling for space around my friend's bed. Choosing a few from between her wilting flowers, she passed them to me. As I scanned the cards, I read phrases like:

I hope you're feeling better soon . . .
I hope the treatment works . . .
I hope you're not in pain . . .

We use the word hope a lot, but rarely bother to define it, or even ask how we can acquire it. If we pause for a moment, we realize we can't just pull hope out of thin air. It has to come from something, or someone.

In daily life, I gain hope from:

Remembering past successes,
Seeing gradual progress toward a goal, and

Having friends who help me find fresh solutions.

Do any of these things help me face death?

Remembering past successes? No.
Seeing gradual progress toward a goal? Hardly.
Catching a glimpse of a fresh solution? Perhaps.

I've noticed people handle death differently. Some are afraid. Some speak of hope with their lips, but their eyes scream *fear*.

Others seem to be secure, even peaceful. Oh, they still weep. They still hug friends and cling to family members. But in spite of their obvious suffering, they have a light in their eyes, and they smile more.

When my time comes, I want to be like them. I want their peace, their security, and their trust. In all my spiritual wanderings, I've only found this kind of hope in one place, in the promises of one person. In the One who gave me life originally, all those years ago, the One who taught my tiny lungs to take their first breath. Jesus.

Why?

Because he not only created me, but he also has two further attributes that satisfy my need. Firstly, an eager loving desire to save me and secondly, the abundant capacity to do so.

Just as God drew me out of womb-darkness to give me first-life, he can draw me out of tomb-darkness to give me second-life!

He can present me with a glorious gift that no one can steal.

Therefore, whatever storms I face in life,
he's like an anchor of hope for my soul.[3]

He's the one who leads me beyond earth's winter,
to heaven's spring.

Time

As the watery womb is to an unborn child,
time is to us. We are immersed in it.

We experience time at such a deep visceral level that even in a room empty
of clocks we can sense the minutes passing.

Time fascinates us, and we watch it, mesmerized. We pass on this fascination
to our children and teach them to measure time in *sleeps*. As they grow up,
we urge them not to waste it.

When we become adults, we become time-hungry, starved for lack of minutes. Insatiable. We convince ourselves that if we had more time, we would
be satisfied, even successful. Immersed in this myth, we try to tame time and
bend it to our will. But when time refuses to play our games and eludes all
our attempts to control it, we become restless and impatient. Then, to numb
our boredom and appease our frustration, we try to *kill time* instead.

Obsessed with our gloriously puny humanity, we rarely pause to consider that
time is neither ours to tame nor kill.

It is only ours to live.

How often do we consider this? Even when we remember our birth day? How
often do we pause to gratefully acknowledge that another year of *life time* has
been our greatest gift?

Until one memorable birthday when a silent inner knowing whispers, "Don't
look now, but your mortality is showing, and your tipping point is coming.
Soon you will have more birthdays in your past than in your future."

And maybe the whisper is right,
and maybe the whisper is wrong.

For how can you measure *midlife*
if you plan to live beyond time,
into the timeless expanse of eternity?

Dusk

Nature herself
eases into night,
then again,
into morning light.

When my grandmother's steps slowed to a shuffle, she moved in with my aunt. As the years passed, the two women became good company for each other. In my school holidays, I loved to visit them. Their gray stone cottage was almost three hundred years old, and like the gnarled apple trees in the back garden, it seemed to have grown its own roots deep into the earth.

In summer, after I had made my bed and washed up the breakfast dishes, I was free to roam wherever I pleased. To escape the low-ceilinged kitchen with its dark oak beams and run in the open air. I loved exploring the country lanes and wandering along ancient bridle paths, half hidden by elder and ash trees. Each time I came to a weathered wooden gate, there was something new to see: baby chickens scratching in the dirt beside their clucking mothers, young calves nudging each other, then kicking up their heels and tails aloft, racing across the pasture. Horses idly nibbling oats and lazily swishing flies away.

Everywhere I went, I searched among the roadside grasses for wildflowers. When I had a posy big enough to fill a jam jar, I took the flowers home to my grandmother.

In winter, my aunt and I wrapped up in woolly scarves and pulled on furry boots to stomp and slip our way down the snowy, lamp-lit lanes. As the moon rose, we hurried home and blew back into the kitchen, cold-ravenous, to shake the crystals off our coats. When my aunt slid the pan of homemade soup to the front of the old stove, I unwrapped the crumpets. Then I knelt on the hearth rug and toasted them one by one on a long fork by the open fire. After we had eaten, my grandmother, my aunt, and I lingered in the sagging armchairs, licking butter from our fingers in the flickering firelight.

One afternoon, as the winter sun dipped low, I remember tumbling in from the golden garden, brimming with chatter and shivering energy. As my eyes adjusted to the softer light of the warm kitchen, I saw my grandmother quietly peeling apples at the table. I reached up to turn on the light, thinking she would be pleased.

But she simply smiled and said, "Please turn it off." So I did.

Puzzled by her request but calmed by her smile, I silently pulled out a chair and sat down beside her. I noticed, as if for the first time, the tender folds of skin on her cheeks. I saw the wisps of white hair framing her face and the soft bun at the nape of her neck. One of her hairpins was coming loose, and I reached up my finger to push it gently back in.

As we sat together in silence, I watched her veined hands lift the apples, one by one, and place them on the scarred wooden board. With even strokes, she sliced each one, then tumbled the pieces into her oval earthenware dish.

As she worked with practiced skill, the light gradually faded. The contours of her face, and of the room, softened and blurred together. The corners of the kitchen filled with shadows.

When all the apples had been sliced, my grandmother eased to her feet and slid her apple crumble into the old wood stove. Closing the oven door, she straightened up. For a brief moment, her body formed a plump silhouette against the pale gold window. Then she wiped her hands on her floral pinny (apron) and moved to turn on the light.

As a child, I loved and admired my grandmother, and I often sidled close, hoping she would slip one of her round white peppermints into my palm. But as a teenager, I secretly thought I was smarter than her. I was more educated, more in tune with real life, and of course, I would never, ever, let myself grow wrinkly and old.

Now I realize how wise my grandmother was. In raising four youngsters and living through war and loss, she had learned to move gracefully in response to nature's rhythms.

She knew the pattern of each day, the brisk and busy jobs to do in sunlight, and the tasks to ease you gently into night. She knew when to bring the washing in before the dew fell, and sensed the hour to feed the chickens and shut them up for the night. She knew when to call her grandchildren in from play to wash for supper.

And when to light the candles.

BALANCING ACT

Life's sinking sun
calls out to you,
 "Relax, ease into twilight.
 Release your goals.
 Seek slippered comfort!"

Yet from within,
a raw and primal
voice protests,
"Rest comes too soon.
Live while you can!"

And so you do!

BEDTIME

We act like children
called in too soon
from play.

Of course I pretended I hadn't seen the shadows crawling across the grass nor felt them creeping, with cool stealth, over my bare toes. But when the shadows reached the rose bushes and inched their way up, branch by branch, then thorn by thorn, I knew the call would come soon.

"Lorna, it's time to come in now."

I skipped faster, leaping high, as if I had not heard.

But then my Father's voice sang out again, more loudly than before, "Come on, Lorna. It's your bedtime."

And I knew it was.

Sooner or later, it is bedtime for us all.

Time for sleep. Time for us to let go of all we cling to so tightly. Time to die.

As the shadows of illness or age lengthen across our path, it becomes so dark we can hardly see to walk. Yet we push on faster and stumble on with determined haste. We distract ourselves with busyness and noise.

We are desperate not to notice that our sun is sinking lower.

We have so much still to do, a lifetime of words to say.

Surely, if we ignore the shadows, they will go away.

And if we refuse to name them, they will not exist.

And silently, with prayer and pleading eyes, we beg to stay up just a little longer . . .

please . . .

BEYOND TABOO

When you know I have to leave,
and you store up memories of my face,

I ask, in love, just one more thing.

Please, have the courage to be kind
and tell me what I need to know.

Say the words your heart already hums.

In my family, and in England as a whole, no one mentioned death, especially in front of children. So to protect me, no one told me my mother was dying.

No one took my hand and led me to her bedside in her final weeks of life.

This meant that while she was still alive, I was denied the chance to wrap my arms around her neck one more time, to say, "I love you with all my heart." Hospital protocol, which banned children from adult wards, also denied my mother the chance to say goodbye to me. So as her life faded, she could not call me to her side, nor brush the curls out of my eyes and say, "I have to go now, but always remember, I love you."

On the day my mother died, I was sitting at my school desk, copying notes from the blackboard. As she lay in a hospital bed, breathing her last, I was writing neatly on the lines of my exercise book and crossing out mistakes. And while the teacher's voice droned on about verbs and nouns, my daydreams escaped, as usual, and wrote stories in the sky. With all my being, I longed for the final bell, the freedom to run in the green summer woods, my hair streaming out behind me.

A few days later, when my family surrounded my mother's coffin to sing and pray, where was I? I was sitting in school, at the same scarred wooden desk, surrounded by classmates. Alone.

My family meant to be kind in having the funeral without me, but their apparent kindness denied me the chance to say goodbye. I wonder now if the adults around me could have made more healing choices.

I still don't fully know.

When we love someone, especially if we see them as vulnerable, we try to protect them from suffering.

In the short term, my family's actions saved me from several painful experiences. They saved me from the somber agony of attending my mother's funeral and shedding many tears. They saved me from feelings beyond my control. But in the long-term, their choices left me suspended in a kind of disbelief. In a limbo of uncertainly in which I wandered aimlessly for years, unsure how to voice or frame my grief, unsure who I was, or even if my mother had really died.

Now I understand that when we honor a taboo, we may unconsciously be more cruel than kind. We may wait too long *for the right time.* Or we may *keep in the dark* those who need to be enlightened. We may hide our love, and shelve our stories until it's too late to tell them.

Unless we realize the truth that honesty and kindness can coexist.

Even complement each other.

Maybe, one day soon, you and I
will have the wisdom and courage
to reach beyond our fears,

To discover that connection and
compassion are more rewarding
than masked pretense.

Then, in deep humanity and love,
we'll permit ourselves the joy of
embracing the wholeness of each other.

While there's still time.

CIRCLE OF LOVE

You were born surrounded by people
who had lived before you.

You will die surrounded by people
who will live after you.

But in the time between, you are
surrounded by people to love.

Enjoy!

LETTING GO

Once upon a time,
you did not exist.

In some mysterious
way, history was
made without you.

The pyramids
were built and filled
with golden treasure,

Cathedrals raised
their soaring spires
to touch the sky,

Great ships sailed
far across the sea,

And slaves
were freed.

Do you lie awake at night worrying about all this?

Do you feel anxious because you were not present to micro-manage history's great events?

No?

When you read ancient literature, and your name is not on the title page . . . when you look at fading photographs, gathering dust on the shelf, and your face is missing . . . do these omissions make you cry?

No?

Do you tremble and grieve for the long centuries that passed before your conscious self began?

No?

Then why waste time worrying about the time when your conscious self will end?

IN THEORY

In theory, each one of us knows we will die one day.

The signs are all around us.

Handmade signs in childish scrawl on backyard graves above beloved pets.

Churchyard graves in tidy rows, slowly sinking beneath a tangle of grass and fading flowers.

We see these signs, but do we really see them? (Have we the emotional capacity to see them and remain fully invested in life?)

Besides, not one of these signs really prepares us for dying ourselves, however well we can read. For life and death, like faith and love, are understood with a *knowing* far more profound than knowledge.

Therefore, an inner knowing that *this is my time* touches my heart more deeply than attending a million funerals ever can. Because this time, death is no longer about others, however dear they may be. This is about Me.

The Me I have known all my life.

This is personal.

QUESTION TIME

All men should strive to learn before they die
what they are running from, and to, and why.[4]
—James Thurber

Although these words are often used in reference to acquiring material things, I think they take on a more profound meaning here, for we are not talking about possessions or goals. We are talking about the meaning of our lives.

Here on our farm, it's a sunny Monday morning. Outside, summer's flowers are fading, and the birds are singing.

As I watch the fluffy clouds drift by, I am pacing the floor and pondering my own death.

Why am I exploring such a melancholy theme?

Because it's time.

We have followed the butterfly's life for a long time now, and its ragged days are fluttering to a close. It's time to think about its death. About our death.

We are used to death, of course. At summer's end, butterflies disappear. And we idly brush moths from our windowsills at dawn, hardly noticing their finely sculptured dust. But we are not used to talking about dying ourselves because, of all the taboos which have come and gone, this one still lingers.

But today, I want to be brave. I want to think about the unthinkable and speak about the unspeakable.

While I can.

Because ignoring the fact of my own death does not make it go away. It just leaves me unprepared both to live and to die. Besides, several of my school friends have already died, one still in his twenties.

When I first heard he had gone, I wanted to dismiss the news as a fable badly timed and badly told. But the void of his loss cries out to be noticed. So, today, on this sunny morning, I am choosing to wrap my courage around me and enter the screaming void, to face the loss of each friend head-on, to see, and know in my gut, that people just like me and of my age can die.

But even as I step forward into my loss, I feel a surge of rebellion, and in grief-fueled defiance, silently shout, *They were too young!* Then I shake my head at the absurdity of it all and mutter, *He was top of our class. How can all that knowledge, which he took such pains to stuff into his head, just disappear? How can all that lauded potential turn to dust?*

It's impossible.

Except, I realize, it's not. Even the wise die. And the rich. And the beautiful. And the good.

Nothing on earth can save us.

As I take the time to grieve the loss of each friend, I discover, to my surprise, that I am also grieving my own death-innocence. I am starting to accept, deep in my soul, my own mortality.

The thought of dying is confronting, and I want to flee back to naivete, to rediscover my lost innocence. Like my teenage self, believe that I will never, ever become wrinkly or old. But I am a grown-up now, and wise grown-ups face the truth, even when it's hard.

So, as the clouds drift by, I imagine myself as *gone*. But it's not easy. I am used to being here. Here in this kitchen. Sitting by this window. I look around the room. When I am gone, who will wipe the bench and water the tiny pink carnation budding on the windowsill? Who will see my geranium cuttings burst into crimson flower?

My mind wanders from room to room. I think of other people going through my things. Will anyone recognize the tangle of knitting in the bottom drawer as a teddy-bear-in-the-making? Will anyone read my unpublished stories? Rummage through my photographs and recognize faces of family?

My mind wanders beyond our four walls to visit those I love: my husband at work, my sons and my relatives scattered across the globe. How can I leave them? Drag myself away from the people I treasure with all my heart? And when I am gone, who will comfort them? Wipe their tears? Hug them close and soothe their sorrows?

When I am gone, my most cherished roles of wife and mother will also cease. Someone else will slice the bread and ladle out the soup. Others will lean forward and listen to stories of weddings and babies. Fill family mugs with hot chocolate and bake comfort cakes.

There will be nothing I can do about it. Then.

As time passes, and my loved ones begin to live and laugh again, I won't be there to laugh with them or lie upon the floor and help them find the last leafy piece of their jigsaw puzzle. And if I am gone, who will continue our traditions? Hide chocolate in each bag before the children leave for summer camp, to be found later in their tent, half-melted? Who will send cards to celebrate the milestones of their lives?

I wonder.

And as I wonder, I sense another thought lingering in the wings, a question waiting to be heard.

Let it surface! Today's the day. I am ready. But still, the question takes me by surprise,

Lorna, are you filling your mind with fear or love?

Instantly, I know this isn't just a question about dying; it's a question about living. And suddenly, within me, there's a deep soul-calm . . . and I know for sure that amidst all of life's chaos, I can choose love. Because, in spite of loss, mess, and muddle, by God's grace, whether it's my time to live or die, I have nothing to fear.

Outside, clouds are
gathering, and the sun
is fading. The treetops
are swaying in the wind.

But on the lawn below,
in a patch of sunlight,
our young dog is rolling
on the new grass and

Playfully tossing an
old bone high in the air.
As I watch him, I catch
some of his delight.

Joy bubbles up inside me
as I realize, deep in my
gut, that before death,
there is life. My life.

DEATH

Sooner or later, even a butterfly,
master of many changes,
must fold its azure wings and rest,
must die. And so must you.

You will die shrouded in as much mystery as when you were born. (For whom among us really understands miracles?)

When you were born, you were squashed and squished and pushed from your mother's womb or lifted free. But, looking back, can you even remember passing from darkness to light?

And what about now?

Do you sense, deep in your gut, that your time has come? That soon you will have to say, "Goodbye" to life? Perhaps not. Maybe you are young and fit, and you plan to outwit death and live forever. Good for you. That's a natural and noble desire. One God built into the human psyche at creation.

But what if your life is winding down? What if you've heard someone whisper the word "terminal" almost out of earshot? Then you may feel like your world, and even your body, are betraying your trust. Casting you adrift and banishing you from all that is safe and secure.

And if death is imminent, they are.

For it's your time to die to all that's familiar.

To farewell the hours and let time itself slip through your fingers.

To slide in silence, or with a primal cry of protest, naked and defenseless into the unknown.

To die.

To rest.

To sleep. Sense by sense.

To let your eyelids fall, even as the sun rises. To close your ears as the magpie opens his beak in song. To leave another mortal mouth to savor life's warm milk and find comfort in fresh bread. To lay your golden perfume on the shelf to gather dust or be dabbed, with the kiss of memory's fingers, on another's neck.

So you can sleep undisturbed. Sense-less. Serene.

Giving up, as you do, with a lingering sigh,
your most prized skill, a skill your aquatic self has
cherished since the moment of your birth:
your precious, God-given ability to breathe.[5]

Interlude

How long will
you sleep?
How long will I?

God only knows.

He also knows
the hour of
Son Rise.

Paul wanted to comfort some grieving friends in the Greek city of Thessaloniki. Because he was too far away to embrace them in person, he wrote them a letter.

In his letter, Paul does not gloss over the reality of death or the pain it causes. Nor does he mock their grief with glib phrases. Instead, he says, "I understand how much you are grieving, and I'm so sorry. But please, don't let sadness overwhelm you. Jesus has promised that if two people know him they can never be permanently separated. One glad day they will live to see each other again."[6]

When the funeral music fades, and I stand in heart-sore silence by the graves of those I love, his words have often comforted me and given me hope.

Beyond Christmas Morning

Go to sleep now; it will soon be morning.
Then you can open your present.

How many parents have soothed their children with words like this? Tucked them into bed full of hopeful trust, based only on their promise? And in response, how many little ones have settled down to sleep, even when they are atingle with wakeful anticipation?

I don't know. But I do know that God, Our Father, says something similar to us:[7]

Don't worry,
My Precious Child, it will soon be morning.

Go to sleep now while I prepare your eternal gift.
Jesus is coming to earth again soon
and he will bring it for you.
When I wake you up, it will be all ready!

It's even more exciting than the gift I gave you
the first time I came to earth. The time when
the angels burst into song and I brought
hope and life to you on Christmas morning.

ETERNITY

Gift-wrapped in mystery
and tied with ribbons of
time by royal hands,
Eternal Life lies ready
for us to unwrap.

As earthbound human beings, we can become so busy obsessing over time
that we may miss what *the end of time* really means.

While it's true that *the end of time* means the end of days and minutes, it also
means the end of measures and limits. And as I write this, I feel a tingle of
wonder. For, when time finishes, time-less-ness begins and eternity com-
mences. And eternity is where God lives![8]

Unbound by hours.

Unshackled by years.

The Source of All Life.

Boundlessly dynamic and forever free.

But can you and I even imagine eternity? Sometimes I like to try. When I do, I instinctively look up to the wide blue Australian sky. I picture myself playing there among the clouds, flying high without fear on the borders of endless space, loving every minute! Bouncing like a child on aerial puffs of gold-brushed cotton wool, laughing with glee as I slide down towering thunder-heads, bumping my way to the bottom. Then, surging with energy, soaring up on wings of joy eager for another try.

Liberated at last from grave and gravity.

Loving life.

But perhaps you think, *All this talk of eternity is airy fairy stuff, insubstantial nonsense.*

And, of course, it is . . .

But only if the moon, which has the power to pull the pounding tides, is just a disc of crumpled silver paper.

And only if the sun, which gilds the grain on countless hills, which fuels and feeds all living things, is just a golden coin taped to an upturned bowl of earthen blue.

And only if the universe, which stretches to infinity, is just a roll of ebony velvet scattered with star-paper stickers,

Then eternity, too, is a mirage.

But only then.

Section 6: Eternity

Awe, Love, Joyful Celebration

The One Who Paints the Butterfly's Wings
offers us one more stage.

MYSTERY

To a child, holy mystery does not
lie beyond the circle of *what is*.

Instead, wonder is cherished and
embraced within the circle of *what is*.

In this sense, may a child have
longer arms than an adult?

On the day you were born, you unconsciously learned many things about mystery and awe that your adult self has forgotten.

You learned the limits of attachment. That the umbilical cord, which symbolized life and safety, was the very tether you needed to release, to live.

You learned to expand the scope of your imagination, because nothing you imagined in darkness could prepare you for the glory of everything you saw in the light.

You learned that the unknown could be more tangible and desirable than the known. That being wrapped in your mother's arms was more wonderful than the solitary confinement of the womb, the limited space you so reluctantly left.

And above all, you learned about love.

And so did I.

Now, as I approach the mystery of eternity, I choose to remember my birth day. I choose to hope once more in all that's beautiful and good, to become, again, a wide-eyed learner.

Innocent of prejudice,
open to awe and
ready for love.

Eager to step, with undimmed intelligence and heart aflame, into this glorious New Earth My Father has prepared for me.[1]

Into the holy, healing
space my soul's been
seeking all along.
The home, where I belong.

Where no one's ever
lost, lonely or scared.
Where I'm free to play,
explore and hug.

The place where hope
and love leap over fear
and God, in tender joy,
wipes every tear.[2]

To hang up a banner like this you need nails. Nails in your hands.

Footnote 3

The Earth

Everywhere I look I see beauty, joy and new life.

Footnote 4

The Water

The clear water bubbles and sparkles with life

The Air

The fresh air shimmers with light and the flutter of wings

Our Invitation

God invites us to be honored guests at His banquet

Footnote 5

We Accept!

We say . . .

Yes,
& forever

The Great Banquet

Jesus has reserved a seat for you, and the meal's about to begin!

Eternal Peace

Settled and at home, at last you have time and space to enjoy peace!

Footnote 6

ENDURING LOVE

Finally, your deepest longings are met.
You begin to understand personally
the height and depth and breadth of God's love.[7]

THE END?

How your story ends depends on where you draw the finish line,
because in God's great plan *everyone's story has a happy ending*.[8]

References

Songs, Sources, and Sacred Texts

If you are an explorer at heart, you may enjoy dipping into this section.

I love reading and have discovered many wonderful authors. I couldn't resist including a few of their thoughts in this book as they have so much wisdom to share. I've included the links to their works below so you can explore their ideas for yourself.

I also refer to several Bible stories because I've discovered they're so rich in spiritual insight. These references are also included. I mostly used the New International Version of the Bible, but feel free to use your own Bible or access an online Bible in a language that suits you.

Section 1: The Egg

1. Womb. "In him we live and move and have our being." Acts 17:28

2. Birth. Celebrating the joy of seeing God's face. Numbers 6:24–26. 2 Corinthians 4:6,7

3. Change. God gives life and breath to everyone on earth. Acts 12:24–25

Section 2: The Caterpillar

1. Family Tree. One ancient historian, a doctor called Luke, wrote a brief genealogy of humanity that has a surprising twist in its tail. He traces our ancestry back beyond Adam and Eve to God Himself. Whenever I read Luke's record, shivers run down my spine. What status! What genetic potential! Luke 3:38 Later, in an ancient letter to the people of Ephesus, Paul suggests an intriguing idea. He says that, before we all adopted different family names, we were all children of The Father, God. As God is called Love, does this mean that, originally, we all had the same surname, *Love*? This idea is at the heart of one of the most splendid biblical prayers! Ephesians 4:13–21

2. Labels. In his letter to the people of Colossae Paul tells us that we are "beloved" (NKJV) or "dearly loved" (NIV). Secure in God's love, we are free to love others, and show compassion, forgiveness and kindness. Colossians 3:12–14

3. Labels. The song which I find really moving is by Jason Gray, *Remind Me Who I Am*. https://www.youtube.com/watch?v=QSIVjjY8Ou8

4. The Garden Path. To paraphrase the words of Jesus, "I've come to offer you a precious gift, *real inner peace*. The genuine article. My peace is not shallow or fickle like the peace the world demands you buy. My peace is free. It eases your worries, fills your soul and leads you to eternal rest. So don't be sidetracked by fear. Your heart is safe with me." John 14:1, 27

5. The Apple Law. The law of cause and effect is first mentioned by God in connection with Creation and the wonder of seed–bearing plants. Genesis 1:11–13 A later writer, named Paul, comments that you can't fool God! If you sow evil, you'll reap evil. But if you sow good actions that please God, and are kind to others, he will give you the *harvest* of eternal life. Galatians 6:7–10

6. Self Nurture. In celebration of life, nature and the beauty of our world, God designed the seventh day of each week to be a holiday, or *holy day*. A day to rest, re-group and remember his goodness. The first mention of this is in the book of beginnings, Genesis. Genesis 2:1–3 Later the idea was expanded to include liberation, equity and respect for all living things. Exodus 20:1–2, 8–11 and Deuteronomy 5:6,12–15

Section 3: The Cocoon – Part 1, Loss, Grief

1. Loss. In his letter to the his grieving friends in Rome, Paul honors their pain as they wrestle with grief. He says all nature is out of balance waiting for healing. Romans 8:22

2. Rest. Matthew, a close friend of Jesus, recorded his gentle, timeless invitation to Divine Rest. Matthew 11:28–30

3. Comfort. John wrote his gospel in the Greek language and the special name he calls the Spirit of God is translated into early English as the

Comforter. (KJV) and later as the Counselor. The original word means someone who comes along side us to travel through life with us. Jesus also promised not to leave us "comfortless" but to come to us so we do not need to be anxious or afraid. John 14:15–18, 25–27

4. Comfort. Paul writes about the *God of Comfort* in his second letter to the people of Corinth. 2 Corinthians 1:2–4

5. Comfort. John, a disciple of Jesus, wrote one of the gospels and several letters to his friends. In the first letter, he assures us that God loves us, and he encourages us to love each other. 1 John 4:7–12

6. A Father's Arms. In one of his stories, a biblical prophet called Isaiah describes Jesus as the ultimate Grief Carrier. He pictures him shouldering our sins and sorrows and bearing in his own heart, all our grief. Isaiah 53:1–6

7. Prayer. You can find Paul's encouraging words about God forming our prayers in his letter to his friends in Rome. Romans 8:26–27

8. Prayer. The story of the golden bowls is in the Book of Revelation, the last book of the Bible. Revelation 5:7–14. In this regal setting, Jesus is referred to as The Lamb because, like an innocent lamb, he died for our sins. An earlier prophet announced Jesus' ministry to the people with this name. John 1:29 (The idea that Jesus is the Lamb of God is woven into stories throughout the Bible.)

9. All There is to Know. In this poem I present God as a warmhearted and engaged Father who is eager to be with us. In his letter to his friends in Rome, Paul calls God Abba or "Daddy." Romans 8:14–16. The Gospels tell us that Jesus often strolled by the seaside, he sometimes ate breakfast at the beach, and he nestled children on his lap. Luke 18:15–17, John 21:7–13. You may have pictured Jesus and God as quite different, but Jesus challenges that assumption. He says to Phillip, "If you have seen what I'm like, you already know what God's like". John 14:9 Paraphrased.

10. Broken Heart. When Jesus reads in the temple he uses a scroll written several centuries before by the prophet Isaiah. Luke 4:18 and Isaiah 61:1

11. Healing Words. In his first recorded public speech, Jesus said he had come to heal the brokenhearted. Luke 4:18–19

12. Fear Less. The idea of honoring and soothing our fears comes from a TED Talk called *Fighting with Nonviolence* by Scilla Elworthy. Scilla has spent a lifetime exploring ways to respond to violence and injustice in peaceful ways. I found some of her wise and gentle insights very moving. Scilla Elworthy, TEDxExeter, 2012. Used by permission.

13. Fear Less. Anxiety and fear have plagued humanity in every generation, so several biblical writers address the topic. For instance, Paul assured his protege Timothy that "God did not give us a spirit of timidity, but a spirit of power, of love and of self–discipline." 2 Timothy 1:7 And Isaiah recorded God saying, ". . . do not fear, for I am with you; do not be dismayed, for I am your God. I will strengthen you and help you; I will uphold you with my righteous right hand." Isaiah 41:10

14. Taboo. The short poem about the comfort of friendship is from the works of Dinah Maria Mulock Craik an English writer and poet born in 1826.

15. Restore Me. After David met and conquered Goliath, the women lined the streets to dance and sing his praises. 1 Samuel 18:5–7

16. Restore Me. God sent the prophet Samuel to David's clan to choose the next king. But his father and brothers did not consider David worthy of the honor. They left David out in the field, until Samuel asked for him. The story is recorded in 1 Samuel 16:1–13, See also Psalm 23 where David says that God restores his soul.

17. Restore Me. David's song is often known as the Shepherd's Psalm. Psalm 23

18. To Forgive? I have included two quotes from Henry Wadsworth Longfellow. The second one is based on words spoken by a character in one of Longfellow's books which explored the theme of grief. It was written after his wife died at 23 years old.

19. The Grace Cascade. Paul wrote to his friends in Ephesus that God is "ten–derhearted" and you can be too. (Though it does not always come natu–rally to us!) I have used his theme to create this poem. Ephesians 4:31–32,

5:1–2 Jesus also urges us to forgive in the passage which many call *The Lord's Prayer*. Matthew 6:9–15

20. Best Friend? In the first of John's three letters he emphasizes love. 1 John 4:7–12. Other authors confirm this. For instance, Matthew concludes his account of Jesus' ministry, and quotes him saying, "I am with you always, to the very end of the age." Matthew 28:20

21. Music. The story of the prisoners of war who were asked to sing comes from ancient Babylon. I have paraphrased the conversation between the captors and the captives. Psalm 137:1–4. The illustration I have painted includes some lines from the score of Ode to Joy by Ludwig van Beethoven.

22. Music. I have blended the themes from two songs, or Psalms, because both of them speak of restoration, music and laughter. David's song of restoration, and a psalm by an unnamed author. Psalm 40:1–3 and Psalm 126

23. Long Weekend. John describes the events of the original Easter Weekend. John chapters 17–20. One of John's contemporaries, Paul, also boldly states that the resurrection of Jesus was verified by at least five hundred witnesses.1 Corinthians 15:1–7, 51–57

24. Passionate Motives. John says that Jesus died for us because he loves us. John 3:16–17. I was surprised to discover that Jesus didn't die only for his friends. For people he liked, or people who liked him. Instead, *he died for everyone*. For those who hated him, and those *who were killing him!* Because his love was greater than their hate. Because he wanted to give each person on earth every opportunity to be saved from eternal death and receive instead eternal life. Romans 5:1–8

25. Home. The original tale of the wandering son is recorded by Dr Luke in his biography of Jesus. It is one of three "lost and found" stories Jesus tells. After each story, Jesus pictures a grand celebration where friends, angels, and especially God overflow with joy! All three stories are in Luke chapter 15.

26. Home. Paul writes that because of Jesus, anyone, however far away from God they are, and whatever they have done, can be brought near again.

Welcomed with open arms. Ephesians 2:12–13 This whole chapter explores the theme of separation, reconnection and reconciliation.

Section 3: The Cocoon – Part 2, Resilience

1. Courage. This tale is inspired by a first century writer named John. In his stories, a great knight named "Faithful and True" defends humanity against a wily red dragon. This evil dragon hides behind many names, for instance, "The Father of Lies", "Ancient Serpent", "The Devil", and "Satan". John 8:44, Revelation 12:3, 7–9 In contrast, John lauds the Knight as, "The Lion of the Tribe of Judah", and "King of Kings". He is also called Michael, the warrior name of God. John's dramatic stories lead to the thrilling finale of the entire Bible. Revelation 5:5, 12:7–9, 19:11, 16 and 21:1–6 In view of the intense spiritual battle that John describes, Paul recommends we all put on a kind of soul–armor. Ephesians 6:10–18

2. The Making of a Brave. The short poem is by Amelia Earhart. I first read it many years ago from an unknown source.

3. Encouragement. The idea that "it is more blessed to give than receive" comes originally from the words of Jesus, as quoted by Dr Luke in Acts 20:35.

4. Mirage or Miracle? The only perfect place to live is the beautiful city designed by God! Hebrews 11:8–10, Revelation 21:1–5, 22:1–6

5. The Whole Truth? You can find the story about the lady who gathered thorns instead of flowers in the final chapter of a little book called Steps to Christ. Ellen G. White, *Steps to Christ* (Nashville Tennessee: Southern Publishing Association, 1892) 121 Please note, this book has been reprinted many times and later editions with different page numbers are now available.

6. The Whole Truth? These wonderfully cheering words are a paraphrase of Paul's advice to his friends in Philippi. Philippians 4:4–9. Also adapted for the topic Rocks and Mountains.

7. Ruminating. The idea that God is our nurturing Shepherd comes from a psalm of David. Psalm 23

8. Entitled. A.B. Facey, *A Fortunate Life (Fremantle, Fremantle Press 1981)*. Albert was born in 1894 and died in 1982, shortly after his autobiography was published. He describes his early life in Western Australia, when the raw bush country was being cleared for farming.

9. Entitled. Colin Thiele, *Sun on the stubble* (Adelaide, Rigby Limited 1964) This amusing and dramatic book has been reprinted many times, and more recent editions are available.

10. The Shield of Good Humor. I had fun creating this topic, and later realized I instinctively blended several biblical themes. In a letter to his friends at Ephesus, Paul writes about a kind of spiritual armor, including a shield. Ephesians 6:10-17 He also says we are sons and daughters of God. Romans 8:14-16 and 2 Corinthians 6:18 Peter exults that God has called us out of darkness into his marvelous light and called us as royal! 1 Peter 2:9

    There's also potential to take this topic far deeper, because Paul says that Jesus was able to despise the ultimate shame using a kind of *joy shield*. This refers to a magnificent story worthy of closer study! See Hebrews 12:2

Section 3: The Cocoon – Part 3, Transformation

1. The Chatty Caterpillar. God listens and cares about us when we cry out to him. Psalm 55:16-18, Ps 61:1-3

2. The Chatty Caterpillar. The Spirit of God is like the wind whispering. Jn 3:8 1 Kings 19:11-12

3. The Chatty Caterpillar. God offers us a glorious transformation. 2 Corinthians 3:17-18 and 4:7

4. The Ten to One Ratio. It's hard to give long term, especially when no one says "thank you", as Jesus himself discovered! You can read the two stories, which I have blended to together, in the Gospels. Matthew 8:1-3, Luke 17:11-19

5. The Ten to One Ratio. As we receive God's lavish love, we're empowered and inspired to pass it on. Matthew 10:8

6. Grace. God says he loves everyone equally, whether or not they respond. You may even need an umbrella! Matthew 5:43–45, John 3:16–17

7. The Journey of a Lifetime. You can read the *Lord's Prayer* beginning with "Our Father" in Matthew and Luke. Matthew 6:9–13 and Luke 11:1–4. The concept that God is Our Father, is astounding enough, but there's more! Jesus also identifies Himself as our brother and welcomes us as joint heirs. Did you hear that? In heaven, you and I will be considered royalty! Perhaps, according to God's promises, *we already are!* Romans 8:14–17, 1 Peter 2:9

8. The Journey of a Lifetime. In his gloriously inclusive prayer of grace, Paul hints that, as Children of God, our original surname should really be "Love"! Ephesians 3:14–21

9. A Credit to the Family. If you search online, you can find several singing wells. In some film clips you can even hear the people chanting. For instance, The Singing Wells in Samburu Kenya.

10. A Credit to the Family. Jesus said how much he valued those who helped their "brothers". Matthew 25:34–4

11. Dalmatians. These lines in various forms have been attributed to several authors, including, James Truslow Adams, Edward Wallis Hoch, Edgar Cayce, and Robert Louis Stephenson. Take your pick! It sounds like the themes of tolerance and understanding resonate with a few folk!

12. Dalmatians. In his letter to the people of Rome, Paul wrote with deep conviction, "God loved us and came to save us before we were good or beautiful. While we were still spotty, and before we had our "act together." Romans 5:6–8, paraphrase mine.

13. The Game of God. There are several references to hide and seek in the Bible. You can read about the time God first called out, "Where are you?" in Genesis. Genesis 3:8–9 A later writer named Jeremiah paints a different picture of God. In his story, it's God who is lingering in the wings, hoping we will find him. Jeremiah 29:11–13 Other authors picture him eagerly stepping into history because he wants to be with us. Matthew 1:23 Or record the three significant stories Jesus told about lost coins, sheep and people. Luke 15 There's certainly plenty to explore! In one amusing and

inspiring story, a very little man acts like a boy and climbs a very big tree. He thinks he's the only one playing hide and seek, but is he? Luke 19:1–10

14. Ice, Eggs, and Grass. Paul states that God is eager to free and transform us. 2 Corinthians 3:17–18 And angels have been commissioned to assist him in the joyful task. Hebrews 1:14

15. God's Eraser. If you ask Him to, God says He will forgive you abundantly. He will search for a big thundercloud to wipe the sky clear of your mistakes. Then throw all your sins into the deepest part of the sea! Isaiah 44:22–23, Micah 7:18–19

16. In Deep Water. Do you want a fresh take on forgiveness? Take a look at one or two of these biblical references. You'll discover the cost, and the glory. The suffering, and the liberation! *Go on, it's worth it!* Micah 7:18–19; Isaiah 53:1–6, 11; John 8:36, 1 John 1:8 – 1 John 2:2

17. Transforming Love. This poem has been attributed to various authors, including Roy Croft. However, according to an entry in Wikipedia, "Roy Croft" is a pseudonym and the most likely author is Mary Carolyn Davies.

Section 4: The Butterfly

1. My Normal Self. Bursting with lyrical insight and gratitude, David praises God for his life and body. Psalm 139. In verse 13, he even mentions "knitting"! He also asks God to remember him when he grows old and help him create an enduring legacy before he dies. Psalm 71:17–18.

2. My Normal Self. Isaiah writes in glowing terms about God's life-long care. Isaiah 46:3–4

3. Shy. If, like me, you have a scar or two, there is a song which may both soothe and move you. It is called, *Scars to Your Beautiful* and it's sung by Alessia Cara.

4. Box of Scales. The Golden Rule has been with us for thousands of years, ever since Dr Luke recorded it in his stories of Jesus. John also recorded Jesus' command to love each other. Luke 6:31, 36. John 13:34–35. Micah recorded an even earlier scale for living a good life. It's sometimes used

by charities today and called The Micah Code. Micah 6:6–8. You may also have heard of a set of scales given to a newly liberated people called the Ten Commandments. Exodus 20:1–17

5. Shoulds. Mathew records this summary of the core values of Jesus. Matthew 22:34–40

6. The Fear–Love Continuum. The pivotal verse about good and evil is in John's biography of Jesus. John 10:10, which I have paraphrased. For the Jesus as the Truth and Way, John 14:6, for peace, John16:33 and Philippians 4:6–8.

7. Mirror of Truth. Jesus spoke about "the truth setting us free". He implied *that he was the one who could liberate each human heart.* John 8:31–36

8. Transforming Truth. There are several descriptions of the golden chest and the tent where it was housed. Try, Exodus 25:10–22 for the chest, (also described as an "ark") Exodus 25:31–39 for the golden lamp and Exodus 26:1–6 for the curtains. In one of the earliest psalms, the Sons of Korah sing to God. They remind him how much he loves them, and say that in him, mercy and truth kiss each other. Psalm 85:7,10 (See KJV) Years later, in the Gospels, John said that Jesus did not come to condemn the world, but to save it. John 3:17

9. Legacy 4: Creating Beauty from Brokenness. The song Something Beautiful was written by Gloria Gaither and is sung by Gloria and Bill (William) Gaither. A creative and devoted couple who have dedicated their lives to blessing others through their music and ministry. You can find the full version of their song, and many more of their glorious melodies, online.

10. Legacy 7: Gallant Happiness. This includes a version of the Toc H Prayer. Talbert House, where this prayer was created, was founded in December 1915 to encourage hope, equality and good will during the First World War. As the motto above the door stated, 'All Rank Abandon, Ye That Enter Here'.

11. Legacy 7: Gallant Happiness. Ah ha, so you know there's no mention of a red carpet in heaven? Perhaps not, but the Bible certainly refers to God giving certain people "a red carpet welcome"! Especially those who serve others in simple, practical, ways. Jesus repeatedly noticed people who

quietly cared for others. He said they were already living like citizens of his kingdom, and he took their kindness to heart, as if they had given him a personal gift. See Matthew 25:34–36 for his welcome and Matthew 10:42 for handing some one a drink of water. See Mark 12:41–44 for the generous–hearted widow. And Revelation 21:21 for the golden streets and pearly gates!

12. Legacy 8: A Greater Vision. From shepherd to savior–figure. When God called Moses to save his people, he showed him to begin by using what he already had. Exodus 4:1–2

13. Legacy 12: Love. You may think, "I'm not sure about God." But if you know how to give and receive love, you already know Him, *because God is love.*" 1 John 4:7

You may also enjoy this song about living a life of loving commitment. It's by Wynonna Judd and called Testify to Love. https://www.youtube.com/watch?v=2Kd5ehaYE8Y

14. Legacy 13: Extra. Throughout the Bible there's a sense of eager urgency with reference to God's saving plan. The excitement peaks in The Gospels and is splendidly brought to life in the final chapters of the book of Revelation. (It's as if Jesus can't wait to give us eternal life.) I therefore tried to capture some of his excitement when I wrote this topic. Feel free to explore the following references which provided the raw material

For the original plan see John 3:16–17 and for The Spirit's commitment see Romans 8:1–2, 14–17. For the angel helpers see Luke 2:8–14 and Hebrews 1:14. And finally, for Jesus' warm–hearted invitation and legacy see Matthew 25:34–40. Note: I used the word enthusiasm for the attitude of The Spirit because it means *inspired* or *God breathed*. I love this word. Sometimes, when I feel a surge of enthusiasm and gratitude welling up inside my heart, I remember that The Lord of Life wants me to feel fully alive like this on a daily basis!

Section 5: Interlude

1. Conservation? Our fear of death casts a shadows over all our lives and relationships. Hebrews 2:15

2. Conservation? As with most things, the wonderful gift of eternal life comes with *terms and conditions. But* unlike most earthly *terms*, these terms have not been designed to trip you up! In them God simply invites, "won't you let me spring clean your heart? Empty out all the sorrow, sin and brokenness that's lingering there? All the regrets and mistakes that are weighing your soul down?" If you answer "Yes please. Take them away!" Then he's free to get to work! Cleanse your soul, and with great delight pour all his divine hope, joy and love into your heart instead!

   So how did he get these priceless soul-gifts? Ah, that's the wonder of it! Jesus walked on foot all the way to the cross to buy them for you. Then he arranged everything and filled in all the legal paperwork. This means that the moment you say "Yes" to God, he has the right to adopt you into his royal family and throw a great party to celebrate! From that moment on, everything changes, because you have access through his Spirit to all the resources of the royal court – why? Because you're family, that's why! New life John 3:16-17, Heavenly celebration Luke 15:1-7, Becoming a royal heir Romans 8:14-16 and Galatians 4:4-7. Enjoy!

3. A Secure Hope. The idea that Jesus will save the world in the future is familiar to many people. But his actions also give us hope *now*. And, his sure promises act like an anchor for our souls. 1 John 5:11-12, Hebrews 6:17-20

4. Question Time. The quote about knowing our values comes from James Thurber, an American writer and cartoonist. Original source unknown.

5. Death. In many Christian traditions, people believe that the soul goes to heaven instantly when a person dies. Some grieving families find this comforting, but, when I explore the Book of Beginnings, Genesis, it tells a different story. There God actively unites body and breath to make a "living person" (Genesis 2:7). Therefore, when the "breath" leaves, only the body remains. Paul agreed with this and wrote to his friends in Corinth that "death is like a sleep" and those who die are resting until Jesus comes. (1 Corinthians 15:51-52, 1 Thessalonians 4:13-17) To me, this is a great comfort. How wonderful that loved ones who have died, know nothing of their loss. Know nothing of the grief they leave behind or the actions of successive generations. Instead, they literally "rest in peace". Then, when Jesus comes, they wake up, and all of us get to begin our new life together! What stories we will have to tell! John echoes the idea of sleep in

the Gospels, where he tells a story of Lazarus, one of Jesus' friends. When Lazarus dies, Jesus goes to visit the family, but his comfort goes beyond what anyone expects. You can find the story in John's Gospel. John 11.

6. Interlude. You can read Paul's encouraging message to his grieving friends in his first letter to the people of Thessaloniki. 1 Thessalonians 4:13–17

7. Beyond Christmas Morning. In his Gospel, John says that Jesus is preparing a place in eternity for us and his joy overflows as he writes (emphasis mine), "and He is coming again so we will *see Him.*" John 14:1–3 Because Jesus already came once, at Christmas, many say this promise refers to "The Second Coming." Revelation 22:20–21

8. Eternity. An ancient sage called Isaiah pictured God as "living in eternity", but also living so close to us that he can reach out to revive our flagging spirits right now! Another wise man wrote to his protégé, Timothy, that God lived in dazzling light. Can you imagine what a splendid home that would be? Isaiah 57:15 and 1 Timothy 6:16

Section 6: Eternity

1. Mystery. We may think that the biblical writers understood everything but, just like us, they were spiritual explorers. Life puzzled them too! Yet they did not become cynical, lose momentum, or lose their zest for wrestling with big ideas. Paul touched on the theme of mystery in his letter to the people of the Greek city of Colossae. Colossians 2:1–3. See this in the New International Version (NIV), or verses 1–4 in The Message. (MSG)

   David, the Shepherd King, was filled with awe when he pondered the magnificent acts of God. David imagined God as a hand's on God, shaping the glowing moon, and sparkling stars, with his fingertips! Psalm 8. When we stroll through a beautiful garden, or hike among majestic mountains, we sense that's how the earth was designed to look. But, God knows, often this earth looks tatty and threadbare. Scarred, abused and bruised. That's why God has promised to restore it and make everything new. Revelation 21:1, 22:1–5

2. Mystery. John, the friend of Jesus wrote about eternity and what it would be like. He said that everything would be made new. Even you and I.

And all our tears would be wiped away for good. Oh yes! Revelation 21:1, 4Welcome Home. Matthew records these words of Jesus (para-phrase mine):

3. "Welcome home! Come on in, the Kingdom's yours!" Matthew 25:34. This glorious welcome cost Jesus dearly, as the lingering nail-scars in his hands reveal. John 20:25

4. The Earth. Revelation 21:1

5. Our Invitation. The Bible sometimes uses imagery to illustrate a spiritual truth. When Jesus (described here as The Lamb) welcomes those who love Him into eternity, He says the first meal will be full of celebration. Like a wedding banquet where everyone is considered to be family and invited to come! Revelation 19:6-9

6. Eternal Peace. This picture was inspired by Isaiah's descriptions of the New Earth. Isaiah 11:6-7 and 65:24-25

7. Enduring Love. For a glorious prayer about God's love see Paul's letter to the people of Ephesus. Ephesians 3:14-21

8. The End? According to John, God wants everyone's story to have a happy ending. John 3:16-17

List of Topics

SECTION 1: THE EGG

Womb. The creative wonder of life in the womb. 11
Birth. Our first breathless view of mother's face. .11
Change. Our senses awake to light, taste, and color 13
The Greatest Gift. The God-given treasure of life itself. 15
Wonder. Appreciating and exploring nature's beauty 16

SECTION 2: THE CATERPILLAR

The Secret Nursery: Discovering where butterflies come from 18
Family Tree. Identity and belonging 19
Labels. The names we bear and live 28
Hall of Mirrors. Understanding and processing distorted feedback 31
Fantasy. Hiding in others' stories, then beginning to create our own 38
Great Timing. Predicting how our day will turn out 41
The Storyteller. Evaluating the stories we tell children (Story topic 1) 42
My Story. The stories we tell ourselves (Topic 2) 45
Running a Story Audit. Monitoring the stories we tell ourselves (Topic 3). . . . 52
Painting into a Corner. Avoid trapping yourself or others (Topic 4) 54
The Garden Path. Be careful whose tales you believe and who you follow
        (Topic 5). 57
Roles. The roles we play which reveal our inner story (Topic 6) 60
Typecast? Living beyond typecast roles (Topic 7) 61
Teaching Others the Ropes. Being patient with beginners 64
The Composite Bug. Comparison, desires, and expectations 65
Resentment. Releasing a grudge 67
Our Club of Choice? Moving from being victims to being friends 69
The Apple Law. The law of cause and effect in our own lives 71
Self-Nurture. Initiating self-care and having a regular day off 72
Nurturing Others. Recognizing and healing past hurts 75
Curiosity. Remaining curious, even as adults. 77
L Plates. Remaining lifelong learners 78
My Place. We all need some personal space to call our own. 82
Self-Confidence. A story of eggs and gaining life skills 83

Confident Together. How community helps build confidence 85
Footprints. Learning life lessons from older women. 89
Growth. Short poem 91

SECTION 3: THE COCOON – PART 1, LOSS AND GRIEF

First Response. Each person's response to loss is unique 93
Loss. Two lambs and grief in nature 96
The Unknown. Grieving for people and unmet goals 97
Refuge. It is natural to seek a safe place to hide 99
Numb. Short poem on self-protection 100
In Shock. Grief makes us temporarily dumb 101
Safe People. Some people are trustworthy; some are not 102
Rest. Short poem on coming to Jesus for rest 103
Comfort. The healing role of The Comforter 104
A Father's Arms. Being embraced and comforted on God's lap 106
Touch. The healing power of touch, which is beyond words 107
One Mother. Building a sand village and the power of memories 108
Two Mothers. The value of maternal and family nurture 111
Latent Power. Even after loss, some choice remains as we move forward . . . 114
Prayer. God speaking up for us 114
Why? Questioning why things happen as they do 116
All There Is To Know. A father and child walking on the beach 117
In Memoriam. Options for dealing with painful anniversaries 118
Creating Meaning? Finding ways to use grief for good 121
Values. Holding on to our values in turbulent times 123
Broken Heart. God comes to heal our broken hearts 125
Healing Words. Jesus's brief speech in Luke's gospel 126
Adoption. We may subconsciously adopt fears, then raise them 126
Fear Less. Hearing the stories fear tells and easing anxiety 127
Taboo. Each culture creates taboos. Many leave us lonely 131
Restore Me. When we take a tumble, God picks us up 136
Recovery. We can't rush grief recovery. Healing takes time 142
Guess Work. Friends are not mind readers. If you need help, say so! 145
To Forgive? Exploring the healing power of forgiveness 146
The Grace Cascade. Passing on God's grace to others 151
Friends. In times of crisis, some friends leave, and others stay 152
Best Friend? Be kind to yourself and shelter in God's care 156
Music. Comfort and being inspired to sing a new life-song 158

Long Weekend. Reflections on the origin of Easter 162
Passionate Motives. Reflections on Jesus's decision to die for us 163
No Contest. Children competing for their mother's love. 167
Home. Welcome, forgiveness, and restoration 167

SECTION 3: THE COCOON – PART 2, RESILIENCE

The Seed. Using life's troubles as compost to nourish growth 175
Courage. Tale of a brave Knight fighting a dragon 178
Our Arena of Courage. Living with courage on life's messy days 184
The Making of a Brave. Paying myself to act with courage 185
The Master Artist. Noticing the good in others and helping them shine. 187
Encouragement. Mentoring others. 188
Two Gifts. When all you have to bring is a broken heart 188
Shame and Hope. Real education and the building of confidence 190
Impossible. Remembering past achievements and gaining courage 194
The Merry-Go-Round. Slowing down and simplifying life. 198
One in a Hole. Appreciating the value of good questions 203
Two Emotional Paths. Choosing how we act when life is unfair 204
Sink or Swim? A person who feels overwhelmed is rarely polite 205
The Tally. Adding up a person's flaws or good qualities 208
101 Ways. We say, "You hurt me" in lots of ways 209
The Lamp. A teenage daughter and her father start to understand 211
Mirage or Miracle? Seeking perfection makes us restless. 216
Half a Mind? Being selective about what we store in our minds. 220
Mind Travel. Choosing our mental "destination" with care 222
Perspective. How it affects our mood, emotions, and decisions 224
The Whole Truth? Being randomly selective or holistic 226
Thorny Moments. Who we are is greater than a single setback 231
Ruminating. Repeatedly dwelling on past hurts 234
Entitled. Believing the world, and others, "owe" us compensation 238
Spring Clean? Clearing out mental rubbish 246
The Honey Pot. Treasuring good memories. 249
Cultivating Joy. A few lines about sowing and reaping joy 251
Speaking Up! Your voice matters because you matter 251
The Hearing Test. Really listening to each other 254
The Shield of Good Humor. Deflecting barbed comments. 255
Play. Recognizing the value of play for all ages 257
Two Doors. Moving on and re-investing in life and adventure. 260

SECTION 3: THE COCOON – PART 3, TRANSFORMATION

Magic Wand? Craving transformation without change 262
Beyond Self. Self-help is often really "other-help." 263
Transformation? Polishing shoes 264
The Chatty Caterpillar. A caterpillar seeing what's possible 265
Baby Steps. Being willing to grow slowly, like a tree 268
Ambivalence. In all relationships, we experience mixed feelings 270
Integrity. Bus ride and the price of integrity 272
Free to Be Human. Not allowing ourselves to be enslaved by things 274
Enough. Short poem on being content with what you have. 275
Ten Percent Tears. Grumbling or gratitude? 276
Do You Like It? The vulnerability of giving 277
The Ten to One Ratio. The risks we take when we offer help 280
Grace. Appreciating the blessings that rain down on us 284
Interior Design. Becoming more aware of my mind's "interior design" 287
The Journey of a Lifetime. Traveling toward belonging and inclusion 287
A Credit to the Family. Encouraging other members of our human family. . 291
Joy. Short prayer 293
Alchemy. Turning the "base metal" of adversity into love and wisdom 293
Dalmatians. We are all a mixture of good and bad, in need of grace 294
The Bridge. Taking the initiative to meet new people. 298
The Bridge of Hope. Role modeling a way forward for others 301
The Game of God. Playing spiritual hide-and-seek. 301
Ice, Eggs, and Grass. Transformation involves costs and rewards 304
God's Eraser. God's desire to wipe out our sorrow, sin and grief 306
In Deep Water. A story about God casting our sorrows into the sea 307
Transforming Love. A poem about how we use the lumber of life 310

SECTION 4: THE BUTTERFLY

New Year. Seeing each day as a new beginning .313
Launch Day. Don't wait for the perfect conditions; live by faith. 313
Freedom. Using the small freedoms we have 316
My Normal Self. Appreciating and relishing every stage of life 317
My Normal World. We cannot own normal, but we can help create it 319
Butterflies Can't Eat Cabbage! Making peace with regret 325
Shy. Living beyond our limitations 327

Tall Poppy. Having the courage to be creative. 329

Good Company. Everyone has something unique and valuable to offer 332

Wing Wardrobe. When your life changes, seek advice without shame. 335

Treasure Hunt. The love of learning is caught more than taught 337

Vocation. Making a meaningful contribution, whatever we do. 337

The Box of Scales. Exploring our inherited values, Part A. 338

Shoulds. Exploring our inherited values, Part B. 342

In a Flap. Balancing rights and responsibility. 348

Scorn Power? Short piece about values and tolerance 350

The Store of the World. Short poem about values. 351

The Gap. Creating a bridge between the ideal and the real. 351

The Visionary. The benefits and costs of idealism. 354

Capacity? Short poem about our vision exceeding our capacity. 360

Gap Fatigue. Idealists need rest, and to be replenished. 361

The Fear–Love Continuum. Living more from love than fear. 367

Expectations. How are hidden expectations shaping your life?. 369

Bread. We can only give what we have, so can others. 371

Expectation Training. We teach people what to expect of us. 373

Amore. Living motivated by love 375

A to B. Life takes us on many detours. 377

Synthesis, Part 1. After analysis comes chaos. 377

Synthesis, Part 2. Dismantling things and ideas, then rebuilding 382

The Mirror of Truth. Facing what's real about ourselves 385

The Door. Opening our hearts to truth. 389

True Accountability. Empowering ourselves. 390

Demanding Truth. Two stories about a broken platter. 391

Transforming Truth. God honors both truth and mercy 394

Good Question? Questions hold no threat if we are living the answers. 397

Loitering with Intent! Questions always loiter on the edge of knowledge . . . 397

Circles of Knowledge. The more we know, the less we know 399

Willingly Ignorant! Choosing to be ignorant of evil 404

Significance. Bridge to Legacy section 405

Gifted. A story about a river to introduce the Legacy section 405

Legacy 1: Hospitality – Plus One. Welcoming others into your home. 410

Legacy 2: Kindness – The Snow Dome. Creating an igloo 411

Legacy 3: Teach – Mentoring others and passing on your skills 413

Legacy 4: Creating Beauty from Brokenness – Inspiring hope. 416

Legacy 5: Sowing Seed – Choosing what we plant 418

Legacy 6: Light Relief – Simplifying life and reducing our stuff. 420

Legacy 7: Gallant Happiness – Reflecting on buoyancy of spirit 421
Legacy 8: A Greater Vision – Using the resources you already have 426
Legacy 9: Still Valid – Your contribution lingers long into the future 427
Legacy 10: If You're Willing – Having the courage to write a will 431
Legacy 11: Building Hope – Helping young people through tough times . . . 432
Legacy 12: Love – An example of human love reflecting divine love 436
Legacy 13: Extra – This is a legacy for you! 439

SECTION 5: INTERLUDE

Survival Strategy? Our greatest motivator is survival 442
Conservation? In all settings, we long to survive 443
The Peacemaker. We need to make peace with who we are 444
Preparation? We cannot be good at dying 444
A Secure Hope. Where does hope come from? 445
Time. Immersed in time, we have no concept of time–less–ness 448
Dusk. Story of my grandmother and easing into rest 449
Balancing Act. A short poem about the push–pull of living and dying 451
Bedtime. Knowing when it's time to let go of life, and sleep 452
Beyond Taboo. Openly talking about life and death in our families 453
Circle of Love. At both birth and death, we are surrounded by people 455
Letting Go. Don't be anxious that you will not exist 455
In Theory. Knowing we are dying 457
Question Time. How does our knowledge of death help us live now? 458
Death. Relinquishing control and returning your birth–gift of breath 462
Interlude. Having hope in God affects how we view death and grieve 464
Beyond Christmas Morning. Sleeping, then waking to a new life 464
Eternity. The gift of a miracle 465

SECTION 6: ETERNITY

Mystery. Embracing the glorious unknown 468
Welcome Home. Jesus's hands nailing up a banner 472
The Earth. Everything is beautiful and new 475
The Water. The water sparkles with life 476
The Air. The air is clean and clear 478
Our Invitation. Jesus invites us to his banquet 480
We Accept! People welcome the invitation 482
We're Coming! Everyone comes running, letter in hand 484

The Great Banquet. There is space for all around God's table 487

Eternal Peace. Peace reigns, and even the animals feel it. 489

Enduring Love. There is harmony throughout the universe 490

The End? In Jesus, everyone's story can have a happy ending. 490

FINAL PAGE

A Final Blessing. A prayer from me to you! 517

Books You May Enjoy

The following books are filled with stories of hope, healing, and encouragement. When I read them, even in my loneliest moments, I feel like I am among friends!

Nothing Left Unsaid

In her tender and soothing book, Carol Orsborn explores a time of personal significance in her own life. Woven though her stories are short poems and prayers. I have included two of my favorites for you below, with the original italics shown.

Exhausting Yourself
If thoughts of recovery, cures, and miracles consume you,
what of you will be left to heal?

Busy yourself instead with love,
and you create the environment in which
healing will most likely take place.

Fulfill Your True Human Potential
Love can grow so large it breaks your heart.
Compassion for another can set your soul on fire.
Clarity of vision can shatter your everyday illusions.
Life can leave you shivering naked and awestruck
before the mystery.

Who says the spiritual path leads only to happiness?

Carol Orsborn, *Nothing Left Unsaid* (Berkeley, California: Conari Press, 2001), 34, 16 Italics in the original.

Kitchen Table Wisdom

As a child, Naomi grew up in a family of pragmatic doctors who valued academic excellence. At first, she followed in their footsteps but later she found more caring ways to connect with her patients, with her own emotions, and with her colleagues. In these stories, she recounts her quest for personal healing and how she discovered that embracing our common humanity may be the most healing act of all. Rachel Naomi Remen, M.D., *Kitchen Table Wisdom: Stories That Heal* (Sydney: Pan Macmillan Australia, 2010)

Secrets of a Bulletproof Spirit
Both Jillian and Azim experienced significant trauma and loss in their lives, but individually, and together, they refused to go under or succumb to despair. Instead, they teamed up to write this book, courageously and graciously sharing what they have learned on their journey toward forgiveness, healing, and joy.
Azim Khamisa and Jillian Quinn, *Secrets of a Bulletproof Spirit* (Crows Nest, New South Wales, Australia, Allen and Unwin, 2009)

The Gift of Anger
In this book, Arun explores ten spiritual lessons he learned from living and traveling with his grandfather Mahatma Gandhi.
Arun Gandhi, *The Gift of Anger,* (London: Michael Joseph, Penguin Books, 2017)

Beautiful Outlaw
I challenge you to explore this book! John blows away the religious fog that often surrounds Jesus and invites us to look at him with fresh eyes. To experience him as a dynamic, playful and warm-hearted person. Someone worth knowing and befriending in all his glorious humanity. John Eldredge, *Beautiful Outlaw,* (New York, Faith Words, Hachette Book Group, 2011)

365 Prescriptions for the Soul
Daily messages of hope and inspiration to help you live with a kind, courageous, and generous heart. Dr. Bernie S. Siegel, *365 Prescriptions for the Soul,* (Novato, California, New World Library, 2004)

Messiah
In this contemporary adaptation of an earlier work by Ellen G. White, Jerry describes the life of Jesus with wisdom, joy, and life-changing insights.
Jerry D. Thomas, *Messiah* (Nampa, Idaho, Pacific Press Publishing Association, 2003)

Radical Gratitude
When Andrew was a child, his family was forced into exile in Siberia. In this freezing environment, he received his first warmhearted lessons in resilience

and loyalty. In how to keep body, soul, and hope alive. Insights that every gen-eration needs, whatever the weather!
Andrew Bienkowski and Mary Akers, *Radical Gratitude*, (Crows Nest, New South Wales, Australia, Allen and Unwin, 2008)

Jesus Calling
I've found this book very healing and encouraging. It contains short inspiring messages, which are written as if Jesus is talking to us personally. There are several versions of this book, and each one is filled with words of love and hope. Sarah Young, *Jesus Calling*, (Nashville, Tennessee, Thomas Nelson, 2004)

How to Win Friends and Influence People
This classic book explores ways of getting along with other people while still successfully getting along with one's self. Dale Carnegie, *How to Win Friends and Influence People*, (Sydney: Harper Business, Harper Collins, 2000)

It Was on Fire When I Lay Down on It
Robert Fulghum has written several humorous books, and this is one of my favorites. Each story describes something that first amused, then touched and inspired him. I read his books when life gets a little too heavy and I need a lift—or just a giggle or two.
Robert Fulghum, *It Was on Fire When I Lay Down on It* (New York: Ivy Books, 1989)

The Road Less Traveled
This classic book explores many aspects of living a mature life, including love, courage, and finding purpose. M. Scott Peck, *The Road Less Traveled* (London: Arrow Books, Random House Inc., 2006)

Follow Your Heart
This practical book on finding your life purpose is lovingly illustrated with dra-matic and amusing cartoons. Andrew Matthews, *Follow Your Heart* (New York: Price Stern Sloan, Penguin Putnam Inc.,1997)

Your God Is Too Small
This slim book is easy to read, but it explores profound ideas about God, life, and purpose.
J. B. Phillips, *Your God is too Small* (New York, Touchstone, Simon and Schuster, 2004)

The Bible
The Bible has been translated into almost all the world's languages, and you can choose from many English versions. The book is divided into two main sections called The Old Testament and The New Testament. Each section also contains several smaller books.

Three of my favorite books in the New Testament are *John, Acts,* and *Ephesians*. *John* was written by a young man who followed Jesus for three years. It describes Jesus' life and work and John's growing awareness that Jesus is God. *Acts* is written by Dr Luke. It tells the dramatic and inspiring story of the beginning of the Christian Church.
Ephesians is a copy of a letter that Paul wrote to his friends in Ephesus. He speaks of the splendor of God's love and urges them to enjoy it themselves, and share it.

In addition to these books, *Genesis*, which I have sometimes referred to as The Book of Beginnings, tells the luminous story of how God created the world and lovingly shaped the first human beings. This book also introduces the battle between *good* and *evil*, which runs throughout the Bible.

I hope you enjoy exploring these books as much as I have!

A Final Blessing

May you always have a friend,
not least in yourself.

May you stay curious and learn,
enriching yourself.

May you respect all people,
including yourself.

May you know you are saved,
in spite of yourself.

May you abundantly serve,
fulfilling yourself.

May you feel loved and wanted,
because of yourself.

And may all your life be graced
and finally embraced by
The Eternal Himself.

Amen

Coming Soon . . .
Also by Lorna Hardy

The Gift of a Buoyant Spirit

Inspiring stories to lift your soul

Printed in the USA
CPSIA information can be obtained
at www.ICGtesting.com
CBHW061913300724
12440CB00018B/342